Creating a Scottish Church

Manchester University Press

Creating a Scottish Church

Catholicism, gender and ethnicity in
nineteenth-century Scotland

S. KARLY KEHOE

Manchester
University Press

Manchester and New York

distributed in the United States exclusively by Palgrave Macmillan

Copyright © S. Karly Kehoe 2010

The right of S. Karly Kehoe to be identified as the author of this work has been asserted by her in accordance with the Copyright, Designs and Patents Act 1988.

Published by Manchester University Press
Oxford Road, Manchester M13 9NR, UK
and Room 400, 175 Fifth Avenue, New York, NY 10010, USA
www.manchesteruniversitypress.co.uk

Distributed in the United States exclusively by
Palgrave Macmillan, 175 Fifth Avenue,
New York, NY 10010, USA

Distributed in Canada exclusively by
UBC Press, University of British Columbia, 2029 West Mall,
Vancouver, BC, Canada V6T 1Z2

British Library Cataloguing-in-Publication Data is available

Library of Congress Cataloging-in-Publication Data is available

ISBN 978 0 7190 8993 0 paperback

First published by Manchester University Press in hardback 2010

This paperback edition first published 2012

The publisher has no responsibility for the persistence or accuracy of URLs for any external or third-party internet websites referred to in this book, and does not guarantee that any content on such websites is, or will remain, accurate or appropriate.

Printed by Lightning Source

For Colin

Contents

List of maps, figures and tables	viii
Acknowledgements	x
List of abbreviations	xii
Introduction	1
1 Scotland's Catholic Church before emancipation	22
2 Reinventing strategies: coping with change	48
3 The recruitment of women religious	74
4 Constructing a system of education	110
5 Consolidating catholicity: devotion, association and community	149
Conclusion	175
Appendix: the patrons of the Holy Gild of St Joseph and the St Andrew's Mortuary Gild, Edinburgh, c.1849	181
Bibliography	183
Index	199

List of maps, figures and tables

Maps

Geographic spread of religious communities in Scotland, c.1870   119

Figures

1.1	Bishop George Hay	30
1.2	*Sawney's Defence against the Beast, Whore, Pope and Devil*, 1779	32
2.1	Bishop James Gillis	56
2.2	St Mary's Chapel, Edinburgh	62
2.3	Gorbals Chapel	62
2.4	St Andrew's Chapel, Dundee	64
3.1	Group of female boarding pupils at St Margaret's Convent, Edinburgh	78
3.2	Religious novice before profession, Ursulines of Jesus, Edinburgh	79
3.3	Veronica Cordier, co-foundress of the Franciscan Sisters of the Immaculate Conception, Glasgow	82
3.4	Mother Mary of the Cross Black, Franciscan Sisters of the Immaculate Conception, Glasgow	102
4.1	Group of the early teaching sisters of the Charlotte Street Convent, Glasgow	114
4.2	Art Room, Sisters of Mercy's Secondary School, Dundee	120
4.3	Dowanhill Teacher Training College, Glasgow	128
4.4	Group of female pupils at St Margaret's Convent, Edinburgh	139
4.5	Raffy, resident of St Joseph's Convent, Perth	140
5.1	Roderick Grant, son of James Grant	157
5.2	Members of the Children of Mary sodality at St Margaret's Convent, Edinburgh	163
5.3	Pupil at St Margaret's Convent, Edinburgh	164

Tables

3.1	Glasgow professions, Franciscan Sisters of the Immaculate Conception and the Sisters of Mercy	94
3.2	Edinburgh professions, Ursulines of Jesus and the Sisters of Mercy	95
3.3	Superiors, Ursulines of Jesus, Edinburgh	98
3.4	Superiors, Sisters of Mercy, Edinburgh	98
3.5	Superiors, Sisters of Mercy, Glasgow	99
3.6	Superiors, Franciscan Sisters of the Immaculate Conception, Glasgow	102
4.1	Educational provision in Glasgow, 1851	115
4.2	Educational provision in Edinburgh, 1851	115
4.3	Educational provision in Glasgow, 1871	123
4.4	Educational provision in Edinburgh, 1868–69	124
4.5	Statistics for Edinburgh's Catholic schools, 1877–78	136
4.6	Statistics for Glasgow's Catholic schools, 1880–81	137
5.1	Parish organisations in Edinburgh, 1893	158
5.2	Parish organisations in Glasgow, 1893	160

Acknowledgements

This book was inspired by my PhD at the University of Glasgow and was made possible by a postdoctoral fellowship from the Social Sciences and Humanities Research Council of Canada. During the fellowship I was based in the Department of History at the University of Guelph in Ontario and was mentored by Graeme Morton, whose constant support and enthusiasm for this project was inspiring. I would like to thank Graeme, Terry Crowley, the Department and the School of Scottish Studies for providing me with such a supportive working environment and for generously accommodating my need to spend extended periods of time researching and writing in Scotland.

When I first began researching this subject, the History of Women Religious in Britain and Ireland research forum was in its infancy, but over the years it has grown in size and influence and has succeeded in professionalising the study of women in religion. It provides its growing network of scholars with invaluable bibliographic resources, discussion forums and conferences for intellectual exchange. For all of their work in bringing this research network to fruition, I want to thank Carmen Mangion, Caroline Bowden and Susan O'Brien. I am grateful to Irene Maver at the University of Glasgow for her excellent supervision of my PhD and Ted Cowan for his insight and sense of humour. I am also indebted to my two examiners, Maria Luddy and Lesley Orr, who challenge and inspire young women to do history. Much of the material presented in this book is new and I appreciate the help that all of the archivists and librarians have given me. Special thanks must be extended to Andrew Nicoll, Keeper of the Scottish Catholic Archives, because without his help this book could never have been written. The Scottish Catholic Archives in Edinburgh is an indispensible resource for scholars near and far and I can only hope that this book will encourage more people to make use of its excellent collections and library. I am also grateful to Mary McHugh at the Glasgow Archdiocesan Archives and to the women religious who gave me unlimited access to their material and patiently answered all of my questions: Loyola Kelly, OSF; Dolores Cochrane,

OSF (RIP); Annette, RSM; Anne Burke, SND (RIP); Marion McCarthy, RSM; Barbara Jeffrey, RSM; Agnes Gleeson, RSM.

I have been lucky to have been surrounded by a group of friends and scholars who have believed in me and this research and who have supported me by discussing and debating and by reading draft upon draft. Thank you to Mike Vance, David Stewart, Iain MacPhail, Raymond McCluskey, Dara Price, Joanne Akalaitis, Paul Jenkins and Stanley MacDonald. Finally, I want to thank my family: Myles, Katie and Elaine for their strong characters and constant encouragement; Paul, Sarah, Patrick, Kate and Meg for their unending generosity and good humour; Lynn and Rudy for their love and kindness; and Colin, whose patience and support have been unmatched.

S. K. K.
Glasgow

List of abbreviations

AOH	Ancient Order of Hibernians
CDS	*Catholic Directory for Scotland*
CPSC	Catholic Poor Schools Committee
ECL	Edinburgh City Library
EUI	Edinburgh United Industrial School
FSICA	Franciscan Sisters of the Immaculate Conception Archives
GAA	Glasgow Archdiocesan Archives
GO	*Glasgow Observer*
INF	Irish National Foresters
MICA	Mercy International Centre Archives, Dublin
NAS	National Archives of Scotland
RGS	Registrar General for Scotland (General Register House, Edinburgh)
SCA	Scottish Catholic Archives
SMA	Sisters of Mercy Convent Archives
SVP	Saint Vincent de Paul Society
UGSC	University of Glasgow Special Collections

Introduction

Between the Reformation and the middle of the nineteenth century, Catholics in Scotland were confined to small pockets in the north-east, the south-west and in the desolate and isolated villages of the western Highlands and Islands. The only people who received any kind of regular instruction were the aristocratic recusants who employed their own priests. Everyone else had to make do with a handful of inconspicuous chapels and infrequent visits from disguised missionaries. This outlawed, underground church bore little resemblance to the one that emerged in the second half of the nineteenth century to claim a very public place in the nation's religious landscape. This new Catholic Church would boast a host of chapels, schools and religious personnel that stretched from one end of Scotland to the other. During the nineteenth century, it was the wealthy and influential upper and middle class that spearheaded a process of change that would take Catholicism to another level, displacing the 'old order' and instigating modernisation through reform and voluntarism. On a number of levels, Catholics were responding to the broader changes that were affecting Scotland and were participating in the overarching campaign to effect social and moral 'improvement'.

In 1800, when Scotland's population was 1,610,000, the majority of the 30,000 Catholics were concentrated in the western Highlands, whereas fifty years later most lived in urban centres and their number topped 150,000 or roughly 19.3 per cent of Scotland's 2,890,000 people.[1] Thirty years later, in 1880, when the Scottish population reached 3,735,573, the number of Catholics had doubled again to 332,000 and the vast majority were Irish and firmly settled in the industrial west.[2] For much of the century before 1900 the Catholic community was preoccupied with trying to redefine its identity and re-establish itself as a church in Scotland with a more public profile. It is true that in this process of change a degree of insularity and guarded separateness was cultivated, but what also happened was the recognition of an insatiable desire to plug into the national consciousness as citizens and acquire both a Scottish and a British identity, civic or otherwise.³ The mass migration of Catholic Irish was a key stimulant that forced indigenous Catholics to reappraise their relationship with Scottish and British society and come up with a strategy that would allow them to join in with the social, economic and imperial ambitions of the nation and the state.

This study examines the changing nature of Catholicism in modern Scotland by placing a significant emphasis on women religious. It highlights the defining role they played in the transformation and modernisation of the Catholic Church as it struggled to cope with unprecedented levels of Irish migration. The institutions and care-networks that these women established represented a new age in social welfare that served to connect the church with Scotland's emerging civil society. The depth of their commitment and the unrivalled emotional authority that they wielded secured for the church an unprecedented influence over a broader laity, the all too often nameless folk who made up the loose body of the church. Some scholars, such as Mary Peckham Magray, recognise this and credit women religious as being the shapers and transformers of Catholic culture.⁴ The sisters and nuns discussed here were integral educationalists who provided the first systematic education towards the improvement of educational standards in Scotland, but they were also pivotal in the complex, though not entirely successful, campaign to dilute Irish Catholic culture in Scotland.⁵

The history of Catholicism in Scotland has been detached from mainstream scholarship despite the fact that it was the vociferous opposition to Catholicism that anchored the nation's Presbyterian identity. Catholic historians have been as guilty of perpetuating an insular approach to their past as their non-Catholic colleagues have been in failing to include any critical examination of Catholicism in their investigations of Scotland's religious, political and social history. Given the fascinating, if complicated, relationship between Scotland and the United Kingdom, it is crucial that historians engage with this alternate dimension of Scotland's past as they take a more critical look at Scottish identity. This book, which focuses on the themes of gender, ethnicity and class, shows how the Catholic Church developed into a multi-faceted institution on a national scale that worked to secure and safeguard a civil society and a national identity that was distinctively Scottish.

Gallicanism and ultramontanism in the Scottish context

Much of the change that would shape Catholicism in Scotland during the nineteenth century was sparked by the migration of Catholic Irish, whose class, culture and imagined racial characteristics found little sympathy with the native Scots.[6] The differences that existed between Catholicism in Ireland and Scotland was a reflection of the widespread diversity that characterised Catholicism more generally before the middle of the nineteenth century, and seeing it as more of a 'loose federation of local churches' than anything else makes it easier to appreciate and recognise the complexity and variety of the regional and national traditions. Gallicanism was a teaching that originated in France in the late seventeenth century; it elevated the prerogative of the local or national church above that of the Pope and its popularity stemmed from its ability to complement Europe's emerging nationalisms. The French émigré clergy brought it to Ireland with them when they sought refuge during the Revolution, but there it seemed to fork into two paths, one that was traditional and one that was nationalist. Nationalist gallicanism blossomed in the south, whereas a more traditional form predominated in the north on account of the strength of dissenting and established Protestantism. There, the clergy were as much diplomats as they were spiritual leaders and, much to Rome's dismay, fraternised regularly with non-Catholics.[7] The same situation had existed across the Atlantic in Quebec, where the survival of Catholicism relied upon the French bishops' ability to forge good relations with their British governors. Quebec was a colony with a predominantly Catholic population in a growing Protestant empire, and it is useful to draw upon its experience here because it helps to show how Catholic populations functioned in non-Catholic states. Gallicanism or associated sympathies and practices enabled Catholicism to survive in Protestant nations such as England or Scotland because it taught that civil and temporal affairs should be independent of ecclesiastical power and that the church was a 'constitutional monarchy'.[8]

Discerning just how far gallicanism influenced Catholicism in Scotland is difficult but there are some clues to indicate that sympathies, at least, existed. The close relationship between Scottish Catholics and France was a crucial link and a number of French clergy found refuge in Scotland after their banishment during the Revolution and managed to survive by ministering privately to wealthy families, by working as missionaries in underserved districts or by teaching French, Italian and other subjects in places like Edinburgh, Glasgow, Greenock, Paisley and Dundee.[9] Given the range of their distribution and the fact that the French were tremendously adept at exporting language and culture, it is likely that these émigré clergymen exerted a strong influence, particularly upon those patrician families with whom they sought alliances.[10] Another clue concerns how some of the priests were trained, because at the heart of French gallicanism were the Sulpicians, a religious order of men who specialised in the training of clerics, and one of Scotland's most active bishops, James Gillis, had been steeped in this tradition since boyhood, both in

Montreal and in Paris.[11] His Canadian birth gave him an unusual perspective and when his family returned to Fochabers in Morayshire, the birthplace of his father, Gillis was regarded as a 'rising star' in the eyes of many influential clerics and laymen.[12] In Quebec he had witnessed a dispersal of gallican spirituality as the 'ethnic forces' of Scottish and Irish immigrants brought about change to the existing Catholic identity, and in Scotland he would witness a similar shift as the number of Irish increased.[13] What is particularly intriguing is that Gillis, who was a tremendously influential figure in the Scottish Catholic Church, blended old and new traditions and was sensitive to both recusant and ultramontane sympathies.

Gallicanism and ultramontanism converged in their recognition of the authority of state leaders or monarchs over civil affairs but were divided by the issue of papal jurisdiction.[14] Before the middle of the nineteenth century Rome was worlds away from these national churches, but as in-migration and political upheaval began to undermine the preservation of indigenous traditions, the ties with Rome were strengthened. Ultramontanism was a doctrine that promoted the absolute supremacy of the Pope, and it would work to consolidate Catholics across Europe by exploiting their national traditions.[15] The term ultramontane had been in use since the sixteenth century, when it had been used to describe a representative of the church north of the Alps, but from the late seventeenth century it began to characterise the challenge being mounted by religious orders like the Jesuits and the Dominicans against gallicanism.[16] In the late eighteenth century the French Revolution and the evolving political and ideological climate threw the church into a state of flux, with its subordination to the state, the widespread confiscation of its property and the banishment of its bishops, priests, nuns and monks being devastating blows. Nineteenth-century ultramontanism was a reaction to this radicalism,[17] and concerned by the growing power of the working class, the upper and middle classes favoured reviving the authority of the Pope and the church to resurrect an ordered social hierarchy.

Ultramontanism's influence in Scotland came about through the nation's unique position, not because of a dramatic shift towards Roman practices. National sympathies, anti-clericalism and an emerging working-class consciousness had to be accommodated and, as in England, there was reluctance in Scotland to sever ties with the old church, but by 1870 much of the resistance to ultramontanism in Scotland, Ireland and elsewhere had been checked. This is not to say that national sentiments disappeared or that a cohesive Catholic identity had been forged, and Bernard Aspinwall points out that in fact most of the chapels built before the First World War were given Scottish, Celtic or Anglo-Saxon names, which indicates the survival of an allegiance to national as opposed to Roman traditions.[18] In Scotland the ethnic tension between the Irish and the Scottish Catholics had delayed the restoration of the church hierarchy until 1878, some twenty-eight years after England, but even after this point friction still bubbled away under the surface. Although ultramontane waves could be felt in Scotland after 1830, its adoption was slow, much slower than in England, despite the fact that it too experienced a division between the ultramontanes and a teetering recusant aristocracy. In England the transition process had been greatly influenced by the Oxford Movement, a Catholic revival in the Church of England that originated at Oxford's Oriel College. It had sparked a radical change in both the Anglican and Catholic churches and while Scotland had certainly been affected, it experienced no equivalent movement. Oxford had been 'academic, clerical and conservative' and with the influence of prominent converts such as John Henry Newman and Henry Edward Manning, ultramontanism's hold was virtually guaranteed.[19]

In Scotland, like France, ultramontanism was channelled through an intellectual and educated laity. Men such as Robert Monteith, James Augustine Stothert and the exceedingly eccentric John Patrick Crichton-Stuart, the third marquess of Bute, were strong proponents who believed that it would unify the Catholic body. It was the aim of the ultramontanes to 'produce good Catholics, but also to produce a body of loyal, respectable working-class Catholics . . . of limited social mobility'.[20] Many of the leading ultramontanes were in fact converts whose religious enthusiasm had been soldered to their own sense of Britishness. In a book that investigates the concept of unionist nationalism in mid-nineteenth-century Scotland, Graeme Morton emphasises that the experience of Britishness was diverse, that there was no 'coherent' sense of it because each of the four nations had constructed a distinctive civil society. He points out that many Scots saw themselves as Scottish *and* British.[21] There was more to the Catholic Church in Scotland than ultramontane converts and it is clear that many outwith this circle prioritised their Scottish identity. The recusants, the old Catholic families, had survived the Reformation with their faith intact and saw themselves as more pure in their catholicity than either the new converts or the Irish migrants. They were also the group most resistant to change. National attachments could not be extinguished among a people who feared that the Scottishness of their church was being abandoned. This dichotomy reflects what Lindsay Paterson proposes in his study of Scottish identity in Britain – that there were two competing forms of nationalism in Scotland: one that was liberal, universalising and eager to adopt the English models that would enhance its cultural prestige and another that was Tory and inclined to 'preserve ancient Scottish institutions'.[22]

The rise of liberalism was crucial to the transformation of Catholicism in Scotland and elsewhere in Europe. It was an ideology that promoted freedom of conscience and personal liberty and came to reflect the growing belief that people should have more autonomy in their everyday lives. It dominated the middle-class consciousness and transcended religious and national boundaries, and the tendency for the middle classes to 'behave alike' meant that they worked to secure social unity and preserve the social order across Europe.[23] Although a serious ideological conflict developed between liberalism and Catholicism, it is important to recognise that ultramontanism could never have been implemented without it. Ultramontanism could accommodate liberalism in as far as it established the machinery that instituted and protected increased freedoms for Catholics and the liberty to construct and implement Catholic institutions. This occurred across Britain and Europe, and in Ireland and in parts of the Netherlands, Catholic nationalists tended to align themselves with secular liberalism. Once greater freedom for Catholics had been achieved, however, liberalism became an obstacle to ultramontanism because it threatened the extension of papal authority. In 1864 Pope Pius IX published *Quanta Cura*, an official church dictum attacking liberalism, and in it he declared the idea of legally proclaiming 'liberty of conscience and worship [as] each man's personal right' to be as erroneous as the notion of giving people 'absolute liberty ... restrained by no authority whether ecclesiastical or civil'.[24] Thus the 1853 Catholic-Liberal coalition that had succeeded in restoring the Catholic hierarchy in the Netherlands had broken down by 1870 and, influenced by *Quanta Cura*, the break had been led by clerics who focused on the autonomy of Catholic education.[25] The reason why liberalism and ultramontanism collided most spectacularly over education was because it was the church's most important tool for implementing its authority, and in nations like the Netherlands and Scotland, where the church was unable to monopolise the state system, it had to construct a separate one if it wanted to ensure the transmission of a common Catholic culture. In Scotland, the desire to develop and impose a more uniform Catholic culture increased as the number of Irish migrants grew.

The Irish factor

During the nineteenth century the Irish in Britain endured a deluge of negative publicity. Simianised caricatures littered the pages of popular weeklies like *Punch*, while social commentators such as Thomas Carlyle declared them to be Britain's 'sorest evil', 'sunk from decent manhood to squalid ape hood'.[26] In Glasgow, they were compared to vermin by commentators who wrote that once they settled 'it is nearly as difficult to expel them as to hunt rats out of a city drain'.[27] They were blamed for contaminating society and for endangering native traditions by both the state and the voluntary sector, which classed the vast majority as drunkards, criminals and beggars.[28] James Handley's *The Irish in Modern Scotland* paints a dismal picture of an impoverished people whose attempts to forge better lives for themselves were confounded by civil authorities that considered them to be little better than 'human flotsam and jetsam'.[29]

Class conflict among the labouring population in the west of Scotland played a key role in both the anti-Irishness and the anti-Catholicism that arose and solidified. While the Irish were recognised as having made a consistent contribution to the Scottish economy as seasonal harvesters in places like Ayrshire and the Lothians and as railway navvies, the growing number deciding to settle in industrial centres like Glasgow and work in industry sparked a fear for the security of the native Scottish labourer. As cities and towns struggled to cope with rapid industrialisation and population explosion and as the Famine took hold in Ireland, the Irish in Scotland came under increasing attack. Famine victims received little sympathy as correspondents from papers such as the *Glasgow Herald* scolded that 'it would be well that our poor Irish friends should understand that the city of Glasgow is at present overrun with poor, and that by flocking hither in droves they are only exposing themselves to certain misery.'[30]

A factor influencing the development of both anti-Irishness and anti-Catholicism was the class conflict among the west of Scotland's labouring population. Industrialisation represented the introduction of technological advances that displaced manual skills and changed the structure of the labour force and sections of the economy. In the late eighteenth century, the labour market began shifting from one that was focused on primary production to one that prioritised secondary production, and this change necessitated a larger pool of unskilled, low-wage workers. After 1820 especially, there were significant employment opportunities for unskilled labourers in the industrial west and this attracted a growing number of Irish migrants. This led to a degree of employment competition between the Irish and the native Scots and contributed to a growing tension between the two, but scholars such as Elaine McFarland rightly stress that 'most of the labour performed by them [Irish Catholics] was actually created by the Industrial Revolution and was not sought as employment by Scots'.[31] Antagonism in the mining districts was particularly acute and in his study of Irish Republicanism in Scotland, Máirtín Seán Ó Catháin notes the residential segregation along sectarian 'ethno-religious' lines and suggests that this might have strengthened the local

Irish Catholic community's 'internal context and the borders with the external Scottish context'.[32]

Part of the reason why the Irish seemed to cause so much offence to Scottish sensibilities lay in the self-perception of Victorian Scots. By the end of the eighteenth century Scotland had begun to enjoy unprecedented economic stability and industrial strength, and for many this represented a Protestant triumph over 'popery'.[33] The parliamentary union between Scotland and England in 1707 was fundamentally anti-Catholic and enshrined Protestant succession as a pillar of Britain's unwritten constitution.[34] Catherine Jones, whose study of immigration and social policy in Britain includes a chapter on the Irish, argues that despite industry's reliance upon Irish labour, they were blamed for impeding the natural progress of Scotland and England.[35] As Scotland's economy continued to expand and its connections with and influence upon empire grew more distinctive, Scots embraced their Britishness so enthusiastically that some believed themselves to be more 'purely English' than the English themselves.[36] The appropriation of the term English was, according to Graeme Morton, nothing new and points to David Hume, 'that towering intellect of the Scottish Enlightenment', as a pioneering example.[37] Colin Kidd asserts that the Irish were essentially placed at odds with a host society that was preoccupied with projecting a Teutonic, Saxon racial identity.[38] On most levels, then, the issue of race and racial difference was a dominant theme among Scottish intellectuals and not simply because it justified imperialism. It offered Scots the opportunity to re-imagine their history as one of triumph, the victory of the Saxon race over the Celtic one, thereby making their claim to a British identity stronger.[39] Declared the contaminants of 'Saxon soil', the Irish faced an uphill struggle as they attempted to settle in Britain's large cities, but in this they were not alone and they shared the experience with their fellow Celts, the Highlanders.[40]

Ireland's nationalist politics conflicted with Scotland's pervasive unionist culture and many Scots feared that the political radicalism and 'alien' religion of the Irish would undermine the stability of Britain and its empire. Catholic authorities in Scotland (clerics and wealthy laymen) wanted to participate as equals in this culture of British and imperial progress but because many Scots failed to make a distinction between Catholic and Irish, they were deeply unsettled by the rising number of migrants. They were acutely aware of the precariousness of their position, being Catholic but not Irish, and felt frustrated by the negative impact that perceptions of the Irish were having upon their status. One contemporary, Glasgow's Bishop John Gray, reported that indigenous Catholics viewed the Irish with 'distrust, if not aversion'.[41] The tendency to equate Irish with Catholic had, as John Belchem explains, become the norm across Britain:

As English anti-Celt prejudice concentrated into enmity of the Irish, hostility was reinforced by a redefined anti-Catholicism, in which the presence of the Irish, rather than the cunning wiles of European emissaries of Rome, became the main cause of alarm.[42]

Many of the pre-1840 Irish migrants had been Protestant, but Catholics dominated among those who came after. This shift sparked concern from both non-Catholic and indigenous Catholic quarters because, while there were fears in Presbyterian circles that the influx was altering the religious dynamic of Scotland's cities, recusant Catholics resented that the heart of their church was being pulled into the urban west by these newcomers, who had no 'rigid concept of religion'.[43] Thus, the Irish were problematised as subversives and as a people who belonged to an inferior race and clung to a corrupt religion.[44] To many Scots they also represented radical politics and were widely perceived as a people whose nationalist baggage upset the native tradition of quiet and conservative living.[45] In reality, most of the Irish were not politically conscious and were more concerned with the basics of everyday survival than they were with securing an independent Ireland. According to Alan O'Day, who publishes widely on Irish immigrant communities abroad, it was the Irish priests who were the real protagonists of nationalist sentiment, and Martin Mitchell's *The Irish in the West of Scotland* confirms that this was the case in Scotland.[46] Those Irish clerics who were unable to contain their nationalist sympathies came under fierce and sustained criticism from the Scots Catholic clergy, particularly the bishops in the Western District and wealthy members of the laity. In contrast to the Eastern District, where there was significant cooperation between the clergy and a highly connected and influential laity, the ecclesiastical positions in the Western District, at least until the late 1860s, were occupied by priests rooted in a strongly recusant tradition who were intensely resistant to outside interference.[47]

The tension that existed between the Irish and Scottish Catholics, particularly at a clerical level in the Western District, was counterproductive to Catholicism's development in Scotland, and John F. McCaffrey, who has carefully examined the history of Catholicism and the Irish in Scotland, speculates that the 'Scottish attitude' and the unwillingness to accept the Irish as permanent members of Scotland's Catholic community were particularly damaging.[48] An interesting appraisal of the situation is provided in H. J. Hanham's *Scottish Nationalism*, which was published in the late 1960s. Interlinking this ethnic tension with nationalism, he observed that:

> The story of the Catholic Church in Scotland is . . . the story of the fight of the native Scottish clergy to retain control over their own church – if you will, one of the earliest struggles of Scottish nationalism against domination from outside.[49]

Hanham goes on to say that what is most important is that 'the native Scots won their battle'.[50] But did they? Hanham claims that although Irish names predominated in senior clerical ranks by the middle of the twentieth century, the fact that they had been born and raised in Scotland meant that they were steeped in its traditions. His argument inspires a deeper consideration of the authenticity of Scottish Catholic identity and its associated traditions. By the turn of the twentieth century the church had been almost entirely transformed and bore little resemblance to that which existed before 1850. Many of the 'traditions' that came to define nineteenth-century Catholicism, such as devotions,[51] had in fact been invented or introduced by those middle- and upper-class Catholics who were desperate to embrace reform and redefine their image as respectable and loyal. Much of the transformation involved the introduction of educational and social welfare institutions, and through these initiatives Scottish Catholics participated in civil society and helped to extend a sense of national identity for, as Morton points out, at a time when parliamentary political nationalism was absent, civil society filled an important and defining gap.[52] What is more, those most responsible for transmitting this new culture of religiosity to the wider Catholic community through education and social welfare were the religious communities of *active* religious women and men.

The centrality of women religious

The French Revolution reinvigorated the religious life, and women, like never before, flocked to the convents and proceeded to stretch and redefine its boundaries. The vast majority of those who entered were from the middle class and were confirming the bourgeois commitment to the moral improvement of society. France and Belgium were the cradles of this rejuvenation and many of the women who helped to rebuild, reinvent or construct religious communities and congregations there would go on to play pivotal roles in the expansion of the church in Britain, Canada, the United States and Australasia. The first two communities of nuns to come to Scotland were French: the Ursulines of Jesus, founded at Chavagnes-en-Paillers in the Loire Valley, had come to Edinburgh in 1834, and the Franciscan Sisters of the Immaculate Conception had been founded in Glasgow in 1847 by two nuns from the Notre Dame des Anges community in Tourcoing, an industrial town in France's north-east near the Belgian border. Once in Scotland, these communities expanded rapidly, and before the turn of the twentieth century the Ursulines had set up three additional houses in Edinburgh and Perth. The Franciscan Sisters had filled two more houses in Glasgow and set up other communities in Inverness,

Aberdeen, Lanark, Innellan, Greenock, Bothwell, Edinburgh, Girvan and Bishopbriggs.[53] Like France, Ireland had also witnessed an explosion in the number of women entering the convents and over the course of the century it is estimated that the figure was as high as 8,000 or roughly 64 per cent of the country's religious personnel.[54] One of the largest congregations was the Sisters of Mercy that was founded by Catherine McAuley in Dublin in 1832, and through their house in Limerick, the Mercies established Scotland's third community in Glasgow in 1849 before setting up another in Edinburgh in 1858; by 1900 there were eleven Mercy communities in Scotland.

That the number of women religious rose so dramatically and expanded throughout Protestant nations like Scotland was the result of Pope Benedict XIV's *Quamvis Iusto*, a 1749 papal bull that reversed *pericluso*, the dictum first issued in 1299, and reaffirmed by the Council of Trent in 1536, that ordered the enclosure of all nuns. Although *pericluso* had been circumvented by some who had devised ways of taking simple, annual vows rather than the solemn, lifelong ones of nuns, church authorities punished these dissidents with imprisonment or excommunication.[55] *Quamvis Iusto* was a radical but necessary shift in church policy that succeeded in opening the floodgates for an unenclosed, active female apostolate. By no means were enclosed or contemplative communities of nuns eliminated, but they did become far outnumbered by unenclosed sisters eager to undertake a more public role as social welfare providers. In France, the growth of the religious life is described as a 'powerful movement by women to re-Christianise French culture and society',[56] but the international, missionary dimension of this life also made it imperialistic. The personal outlook of these women was crucial and, as Carmen Mangion explains, the decision to enter the religious life was not a passive one and entrants opted for the life path that best suited their needs.[57] In fact, many women entered the religious life for the chance to live and undertake meaningful work abroad or to avoid marriage and childbirth. Not only were they designing a new personal identity but they were negotiating a new direction for religious culture through collective female action. Despite having to undergo the formality of being recruited or invited into a parish by bishops and priests before they could begin their work, sisters and nuns were adept at establishing foundations around the world, from England and Scotland to Canada, the United States, Australia and India. What is more, they did this because of their own 'sense of mission'.[58]

While there is a need to examine the influence and experience of those British and Irish sisters who worked as missionaries abroad,[59] it is important to remember that Britain was itself a mission and those sisters who lived and worked in nineteenth-century Scotland, for instance, need to be appraised critically within that context. In a groundbreaking study of sisters and nuns in Ireland between 1750 and 1900, Mary Peckham Magray argues that women religious were the protagonists in the transformation of Catholic culture. Critical of Emmett Larkin's theory of a post-Famine devotional revolution, Magray proposes a more gradual process of religious change, one that was intimately linked with the broader cultural transformation that had been actively pursued since the mid-eighteenth century by an ambitious and increasingly influential Catholic middle class. In Scotland, despite rapid population growth in the nineteenth century, Catholicism was never in a position to realistically challenge Presbyterian hegemony, but Magray's emphasis on the ability of women religious to effect social and religious change by influencing the development of a 'new style of religious devotion and social behaviour' establishes an important precedent that helps to contextualise the role of women religious in nineteenth-century Scotland.[60]

Sisters and nuns were conscripted to Scotland in an effort to dilute Irish Catholic culture. Their identity as pious women with religious authority complemented the broader middle-class preoccupation with the resurrection of a Christian society through social and moral improvement. Callum Brown emphasises the pivotal role that Protestant women played in the 'moral revolution' and notes how the evangelical emphasis on female piety was used to reverse, or stem, the effects of 'moral weakness and [the] innate temptations of masculinity'.[61] Although he included only a few generalised comments about Catholicism and remained entirely silent on women religious, his points about the extension of the female role for the improvement of society are crucial because they can be applied across the denominational spectrum.[62] Scotland's civic atmosphere permeated every level of society and relied upon the moral responsibility of women. The Catholic Church needed sisters and nuns to transform their fellow women into models of Christianity, virtuous and pious 'angels' of the home. Women religious were responsible for transforming Catholics into respectable, obedient and loyal Scottish and British citizens and for facilitating church expansion.

The tendency for scholars to focus on the clergy or on wealthy members of the laity has meant that an entire dimension of the Catholic experience in Scotland has been overlooked. What this book does is show how important it is to examine the role of women in the church, those who did not and could not hold titled ecclesiastical posts.[63] Overall, and unfortunately, scholars have been reluctant to engage with the agency of Catholic women. While Bernard Aspinwall, who is a prolific and influential scholar of Catholic history in Scotland, acknowledges their work in some of his writings, other scholars of religious history such as Brown ignore them entirely. Given Brown's more recent attempts to incorporate a gendered analysis, for example in *The Death of Christian Britain*, it is disappointing that women religious were overlooked. Much of the work done on women religious in Scotland to date centres around education, and although Jane McDermid only briefly mentions them in her study of working-class female education in Victorian Scotland, she notes the absence of Catholic women's experience and calls for more research and writing to be done. Very little work has been done on Catholic education in nineteenth-century Scotland apart from T. A. Fitzpatrick's book on Catholic secondary education before 1972, which can only act as a basic reference point, his article on Catholic elementary education in south-west Scotland before 1872, Ian Stewart's article on the careers of teachers in Edinburgh's early Catholic schools, and the work of Francis J. O'Hagan.[64] O'Hagan wrote two books, *The Contribution of the Religious Orders to Education in Glasgow during the Period 1847–1918* and *Change, Challenge and Achievement: A Study of the Development of Catholic Education in Glasgow in the Nineteenth and Twentieth Centuries*, and while both focus on the work of the religious orders in Glasgow, their lack of archival material makes for an extremely limited analysis.[65] However, the article he co-wrote with Robert A. Davis, entitled 'Forging the compact of church and state in the development of Catholic education in late nineteenth-century Scotland', has significant value.[66] Outwith the realm of education, very little exists apart from John Watts's *A Canticle of Love: The Story of the Franciscan Sisters of the Immaculate Conception*, which is a well-researched, general history of one congregation in Glasgow, and two of my own articles. 'Nursing the mission: the Franciscan Sisters of the Immaculate Conception and the Sisters of Mercy in Glasgow, 1847–1866' looks at the formal and informal nursing work undertaken by two communities, and 'The Venerable Margaret Sinclair: an examination of the cause of Edinburgh's twentieth-century factory girl' which links a young nun's candidacy for sainthood to working-class culture and industrial unrest.[67]

Nationalisms and the power they could exert upon religion and religiosity have featured prominently in convent life and in many ways this study brings this to the surface. Studies dedicated to examining the relationship between women religious, culture and identity in Scotland are non-existent but even where they exist elsewhere, apart from Magray's *The Transforming Power of the Nuns*, the analysis is limited. An example is Jo Ann Kay McNamara's book on nuns across two millennia wherein she suggests that sisters and nuns, particularly those in the missions, ignored nationalist claims to 'reinforce the Vatican's ultramontane policies'.[68] This sweeping appraisal becomes problematic when a closer look at the relationship between national identities and Catholicism is taken. The spread of ultramontanism was, as noted earlier, only achieved with the cooperation of the national group or groups. What I argue is that convents were key venues for contesting Catholic culture because it was there that national and ethnic claims were particularly strong. Archival material shows again and again the prevalence of ethnic tension in places where the indigenous Catholic population could not fill its own convents. In Scotland, the composition of religious communities was such that women from a variety of nations found themselves living and working together under one roof and the inability of many to leave their national identities behind them, or the fear that they would not be willing to do so, sparked increased efforts by the hosts to suppress other nationalist claims. In a study that considers the impact that sisters and nuns had upon the shaping of Catholic culture in the United States, Carol Coburn and Martha Smith explain that the survival and expansion of religious communities was ultimately determined by their ability to 'Americanize'. They show that within the congregation of the Sisters of St Joseph, the diverse range of nationalities often led to 'ethnic infighting', which eventually forced an amendment to its rule and constitutions that obliged sisters to avoid 'the spirit of independence, of nationality, and of faction'.[69] Similarly the presence of cultural and national tensions in the French-founded convents in England meant that although many superiors worked to overcome such sentiments, it was not easily achieved. Susan O'Brien's research in this area reveals that these communities tended to remain 'culturally French' despite having an international membership, but she maintains that class was the main determinant in internal convent relations.[70] All of this is relevant to the Catholic experience in nineteenth-century Scotland because the notion of creating the right convent ethos and cultural identity was crucial to the dissemination of a transformed Catholic culture.

Chapter overview

The first chapter considers the state of Catholicism up to 1834 and begins with a brief sketch of Scottish Catholicism in the seventeenth and eighteenth centuries to reveal just how disorganised and divided the church actually was. It shows how the church began to stabilise after the 'Jacobite threat' subsided, and to establish a presence beyond the western Highlands and the north-east. The extension of Catholic relief was a crucial but hotly contested development and vehement opposition from groups such as the Committee for the Protestant Interest help to demonstrate the extent to which Scottish national identity was tied to an unwavering commitment to union and to the Protestant constitution. This chapter shows how the Catholic clergy, inspired by the progress being made to secure greater rights for Catholics but conscious of Scotland's anti-popery past, encouraged their followers to maintain a quiet and conservative profile and dedicate themselves to proving their loyalty to crown and country. It also explains how their efforts to contain political activity among the laity were frustrated by the rising star of Ireland's Daniel O'Connell and how, as calls for Catholic emancipation grew louder, the Scottish clergy, anxious to avoid inflaming anti-Catholic antagonism, reacted with increasing hostility towards the Irish migrants.

The second chapter examines how the church reacted to liberalism, legislative reform, the rise of evangelicalism and the continued growth of Irish migration between the late 1820s and the late 1850s. A mutual aversion to the Irish and a loyalty to nation and state inspired a recusant and ultramontane laity to invest heavily in a programme of church transformation and development. The recruitment of the Ursulines of Jesus, the first community of nuns to return to Scotland since the Reformation, is highlighted as a significant step towards legitimising Catholic respectability, but attention is also paid to other important developments such as the establishment of the first parish schools and new chapels and orphanages, and the founding of relief and friendly societies. Not only did these organisations work to counter Protestant proselytism but they granted the upper and middle classes a more direct role in the Catholic mission by involving them as teachers, community visitors and care workers. This chapter interlinks an embryonic social welfare network with Scotland's developing civil society and uses it to bring into sharper focus female agency and the role that it would play in establishing the authority of the church as it worked to integrate itself into the fabric of Scottish and British citizenry.

Chapter 3 is divided into two distinct sections and focuses specifically on the recruitment and influence of women religious. The first section begins by looking at the expansion of religious communities in Scotland between 1834 and 1860 before considering the experience of the first four teaching communities to arrive in Edinburgh and Glasgow: the Ursulines of Jesus and the Sisters of Mercy, established in Edinburgh in 1834 and 1858 respectively, and the Franciscan Sisters of the Immaculate Conception and the Sisters of Mercy, founded in Glasgow in 1847 and 1849. This section, which discusses their background, recruitment, settlement, ethos, structure and organisation, leads into a discussion on the widespread public anxiety that existed towards nuns as a way of re-emphasising Scotland's anti-Catholic tradition. The second section refocuses attention on the issue of identity by considering how gender and ethnicity influenced the development of these religious communities and how this was connected with the broader campaign to transform Catholic culture in Scotland. Statistics that outline the nationality and family connections of the convent leadership and membership are used as evidence of this. This section also includes a discussion about the clerical control that was exerted over the two key posts in a convent, that of mother superior and novice mistress, and it is argued that the close scrutiny of these positions demonstrates a precise clerical understanding of the ability of women religious to influence those under their care.

The fourth chapter examines the development of Catholic education in Scotland between the late 1840s and 1900 and prioritises the role played by women religious in this process. As industrialisation and urbanisation increased, the upper and middle classes sought new ways to achieve greater control over the working class, and their main focus was education. The extension of state aid, albeit limited, to Catholic schools in 1847 ushered in an era of dramatic change and led to the foundation of the Catholic Poor Schools Committee. This organisation sought to organise Catholic education at a British rather than a Scottish level and is shown to have had an Anglicising influence upon Catholic culture in Scotland. As the number of Catholic schools in Scotland grew, so too did the influence of women religious, particularly in the more populated cities and towns. By the time the Education (Scotland) Act was passed in 1872, the church had implemented a skeletal system of education that was largely under the authority of religious personnel and those they had trained. While this chapter reveals that the provision of Catholic education was central to the ultramontane strategy of consolidation, it also demonstrates that education gave the church a more permanent role in the production of a civil society that forged and supported a Scottish national identity within the British state.

The final chapter is a critical consideration of the relationship between the influence of religious personnel over education and the transformation of Catholic culture in Scotland by looking at the rise of devotional activity and organisational culture between 1870 and 1900. An increase in the number of societies and associations served to enhance people's spiritual commitment to Catholicism and indicated the emergence of a more national and international consolidated church. However, the role of class is carefully considered since much of the devotional activity was introduced and dominated by the middle class. What this chapter also does is challenge the notion of a Catholic 'ghetto' by asserting that while there was a degree of alienation and insularity, the energy that was invested in transforming Catholic culture had succeeded in liberating Catholics, to a greater extent, from the periphery of Scottish society. It is also suggested that, towards the end of the century, although Irish culture was still a prominent element in the character of Catholicism in Scotland, it did not arouse the same level of concern that it had evoked in earlier years because the church and its leadership were increasingly preoccupied with the rise of a united working-class consciousness and activism. Devotional initiatives and associations, the roots of which had been sown by the work of the religious communities through education and social welfare, would serve to connect the local parish more closely with the wider church and it was hoped that they would help combat subversive elements and consolidate the wider Catholic community.

Notes

1. Neil Tranter, 'Demography', in Anthony Cooke et al. (eds), *Modern Scottish History: 1707 to the Present*, vol. 1: *Transformation of Scotland, 1707–1850* (East Linton, Tuckwell Press, 1998), p. 112.
2. John McCaffrey, 'Roman Catholics in Scotland in the 19th and 20th centuries', *Records of the Scottish Church History Society*, 21 (1983), p. 276.
3. *Ibid.*, p. 277, and his 'The Catholic Church and Scottish politics since 1707', in James Kirk (ed.), *The Scottish Churches and the Union Parliament, 1707–1999* (Edinburgh, Scottish Church History Society, 2001), pp. 22–3.
4. Mary Peckham Magray, *The Transforming Power of the Nuns: Women, Religion, and Cultural Change in Ireland, 1750–1900* (Oxford, Oxford University Press, 1998).
5. Bernard Aspinwall, 'The formation of the Catholic community in the West of Scotland: some preliminary outlines', *Innes Review*, 33:1 (1982), pp. 46–8.
6. Mary Hickman, 'Incorporating and denationalizing the Irish in England: the role of the Catholic Church', in Patrick O'Sullivan (ed.), *The Irish World Wide: History, Heritage, Identity*, Volume 5: *Religion and Identity* (London, Leicester University Press, 1996), p. 200.
7. Desmond Bowen, *Paul Cardinal Cullen and the Shaping of Modern Irish Catholicism* (Dublin, Gill and Macmillan, 1983), p. 45.
8. Austin Gough, *Paris and Rome: The Gallican Church and the Ultramontane Campaign, 1848–1853* (Oxford, Clarendon Press, 1986), p. vi.
9. James McGloin, 'Some refugee French clerics and laymen in Scotland, 1789–1814', *Innes Review*, 16:1 (1965), pp. 27–55.
10. *Ibid.*, p. 29.
11. Gough, *Paris and Rome*, pp. 17–18 and 58.
12. Bernard Aspinwall, 'Gillis, James (1802–1864)', *Oxford Dictionary of National Biography*, Oxford University Press, 2004. www.oxforddnb.com/view/article/10750 [accessed 27 November 2007].
13. Terrence J. Fay, *A History of Canadian Catholics, Gallicanism, Romanism and Canadianism* (Montreal and Kingston, McGill-Queen's University Press, 2002), p. 47.
14. Alec R. Vidler, *The Church in an Age of Revolution: 1789 to the Present Day* (London, Penguin Books, 1990), p. 146.

15 Peter Raedts, 'The Church as nation state: A new look at ultramontane Catholicism', *Dutch Review of Church History*, 84 (2004), p. 477.
16 Fay, *History of Canadian Catholics*, p. 69.
17 Eric Yonke emphasises that ultramontanism was favoured by the entire middle class, not just the upper portion. 'The problem of the middle class in German Catholic history: the nineteenth-century Rhineland revisited', *The Catholic Historical Review*, 88:2 (April 2002), p. 264.
18 B. Aspinwall, 'Catholic devotion in Victorian Scotland', Manuscript of paper delivered in May 2003 at the University of Aberdeen.
19 Vidler, *The Church in an Age of Revolution*, p. 52.
20 Mary Hickman, 'Alternate historiographies of the Irish in Britain: a critique of the segregationist/assimilation model', in Roger Swift and Sheridan Gilley (eds), *The Irish in Victorian Britain: The Local Dimension* (Dublin, Four Courts Press, 1999), p. 249.
21 Graeme Morton, *Unionist Nationalism: Governing Urban Scotland, 1830–1860* (East Linton, Tuckwell Press, 1999), pp. 8–9.
22 Lindsay Paterson, *The Autonomy of Modern Scotland* (Edinburgh, Edinburgh University Press, 1994), p. 65.
23 Thomas Megel, 'Ultramontanism, liberalism, moderation: political mentalities and political behaviour of the German Catholic Bürgertum, 1848–1914', *Central European History*, 29:2 (2001), pp. 160–2.
24 *Quanta Cura. Encyclical of Pope Pius IX promulgated on December 8, 1964.* http://papalencyclicals.net/Pius09/p9quanta.htm [accessed 27 November 2007].
25 Herman Bakvis, *Catholic Power in the Netherlands* (Kingston and Montreal, McGill-Queen's University Press, 1981), pp. 60–4.
26 Thomas Carlyle, 'Finest peasantry in the world', in *Thomas Carlyle: Selected Writings* (London, Penguin Books, 1971), p. 171. L. Perry Curtis, *Apes and Angels: The Irishman in Victorian Caricature*, revised edition (Washington, Smithsonian Institution Press, 1997). Roy Foster takes issue with Curtis, arguing that the representations he identifies as being associated with the Irish were also found in caricatures of the English labouring population. R. F. Foster, *Paddy & Mr Punch: Connections in Irish and English History* (London, Penguin Books, 1993).
27 *Glasgow Past & Present*, vol. 1 (Glasgow, David Robertson & Co., 1884). Entry for 15 December 1848.
28 Catherine Jones, *Immigration and Social Policy in Britain* (London, Tavistock, 1977), pp. 48–53. William Pitt Dundas, Registrar General, and James Stark, MD, *Eighth Decennial Census of the Population of Scotland taken 3D April 1871, with Report*, vol. 1 (Edinburgh, Murray and Gibb, 1872), pp. xviii–xix.
29 James Edmund Handley, *The Irish in Modern Scotland* (Cork, Cork University Press, 1947), p. 22.
30 *Glasgow Herald*, 10 August 1846, 21 December 1846, 11 June 1847.
31 Elaine McFarland, *Protestants First: Orangeism in 19th Century Scotland* (Edinburgh, Edinburgh University Press, 1990), p. 101.

32 Máirtín Seán Ó Catháin, *Irish Republicanism in Scotland 1858–1916: Fenians in Exile* (Dublin, Irish Academic Press, 2007), p. 85. See also Terrence McBride, *The Experience of Irish Migrants to Glasgow, Scotland 1863–1891: A New Way of Being Irish* (Lewiston, NY, Edwin Mellen Press, 2006).
33 Colin Kidd, 'Constructing a Civil Religion: Scots Presbyterians and the eighteenth-century British State', in Kirk (ed.), *Scottish Churches and the Union Parliament*, p. 1. See also Stewart J. Brown, *The National Churches of England, Ireland and Scotland, 1801–1846* (Oxford, Oxford University Press, 2001), ch. 1.
34 Kidd, 'Constructing a Civil Religion', p. 1.
35 Jones, *Immigration and Social Policy*, pp. 48–53.
36 Colin Kidd, 'Race, Empire and the limits of nineteenth-century Scottish nationhood', *The Historical Journal*, 46:4 (2003), p. 886.
37 Morton, *Unionist Nationalism*, p. 3.
38 Kidd, 'Race, Empire', p. 877.
39 *Ibid.*, pp. 873–92.
40 Carlyle, 'Finest peasantry in the world', pp. 171–2 and 176. Christopher Harvie, *Scotland and Nationalism: Scottish Society and Nationalism, 1707–1994*, 2nd edition (London, Routledge, 1994), p. 94. Krisztina Fenyő, *Contempt, Sympathy and Romance: Lowland Perceptions of the Highlands and the Clearances during the Famine Years, 1845–1855* (East Linton, Tuckwell Press, 2000).
41 GAA. WD12/43. *Report on the State of Religion in the Western District.* John Gray, 1866.
42 John Belchem, 'Nationalism, republicanism and exile: Irish emigrants and the revolutions of 1848', *Past & Present*, 146:1 (1995), p. 134.
43 McCaffrey, 'Roman Catholics in Scotland', p. 276. Timothy G. McMahon, 'Religion and popular culture in nineteenth-century Ireland', *History Compass*, 4:3 (2007), p. 854.
44 John McCaffrey, 'Reactions in Scotland to the Irish famine', in Stewart J. Brown (ed.), *Scottish Christianity in the Modern World* (Edinburgh, T. & T. Clark, 2000), p. 160.
45 James Walsh, 'Archbishop Manning's visitation of the Western District of Scotland in 1867', *Innes Review*, 18:1 (1967), p. 15.
46 Alan O'Day, 'Imagined Irish communities: networks of social communication of the Irish diaspora in the United States and Britain in the late nineteenth and early twentieth centuries', *Immigrants and Minorities*, 23:2–3 (November 2005), p. 410. Martin Mitchell, *The Irish in the West of Scotland 1797–1848: Trade Unions, Strikes and Political Movements* (Edinburgh, John Donald, 1998).
47 Aspinwall, 'The formation of a British identity within Scottish Catholicism, 1830–1914', in Robert Pope (ed.), *Religion and National Identity: Wales and Scotland, c.1700–2000* (Cardiff, University of Wales Press, 2001), p. 271.
48 McCaffrey, 'Roman Catholics in Scotland', pp. 277–8.
49 H. J. Hanham, *Scottish Nationalism* (London, Faber & Faber, 1969), p. 20.
50 *Ibid.*

51 Mary Heimann, *Catholic Devotion in Victorian England* (Oxford, Clarendon Press, 1995), pp. 38–69. Agnes Trail, *Revival of conventual life in Scotland. History of St. Margaret's Convent, Edinburgh, the first religious house founded in Scotland since the so-called Reformation; and the autobiography of the first religious Sister Agnes Xavier Trail* (Edinburgh, 1886), pp. 136–8.
52 Morton, *Unionist Nationalism*, p. 8.
53 John Watts, *A Canticle of Love: The Story of the Franciscan Sisters of the Immaculate Conception* (Edinburgh, John Donald, 2006), p. 258.
54 Magray, *The Transforming Power*, p. 9.
55 Kathleen A. Brosnan, 'Public presence, public silence: nuns, bishops and the gendered space of early Chicago', *The Catholic Historical Review*, 90 (2004), p. 475.
56 Susan O'Brien, 'French nuns in nineteenth-century England', *Past & Present*, 54:1 (1997), p. 142.
57 Carmen Mangion, *Contested Identities: Catholic Women Religious in Nineteenth-Century England and Wales* (Manchester, Manchester University Press, 2008.), p. 8.
58 Susan O'Brien, 'Coda – missing missionaries: where are the Catholic sisters in British missiology?' Unpublished paper delivered at the 4th annual Consecrated Women Conference, Divinity Faculty, Cambridge University, 16–17 September 2005.
59 *Ibid.*
60 Magray, *The Transforming Power*, p. 11.
61 Callum Brown, *The Death of Christian Britain: Understanding Secularisation, 1800–2000* (London, Routledge, 2001), p. 9.
62 *Ibid.*, p. 68.
63 Bernard Aspinwall, 'The welfare state within the state: the Saint Vincent de Paul Society in Glasgow, 1848–1920', in W. J. Sheils and Diana Wood (eds), *Voluntary Religion* (Oxford, Basil Blackwell, 1986), p. 445. Aspinwall, 'A long journey: the Irish in Scotland', in O'Sullivan (ed.), *Religion and Identity*, p. 164. He is one of the scholars who tends to place too much of an emphasis on the clergy and influential laity.
64 T. A. Fitzpatrick, *Catholic Secondary Education in South-West Scotland before 1972: Its Contribution to the Change in Status of the Catholic Community of the Area* (Aberdeen, Aberdeen University Press, 1986) and Fitzpatrick, 'Catholic education in Glasgow, Lanarkshire and south-west Scotland before 1872', *Innes Review*, 36:2 (1985), pp. 86–95. Ian Stewart, 'Teacher careers and the early Catholic schools of Edinburgh', *Innes Review*, 46:1 (1995), pp. 52–66.
65 Francis J. O'Hagan, *The Contribution of the Religious Orders to Education in Glasgow during the Period 1847–1918* (Lewiston, NY, Edwin Mellen Press, 2006) and O'Hagan, *Change, Challenge and Achievement: A Study of the Development of Catholic Education in Glasgow in the Nineteenth and Twentieth Centuries* (Glasgow, St Andrew's College, 1996).
66 Francis J. O'Hagan and Robert A. Davis, 'Forging the compact of church and state

in the development of Catholic education in late nineteenth-century Scotland', *Innes Review*, 58:1 (2007), pp. 72-94.
67 S. Karly Kehoe, 'Nursing the mission: the Franciscan Sisters of the Immaculate Conception and the Sisters of Mercy in Glasgow, 1847-1866', *Innes Review*, 56:1 (2005), pp. 46-60. Kehoe, 'The Venerable Margaret Sinclair: an examination of the cause of Edinburgh's twentieth-century factory girl', *Feminist Theology*, 16 (2008), pp. 169-83.
68 Jo Ann Kay McNamara, *Sisters in Arms: Catholic Nuns through Two Millennia* (Cambridge, MA, Harvard University Press, 1996), pp. 584 and 588.
69 Carol K. Coburn and Martha Smith, *Spirited Lives: How Nuns Shaped Catholic Culture and American Life, 1836-1920* (Chapel Hill, University of North Carolina Press, 1999), p. 87.
70 Susan O'Brien, 'French nuns', p. 159 and 'Lay sisters and good mothers: working-class women in English convents, 1840-1910', in W. J. Sheils and Diana Wood (eds), *Women in the Church* (Oxford, Basil Blackwell, 1990), pp. 453-5.

1
Scotland's Catholic Church before emancipation

For much of the period between the Reformation and the nineteenth century, Catholicism existed on the periphery of Scottish society, its survival fraught with uncertainty in an atmosphere of institutionalised anti-Catholicism and extreme poverty. The Scottish Mission, a term used to describe the Catholic Church in Scotland between 1603 and 1878, when it had no formal governing hierarchy, had been thrown into complete disarray by the Reformation. Those who remained Catholics went underground, keeping their religious convictions quiet in an attempt to avoid imprisonment, exile or the confiscation of their property. Penal legislation, designed to wipe out Catholicism completely by prohibiting Catholics from entering into the professions, holding public office, voting or purchasing land, had been severe and was implemented across Britain during the seventeenth century. After the parliamentary union in 1707 when Protestant succession was secured, but more towards the end of the eighteenth century, these laws were beginning to be relaxed. Increasingly confident in their security and desperate for a place in Scottish society, church leaders and a number of recusant aristocrats began pressing for greater toleration and increased freedoms. Yet they were wary of the Irish who, after the 1798 rebellion, were migrating to Scotland in increasing numbers and were considered a serious threat to the native tradition of 'quiet Catholicism'.[1] As outlined in the introduction, this is a study concerned with examining the role played by women religious in the re-creation and modernisation of Catholicism in nineteenth-century Scotland. However, to understand the context of their recruitment, a brief examination of the historical background of the Scottish Catholic Mission must first be provided.

This chapter begins with an outline of the state of Catholicism in Scotland during the seventeenth and eighteenth centuries, a period when persecution, priest shortages and incessant financial hardship plagued church development. It highlights the cultural tension that was at play between an indigenous Scots clergy and many of the Irish missionaries who, through their common language and shared customs, had formed strong and definitive connections with pockets of faithful in the remote Highlands. It reveals that as the eighteenth century progressed and the 'Jacobite threat' subsided after 1760, the church began to stabilise and establish roots outside of its traditional strongholds in the western Highlands and in the north-east. Building upon this foundation, the second section examines the evolution of Catholic relief, the process of repealing the legislation that imposed numerous civil disabilities and restrictions upon Catholics and dissenters, between 1779 and 1829. What starts to emerge are ideas about the impact that Catholic relief had on the shaping of relations between the Scots clergy, particularly those in and around Glasgow, and the Irish migrants. This section also concentrates on the cultural antagonism and personal antipathy that would evolve into what was arguably *the* definitive force in nineteenth-century church development. Impressions of the Irish as racially, culturally and religiously inferior fed clerical anxiety and convinced many of the need to transform the migrants into respectable, loyal and obedient Scottish citizens and British subjects because they were undermining the Catholic position in Scotland.

The Scottish Mission in the seventeenth and eighteenth centuries

Catholicism in Scotland had been all but wiped out by the Reformation, but what did survive existed mainly in the western Highlands. Although the process of reformation was protracted and really only reached a 'popular' level in the 1620s,[2] the Catholic Church in the Lowlands had been reduced to a shadow of its former self. The vast majority of the nobility, the aristocracy and a number of priests and monks embraced the reformed church. For example, the canons regular, who were priests living monastic lives, made a greater contribution to the spread of Protestantism than to Catholicism.[3] Edinburgh, for instance, which had once operated as a 'centre of distinct Catholic piety' was transformed into a 'stronghold of "precise" Protestantism'.[4] The fate of Catholicism appeared sealed when James Beaton, the last bishop of the ancient hierarchy, died in exile in Paris in 1603, the same year that the crowns of England and Scotland were united under James VI and I. It was at this point that Scotland became a mission territory.

In the early seventeenth century only a handful of missionary priests worked in the Highlands. The majority were Irish Franciscans and Vincentians (regulars) whose tendency to operate as 'freelance evangelists' had the effect of thwarting organisation, despite the appointment of a Prefect Apostolic in 1653.[5] In the century following the Reformation an acute shortage of missionary clergy ensured that Catholicism in Scotland remained weak, disorganised and vulnerable. The isolation of the Western Isles facilitated its continuation there, but elsewhere it was much reduced, with pockets of faithful surviving in places like the Enzie in Banffshire in the north-east and Kirkcudbrightshire in the south-west. Actual churches were sparse, with a smattering in the Western Isles, but across the country most had been destroyed, forcing masses to be conducted privately in cottages or outside in the open air; some of the Catholic aristocracy, however, employed private chaplains. Although most disguised their Catholicism by attending Protestant worship, a number declined to do so and frustrated ministers with excuses and stalling tactics. Aristocratic women have been credited as the most successful deviants because they were less likely to be fined or have their property confiscated for failing to attend kirk services. The obstinacy of some, like Lady Kinnairdy, who simply refused to abandon 'poperie' confounded ministers who tried in vain to convince her to alter her beliefs.[6] After the Reformation many Catholics simply converted and this apostasy was difficult to avert because of limited resources, a consequence of a failure by the Scots Colleges still operating in Paris, Rome, Madrid and Douai to return clergy to Scotland. By 1627 the Jesuits controlled all but Scots College, Paris and had creamed off many of the brightest prospects by emphasising the security and companionship that membership to their order could offer. In addition, the Continent's more favourable climate tempted others to remain rather than face the harsh reality of life as an isolated, impoverished and persecuted secular priest in the Scottish Highlands.[7] This shortage of indigenous priests meant that the Highlands were dominated by Irish regulars, whose Gaelic language skills afforded them a special connection with the people there. The 'old faith' could not have survived without them, but antagonism between the Irish and Scottish clerics was intense and was characterised by the embedded belief that Scotland would never be 'well-served' until it had its own clergy.[8]

While the regulars, those clergy who were members of a religious order like the Franciscans, tended to dominate Catholicism in the Highlands, the notes of John Geddes, an ecumenist who served as Coadjutor Vicar Apostolic of Lowlands from 1780 until his death in 1799, indicate that seculars were more prominent in the Lowlands.[9] Of the roughly forty-three secular priests identified as having worked in Scotland during the seventeenth century, the vast majority served in the Lowland region.[10] Although this number might appear high, the clerical presence was patchy at best, with many priests constantly on the move between Scotland, Paris, London and Rome and with others simply sojourning on the Continent for extended periods of time.[11] Women religious, having been driven out at the Reformation, remained entirely absent, their attire and forced enclosure making them too conspicuous for Scotland's anti-

Catholic climate. In addition, deaths and apostasies among the male religious were not infrequent, nor were imprisonments and banishments. The fear of capture contributed greatly to the frequency of movement between Scotland and the Continent, and one unfortunate priest, Alexander Burnett, failed to return to Scotland after his post-ordination capture, presumably in England in 1671. He died not long after his subsequent banishment to France. Even Scotland's first Vicar Apostolic, Thomas Nicholson, was consecrated abroad after having fled to Paris in 1689, though he eventually returned to Scotland in 1697.[12]

The consecration of a Vicar Apostolic in 1695 was an important development, but one that yielded no immediate remedy to the mission's inherent disorganisation. The division of the mission into the Highland and Lowland districts in 1732 attempted to better accommodate the regions' cultural and linguistic differences, which in many ways served only to exacerbate existing friction and alienate the Highlands. During this same year two seminaries were established, the Scalan Seminary at Glenlivet (1732–99) and the Highland Seminary, whose continued financial crises forced its closure, relocation and re-opening no fewer than six times between 1732 and 1803.[13] Overall, these developments were indicative of a more concerted effort by Rome to impose ecclesiastical order, but they also reveal the growing strength of the secular clergy, who wished to expand their influence and cultivate an indigenous priesthood that would do away with regulars. Instability, resulting from incessant poverty, persecution, apostasy and an overall shortage of priests, would continue to plague the mission. As the influence of the secular clergy expanded, the regulars were gradually phased out. This shift in power was aided by Rome's suppression of the Jesuits in 1773 and by the growing perception that the Irish regulars were unfit missionaries. The Jesuits were a tenacious order of men founded by Ignatius Loyola in 1540 whose zealous missionary activity had led to an assumption of unfettered influence.[14] While the extent to which an ethnic rivalry persisted between the Irish and the Scottish missionaries in the early modern period is unclear, it is believed that the Scottish secular clergy were the main protagonists. The Scottish Mission's reliance on religious personnel from Ireland would continue throughout the nineteenth century, incorporating Irish sisters and nuns, but as will be shown in Chapter 3, this was accompanied by similar discontent. The tension that characterised relations between the Irish and Scots Catholics had a definitive impact upon the development of both Catholicism and national identity in Scotland, and although this point will be explored more fully below and in the following chapters, these antagonisms became enshrined as part of the memory and imagining of Scottish Catholicism, so much so that when Irish migrants began arriving en masse after 1800 antipathy towards them was already well established.

For their part, the eighteenth-century Scots seculars proved equally divided, as lingering character clashes and petty jealousies boiled over into serious incidents, such as those connected with the Jansenist controversy, which was heightened in Scotland between 1730 and 1760. Jansenism, which is notoriously difficult to define, was a persistent and controversial element in Catholic theology for much of the early modern era. Its followers subscribed to the doctrines of Cornelius Jansen, a seventeenth-century Dutch theologian whose writings, which endorsed predestination and called for church reform, were influenced largely by those of the fourth-century saint, Augustine. Repeated condemnation from Rome on account of its obvious similarity to Calvinism caused deep concern, especially in Scotland, which was renowned for Calvinistic celebrity. Allegations of Jansenist activity in Scotland surfaced in the 1730s and 1740s and caused considerable tension but, unlike on the Continent, there was more concern over financial issues than doctrinal ones.[15] A scarcity of resources spurred two young priests, Colin Campbell and John Tyrie, both of whom were active Jacobites, to allege Jansenist plotting in Scotland. Campbell believed that the anti-Highland attitudes of a number of prominent clerics at Scots College in Paris (where the bulk of the mission's money was kept) had led to the region and its priests being inadequately supported, but he also had a bone to pick with those who had passed him over for a more senior position in the Lowland District.[16] Jansenist influences and sympathies did indeed exist in Scotland, fed from France, but these were neither pervasive nor theological.[17] Nevertheless, the seriousness of Campbell's allegations and the fact that a number of its principals were known supporters, saw the Scots College in Paris implicated as a Jansenist conspirator and led to its being reduced from a seminary to little more than an affluent establishment for the sons of Scottish nobles and, according to some, a 'hotbed of Jacobite plotting'.[18] While Rome itself did not form any concrete opinions about the connection between Jansenism and the Scottish Mission, irreparable damage had been done, and in 1740 James Gordon, Vicar Apostolic of the Lowland District, accused those involved as having placed a 'dangerous stumbling block in the way of weak and ignorant people'.[19]

In addition to these controversies, priest shortage and a lack of funds remained the over-arching problems and in the Highland District, for example, the number of priests averaged around ten until 1768, rising to twenty by 1780, but never exceeding twenty-four before 1828. A number of factors were in collusion to keep the number of active priests low, including the fact that many, at any given time, were abroad or serving as private chaplains to wealthy households. In addition to old age, illness, poverty and scandal, Jacobitism also endangered the availability of priests. Before it was emasculated and re-imagined as a symbol of romantic Scotland, government action and anti-Catholic propagandists like Edinburgh's Presbyterian Society ensured that most Scots saw little difference between Jacobitism and Catholicism.[20] Not all priests were Jacobites, but a significant number were involved either as active participants or as sympathetic supporters.[21] One known participant was James Carnegie, who had been present at Edinburgh at the beginning of the '15 before fleeing to France, and whose charitable biographer described him as 'the very soul of the struggle for the restoration of the Stuarts'.[22] In the 1745–46 rising it is known that at least seven priests were involved as rebels, including the aforementioned Colin Campbell, a convert who died at Culloden, and John Tyrie, an Aberdeenshire native who after a 'scandalous life abjured the Catholick faith' to become an Orkney minister. There was also Allan Macdonald, originally from Uist, and George Gordon, who was among the first priests to be ordained in Scotland at Scalan.[23] In addition to these men there was Angus MacGillis from the Hebrides, who had been trained at Scots College, Rome, James Leslie, another native of Aberdeenshire, and Hugh MacDonald, the 'Jacobite vicar apostolic of the Highland District'.[24] Notwithstanding the deaths and injuries suffered during the rebellion, arrests, imprisonments and the banishment of priests like Alexander Forester, George Duncan and James Grant in the post-rebellion crackdown further reduced the number of active clergy.[25]

Inevitably, the perpetual lack of priests and religious personnel in the form of monks and nuns translated into religious drifting. Isolated communities with infrequent priestly visits did not develop the same formal religious customs as those areas receiving more regular contact, but rather maintained or adopted traditions that suited local needs.[26] What developed on the isles of Barra and Eigg, for example, was a sort of hybridised religiosity that incorporated pagan and Christian elements. This was common in the western Highlands and Islands, where religious rituals often incorporated supernatural elements informed by fairy belief. Circular processions around chapels, standing stones and enchanted wells allowed people to pay homage to saints such as St Christopher, St Katherine and St Barr (Finbar). In the case of St Barr, who was particularly revered, the locals of Barra had placed a linen-clad wooden statue of the patron on the chapel altar.[27] Catholicity at this time was localised since a unified Rome-centred, European Catholic culture did not really exist before the mid-nineteenth century and so customs such as these provided alternative explanations of the world to those who had little or no contact (perhaps on purpose) with church officials. The pervasion of these beliefs confounded countless missionaries who sought to root out local tradition, folk and fairy belief. One English tourist travelling through the region at the turn of the nineteenth century declared that the locals remained 'much addicted to a kind of sorcery and charming'.[28] The persistence of supernatural belief complemented the many magical elements, such as miracles and transubstantiation (the process by which the bread and wine becomes the body and blood of Christ), that were inherent in Catholicism.

Catholic relief

Up to 1800 Catholicism in Scotland had made minimal progress, growing slowly from an underground church with an estimated population of 14,000 in the early 1680s to somewhere in the region of 30,000 by the turn of the century. Despite this growth, Catholics represented a mere fraction of the nation's 1.6 million people.[29] The highest concentration was in the Highland District, where unofficial enumerators placed the number of adherents just below 13,000.[30] Slow growth characterised the Lowland District, where roughly 2,000 Catholics in the 1680s rose to approximately 6,000 by 1780 with the sharpest rise occurring in Aberdeenshire and Banffshire.[31] In Glasgow and Dundee, the towns that would come to define urban, industrial Scotland, the Catholic population was virtually invisible before the nineteenth century. In Dundee there were only thirty Catholics in 1786 and a list for Glasgow for that year noted just fifteen known Catholics and 'some other poor persons' who could be identified as such.[32] In terms of population, Scotland's Catholics represented an insignificant entity, but culturally they had a definitive impact upon society. Anti-Catholicism was a pervasive element in the national consciousness and was as much a consequence of Presbyterianism's divisions and increasing vulnerability as it was of Scotland's changing self-image thanks to empire and industrial enterprise.

The fear of a return to 'popery' was a ubiquitous social concern throughout the eighteenth century, and between 1714 and 1747 a range of reports were compiled by Church of Scotland ministers to show that Catholic baptisms, confirmations and marriages were being regularly performed in the Highlands by priests who 'swarm[ed] like locusts'.[33] The perception that 'popery' was growing rapidly on account of the Jesuits, intermarriage, language barriers, the lack of penal law enforcement and the paucity, poverty and frequent infirmity of Church of Scotland ministers was widespread.[34] While conversions to Catholicism were certainly sought and sometimes achieved,[35] the perception of an 'infesting clergy' and the belief that all non-juring Episcopalians and Catholics were seditious Jacobite menaces whose treachery put the British monarchy, constitution and empire at risk was a blatant exaggeration.[36] One pamphlet, *An antidote against the infectious contagion of popery and tyranny*, alleged that Jacobitism was a 'war for Antichrist and his Members' (i.e. the Pope and Catholics),[37] and can be classed as 'Presbyterian political paranoia' that did nothing but expose a deeper vulnerability.[38] Although installed as a 'pillar of the British constitution', the Church of Scotland did nothing but irritate those Anglicans intent on maintaining a social hierarchy. Efforts to re-invent itself as a 'civil religion' committed to the 'political and social establishment'[39] were hampered by the growing dissatisfaction with union and by the dissent that festered over the issue of patronage that had pitted those committed to the 'doctrine of the Church as the body of Christ' against those who favoured establishment.[40] Dissent, contrasting theological interpretations, the evolving needs of empire and an emerging class consciousness meant that by the 1770s anti-Catholic hostility in Scotland was still strong.

In her book *Britons*, Linda Colley subscribes to the belief that Protestantism was *the* glue that bound the people together. She argues that underneath the linguistic, cultural and geographic differences was an 'uncompromising Protestantism ... [upon] which their state was explicitly and unapologetically based'.[41] As the eighteenth century progressed, however, the realities of empire began to dictate a new direction, one that would, in principle, see Catholics incorporated more fully into the fabric of British citizenry. Confronted with the urgent need to appease a potentially subversive colonial population in Quebec and to access the untapped reserve of Highland and Irish Catholic soldiers in a climate of international conflict, government officials had become convinced at the necessity of Catholic relief; the 'covert enlistment' of Catholics had been happening well before the relief acts officially permitted this.[42] A definitive link between Catholic relief, concerns over internal security and the 'material considerations' (the need for additional troops) associated with the American war has been established by Robert Kent Donovan, but it is important to bear in mind that because the needs of government did not correspond with public opinion, Catholic relief was a protracted, rather than an instantaneous process.[43] The political management of eighteenth-century Scotland, first by the Argylls and then by the Dundases, had enabled Scotland to be consolidated as a keen partner in the British Empire, while remaining socially and culturally remote. The lack of direct governance from Westminster facilitated the development of local alternatives, namely the introduction of local sheriffs, and the further empowerment of Church of Scotland parishes to oversee poor relief, education and general societal morality. What resulted was an enhanced and fiercely guarded Presbyterian identity whose hegemony could never be realistically challenged by Catholicism – despite the widespread fear to the

Figure 1.1. Bishop George Hay, etching, undated. Reproduced by permission of the Scottish Catholic Archives, Edinburgh.

contrary. A movement towards Catholic relief was thus viewed as an abuse by increasingly south-bound elites whose disaffection with Scottish society had alienated them from the grassroots and their deeply valued Presbyterianism. Decadence and Catholicism were, to many Scots, frighteningly similar and posed a very real threat to Scotland's progressive economic transformation. And while some historians may cringe at the thought of it, such perceptions were as much about a collective psychology as they were about religion, politics and economics. Protestantism, it is argued, gave the majority of Britons 'a sense of their place in history and a sense of worth' at the crucial point when momentum was needed to carry forth industry and support a burgeoning empire.[44]

Negotiations for Catholic relief occurred in Scotland when Sir John Dalrymple, an ambitious Edinburgh lawyer and kinsman of the Lord Advocate, Henry Dundas, and George Hay, Vicar Apostolic of the Lowland District, discussed relief in exchange for soldiers. Tellingly, when the first Relief Act was introduced on 25 May 1778 it applied only to England and Ireland; parallel relief legislation was not secured for Scotland until 1793.[45] The ubiquity of anti-Catholic prejudice was one reason for its delay north of the border, but the sympathy many Scots had for the plight of their Calvinist co-religionists in America had fostered a sort of Protestant solidarity. When relief became a reality for England and Ireland in 1778, two tenacious and well-organised groups, the Committee for the Protestant Interest and the Protestant Association, emerged in Scotland to inflame antagonism. They launched petitions calling for the repeal of relief in England and Ireland and succeeded in drawing support from all but one of the Church of Scotland synods. Only Lothian and Tweeddale, led by William Robertson, an influential moderate and Principal of Edinburgh University, refused its support.[46] Their employment of direct action and an expertly executed propaganda campaign involving all forms of available media, from pamphlets and broadsides to public pronouncements and caricatures, resulted in the widespread public opposition to Catholic relief in Scotland. One of the more intriguing examples of their propaganda was a 1779 illustration entitled *Sawney's Defence against the Beast Whore Pope and Devil* (Figure 1.2).[47]

Teeming with evocative imagery, this plate is a good example of apocalyptic rhetoric in Scotland and shows the degree to which American millennialism was influencing Scottish religious and political thought. While Britons tended to equate themselves and their country with Israel,[48] during the 1770s a condemnation of Britain's imperial policies saw American millennialists demonise rather than sanctify the mother country. American anger over the 1765 Stamp Act, which introduced sweeping taxes on most legal, financial and administrative documents and printed media,[49] had instituted a 'symbolic association between British policy and the Devil', but the Quebec Act of 1774 caused deeper resentment and led to American patriots accusing the British government of being in cahoots with Rome.[50] In *Sawney's Defence* the River Tweed's

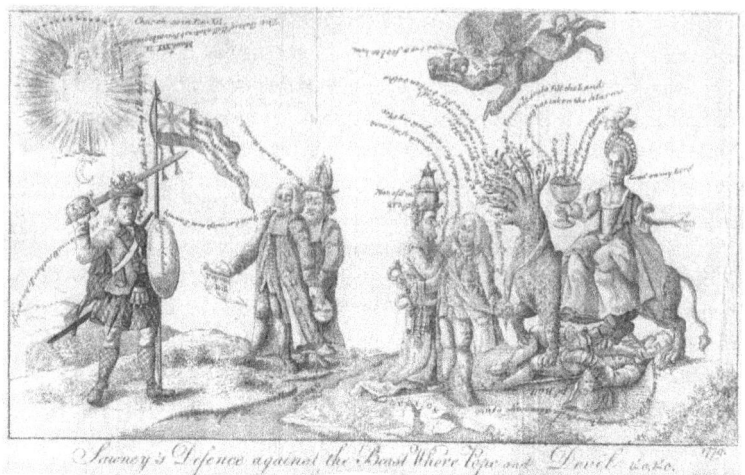

Figure 1.2. *Sawney's Defence against the Beast, Whore, Pope and Devil,* 1779. Reproduced by permission of the Scottish Catholic Archives, Edinburgh.

exaggerated proportions symbolised a growing divide between England and Scotland. England is depicted as a nation where union crumbles, where the 'mad' King George III falls prey to 'popery' and where the handcuffed John Bull is trampled by the Book of Revelation's seven-headed beast. Conversely, the tartan-clad Sawney Scot, the Scottish equivalent of John Bull, appears as the heroic defender of union with his raised sword pointing towards a flag into which the words 'see Articles of Union Claim of Right & Protestant Succession' have been stitched. Usually the brunt of ridicule and contempt 'by many English xenophobes', Sawney Scot is re-imagined here as a noble and dignified figure and is a useful example of the complexities of Anglo-Scottish relations and the impact this had upon Scotland's self-image.[51] By emphasising Protestantism, loyalty, valour, bravery and equality, this illustration brings into sharp focus the fundamental elements of Scotland's developing national consciousness. This illustration, and material like it, had a marked influence on public opinion, a point alluded to in William Robertson's scathing speech to the General Assembly in which he vehemently denied acting as a 'pensioner of the pope, as an agent of Rome [and] as a seducer of [his] brethren to Popery'.[52]

In the winter of 1779 public paranoia erupted into the mass rioting in Edinburgh and Glasgow that would precipitate London's Gordon Riots.[53] For four days in early February Edinburgh was absorbed in chaos and on 9 February the agitation spread to Glasgow, where it lasted for a couple of days before burning out.[54] In a published narrative, Bishop George Hay castigated Edinburgh town officials for failing to offer Catholics adequate protection from the 'mob' as it ravaged businesses, homes and a makeshift chapel. An anonymous respondent accused the Catholic population of bringing the rioting upon itself by having 'grown into confidence from the long indulgence with which they had been treated'.[55] Hay responded by stressing the loyalty of the Catholic population and by asserting that France's position had weakened because of the Catholic relief granted in England and Ireland.[56] This exchange stands as proof of the Catholic leadership's growing confidence in the belief that they were entitled to engage in an open debate about their civil liberties. Times were changing, but Catholicism would remain a sensitive issue for some time, as Hay himself acknowledged when comparing the two nations: England, he said, had demonstrated 'liberal sentiments', whereas Scotland had remained 'unhappy' and 'fanatical'.[57]

A growing class consciousness was beginning to fuse with politics and religion and this would set the tone for how the church operated amidst mass Irish migration during the nineteenth century. The leaders of the Committee for the Protestant Interest, for example, had been criticised for possessing 'neither Rank, nor Learning nor Authority',[58] and yet they had succeeded in preventing Catholic relief legislation for Scotland in 1779. The perception that anti-Catholicism was integral to lower- and working-class identity, the groups most adversely affected in periods of economic booms and busts, is useful because it helps to explain why the Irish were problematised in the nineteenth century.[59] Anti-Catholicism was not rooted purely in economics: there were also fundamental theological and cultural pretexts. Most Scots believed that Presbyterianism had ushered in a new era of imperial growth and economic prosperity, whereas Ireland and the Irish, predominantly Catholic, were poor, backward and ignorant. The re-imagining of the Scottish past as one of Protestant triumph over 'popery' would galvanise the 'downtrodden proletariat' that was emerging as a result of Scotland's, but especially Glasgow's, rapid industrialisation.[60] All of this would, as will be shown, come to impact fundamentally upon how Catholicism in Scotland would develop.

Presbyterian hegemony thus remained an intrinsic element in the developing national consciousness, but the French Revolution forced a dramatic shift in opinion, one that was less acerbic towards Catholics. European Catholicism experienced a revival after 1789 and Scotland was intimately connected with this since works like MacPherson's *Ossian* had served to renew an interest in origins, the feminine and the romantic.[61] The events in France were shocking and their wide publicity helped to reassert the authority of the aristocracy as the main instruments of Catholic influence. In France, the seizure of church property, the suppression of the religious orders, the banishment of secular clergy unwilling to swear an oath of allegiance to the state, and the termination of 'all papal jurisdiction'[62] had left Catholicism battered and bruised, and the effects on the Scottish Mission were particularly devastating since the bulk of its investments had been arranged in France by senior clerics at Scots College, Paris, and were therefore lost. Its Continental properties, including the colleges at Paris, Douai, Rome and Valladolid, had been seized and vast sections of its archives, which included documents like the original memoirs of James VII and II, were stolen, lost or destroyed.[63] In 1793 when Britain declared war on France and extended Catholic relief to Scotland, guaranteeing freedom of worship and property rights, it was not met with the same degree of opposition displayed in 1779.[64] The Highlanders had proven masterful soldiers and were even incorporated into the fabric of a united national image, as an early nineteenth-century chapbook entitled *Sawney and Bonaparte, a dialogue* reveals. The figure of Sawney Scot was once more invoked as Britain's protector and warned Napoleon of Highland retribution should French troops set foot in Britain. Although it is not known who commissioned it, there is the possibility that it was the printer himself, Charles Randall of Stirling, who specialised in printing chapbooks and whose father had been a surgeon in the field during the '45.[65] The passage reads:

> There's no man in a' Scotland, but would fight to the last drop o' his blood for the Land o' Cakes and I m sure I m right, when I say the same for England. We hae a King we love, and a country we love; an' you'll speak o' hurting our King, and taking our country! I wonder what hads me frae kicking you.[66]

Collective assertions like this were welcomed by a Catholic leadership whose growing confidence was helping them to capitalise upon the situation and agitate more publicly for emancipation and social integration. Conscious of the support Catholics provided to Britain during a period of intense warfare, the clergy, led by the tenacious Vicar Apostolic, George Hay, engaged actively in debates for the extension of relief by publishing pastoral addresses, pamphlets and, later, open letters to the people of Britain. Such public validations of themselves and their followers as defenders of king and country established a sturdy platform from which to declare their right to participate, as equals, in Scottish and British society. While acting primarily as directives for Catholics, the pastoral letters contained frequent references to the church's stance on issues of a political nature, suggesting that they were also meant for a wider audience. Publishing was too expensive for the production of vast quantities of material promoting the Catholic interest, so this was the only type of public forum available through which the official church position on matters of national importance could be spread. The pastoral letters written during the Napoleonic wars tended to emphasise loyalty and always included biblical references endorsing deference to 'kings, and for all that are in Authority' and obedience to the country's laws.[67] They also reassured Catholics that the required Oath of Allegiance did not 'in the smallest degree' jeopardise their religious principles, since it was actually a demonstration of their obedience to God. While it is difficult to determine how far these directives influenced public opinion, it is clear that the clergy were keen to remind their followers that anti-Catholicism would not be easily extinguished:

> You know the unfavourable circumstances in which we have hitherto been: You know the mistaken notions that many, through ignorance, may still retain for us ... You ought therefore to consider it as a duty we owe both to our religion and to ourselves, to be extremely cautious not to give the least cause of offence to anyone, but by a modest, quiet, and peaceable behaviour to convince the world that we are not undeserving of the favour bestowed upon us.[68]

The unobtrusive and conservative catholicity that the Scots clergy were trying to establish came under threat when, in 1798, rebellion erupted in Ireland. Almost immediately the Catholic leadership, with limited resources and minimal organisation, embarked upon an aggressive campaign to prevent subversion and to reassert their commitment to the British state while distancing themselves from events across the water. The British Vicars Apostolic branded the Irish radicals 'emissaries of impiety and rebellion' and chastised them for attempting to corrupt a population who had held 'firm and steady' in an atmosphere of catastrophic European crisis.[69] Such statements were, of course, made by members of a class that was becoming increasingly wary of the lower orders' growing political awareness and militancy. A growing disillusionment with agriculture and land tenure, religion, rapid industrialisation and ineffective political management had created an appetite for Irish and Continental radical influences that set Scotland apart from the wider British experience.[70] These differences were reflected in many of its reform-oriented groups such as the Scottish Friends of the People and the United Irishmen. Although sharing many similar social and ideological principles, including the desire to provide 'political solutions' to what they saw as 'political problems', they differed on the issue of Catholic emancipation. The latter accepted its necessity but the former did not. Disappointing to many leading priests, radical activity in Scotland included a number of Catholics keen on the principles of reform, and so discerning how Catholic radicalism fitted into the wider movement, and how it was represented and expressed will shed light on the broader relationship between Catholicism and the Scottish nation.[71]

Irish Catholic involvement in Scottish radicalism occurred from the early nineteenth century in issues such as reform, trade unionism and temperance (there were almost 40,000 Irish pledges by 1844).[72] Not only was such involvement indicative of their organisational skills and their ability to operate outwith church control, undermining somewhat the appraisal of the Irish as a 'hindrance to native radicalism', but this involvement enabled the Irish to become integrated with activities that cut across religious lines and national boundaries.[73] After 1800, as momentum for reform gathered strength and the populations of centres like Glasgow started to engage more fully with radicalism as a means to an end, the Scots clergy found it difficult to convince Catholics, particularly those of Irish origin, of the necessity of abstaining from political radicalism.[74] The fact that the previous relief acts had been passed in relatively quick succession had convinced the church's leaders that if they could continue to prove themselves worthy, the loyalty and support they had shown during times of crisis would be rewarded by their liberation from the periphery. The parliamentary union with Ireland in 1801 was not to be accompanied by Catholic emancipation, despite the resignation of two prime ministers over King George III's stubborn refusal to budge. Initially Britain's bishops regarded the King's obstinacy as impermanent, a temporary setback, but they grew increasingly frustrated as time passed and he remained unmoved. A perusal of the pastoral addresses shows this shift. In 1803 one praised Catholics for their service during the first phase of the war and requested that people pray for the preservation of the constitution so that 'united efforts' would bring 'a glorious and lasting peace'.[75] In addition, all priests in Scotland were instructed by their bishops to ensure that everyone, publicly and privately, recite the Prayer for the King.[76] Ten years later the tone had soured and, presenting an address penned by William Gibson, the Vicar Apostolic of England's Northern District, the Scots bishops endorsed its message of obedience, loyalty and 'attachment to the Civil Constitution',[77] but also its emphasis on the necessity of liberating Britain's Catholics 'from the many penalties and disabilities which they undeservedly suffer'.[78]

As time passed and full emancipation did not materialise, the Irish were increasingly vilified as rabble-rousers whose social, cultural, racial and religious inferiority was undermining the Catholic position in Scotland. Crucially, the debate over emancipation had, by this time, grown more critical as Daniel O'Connell, an astute Irish Catholic lawyer on the cusp of infamy, became involved in the push for legislation that would, if passed, see the authority of the church leadership significantly reduced. In 1813 his negotiation of a Relief Bill that proposed to make ecclesiastical appointments subject to state approval pushed the clergy to take a more 'radical stance' than they would have preferred.[79] Perceiving their authority to be under threat, the English and Scottish bishops expressed their fervent opposition against O'Connell and his concessions:

> The spiritual powers with which the Supreme Pastor, the Bishops and other Ministers of the Catholic Church, are invested, are held by them, for the benefit of their flocks. If then we are anxious to preserve to the Catholic Church the free appointment of the Ministers of Religion, it is not from a spirit of being independent of the State in civil matters, but from our solicitude to provide Pastors, according to the institution of Christ...[80]

Desperate to keep politics under the sole remit of the national bishops, Scotland's Vicars Apostolic cooperated with their English counterparts by sharing pastoral letters, statements and open letters. They developed a pan-British support network and demonstrated a preparedness to mobilise when it appeared that their spiritual authority was at risk. On the one hand their reaction was characteristic of the growing debate over the division of church and state and fears of increased secularisation, but on the other it was a clear indication of their opposition to lay dictates. While threatening the 'severest ecclesiastical censures' against 'subordinate Pastors' speaking out against the government, the 1813 address also established the Scots bishops' particular aversion to the activities of Daniel O'Connell and those Irish priests in Scotland who actively supported him.[81] Tensions flared again in 1823 when the Glasgow Catholic Association was founded to support O'Connell's emancipation campaign. Vehemently opposed to Irish political radicalism and concerned about the threat this might pose to the support they had been receiving from influential Protestants, Andrew Scott and John Murdoch, two of Glasgow's leading clerics, went on the offensive and viciously attacked the Association.[82] This did not build bridges, but some suggest that this reaction was necessary to pacify Glasgow's civic authorities who feared O'Connell's symbolic importance as a champion of reform.

Opposition to emancipation was strongest in Glasgow, a city whose famous cemetery, the Necropolis, still bears a poignant emblem. The towering whinstone Knox Monument, conspicuously positioned overlooking Glasgow Cathedral, was constructed as a symbol of Presbyterianism's triumph over 'popery'. Amidst Daniel O'Connell's growing influence and in response to the 1825 Emancipation Bill that was defeated by the House of Lords, subscriptions were taken by the Rev. Dr Stevenson MacGill, Professor of Theology at the University of Glasgow, for a monument to honour the father of Scotland's Reformation. On 22 September 1825 an estimated crowd of 10,000 gathered for the laying of the foundation stone and were treated to sermons, speeches and prayers. Dr John Burns, minister for Barony Parish, prayed for parliament to remember the 'Rights, the Liberties, and the Religion' of Scotland and urged people to be vigilant against a return to the 'dominion of ignorance, superstition and tyranny', while MacGill stressed the importance of 'well-regulated freedom', a rather interesting contradiction.[83] Those representing the city's business interests, such as James Ewing, the highly influential evangelical West Indies merchant, went so far as to attribute Scotland's commercial prosperity, enlightened clergy and industrious artisans to Knox's courageous attack against the 'errors and impostures of popery'.[84] The Catholic clerics paid close attention to these outbursts and worked diligently to dispel anti-Catholic myths and anxieties. In 1826, for example, Alexander Cameron and Alexander Paterson, the Vicar Apostolic and his Coadjutor Bishop of Scotland's Lowland District, and Ranald MacDonald, Vicar Apostolic of the Highland District, together with their English counterparts, issued a joint declaration addressing the main claims made against Catholicism. Exasperated by the lack of progress, but not disheartened, they responded to criticisms centring on the adoration of Mary, confession, idolatry, the Mass and transubstantiation. They questioned the legitimacy of denying Catholics civil rights on religious grounds when, in their opinion, the civil or social realms were separate concerns. What is more, they countered that because emancipation had not been granted, the so-called tradition of 'liberty of thought' in Britain was an illusion.[85] By the mid-1820s emancipation for Catholics had become a matter of entitlement rather than privilege.

In 1829, the year emancipation was finally granted, public opinion was still largely opposed, and there was significant regional variation. The strongest and most sustained opposition came from the west, the region in and around Glasgow, where the levels of Irish migration had been highest and the effects of industrialisation had been the most striking. The *Glasgow Courier* and the *Glasgow Herald*, both Tory soapboxes, had linked the Bill to the 'Irish Papists' and actively encouraged petitions against it,[86] and although it is difficult to discern how many anti-emancipation petitions were sent from Glasgow, there were an estimated 245 sent from Scotland.[87] Nevertheless, the degree to which anti-Irish sentiments were at play has been questioned by some scholars, who propose a 'native tradition of resistance to Catholicism', what it represented to them and how it had defined them.[88] Evangelical ministers emphasised the threat such a measure posed to the Revolution Settlement, the parliamentary union and the Protestant establishment, and strenuously argued that obedience to the Pope automatically disabled the Catholics' ability to be truly loyal to Britain.[89] None of this entirely explains the marked regional variation in Scotland and it cannot be suggested that people in the east were any less

'Protestant' than those in the west. Class must therefore be considered a key factor. A study of reactions to emancipation in Scotland reveals that the vast majority of petitioners were from the lower classes, particularly those belonging to the industrial workforce of the urban cities, those who would have felt the impact of cheap Irish labour most acutely. In 1829 *The Scotsman* reported that many of the more 'enlightened' people of Edinburgh were appalled at the anti-emancipation petitions being sent to London, since the majority of the signatories were those 'utterly incapable of understanding the nature or bearings, or vital importance of the question'.[90] Yet dismissing these petitions as lower-class rumblings undermines their significance as evidence of social distress and discontent, since notwithstanding the duplicate and illegible signatures and those added by women and children, these petitions represented one of the few options available to this class for recorded political participation. In Glasgow, where there was intense industrialisation and the largest concentration of Irish labourers, the mood was decidedly anti-emancipation, whereas in Edinburgh it was a different situation. In fact, it was there that the single largest show of support in favour of emancipation took place, on 14 March 1829. In the city's Assembly Rooms, a crowd of roughly 2,000 gathered to hear speeches endorsing emancipation, and the speakers included the distinguished orator Thomas Chalmers.[91] He justified his support for emancipation by asserting his progressive Protestantism, stating plainly that his stance was not 'pro-Catholic', but that he was committed to the extension of Protestantism:

> [G]ive the Catholics of Ireland their emancipation; give them a seat in the parliament of their country; give them a free and equal participation in the politics of the realm; give them a place at the right ear of majesty, and a voice in his councils; and give me the circulation of the Bible, and with this mighty engine I will overthrow the tyranny of the Anti-Christ, and establish the fair and original form of Christianity on its ruins.[92]

To Chalmers and others like Sir James W. Moncrieff, an evangelical and leading proponent of reform, Protestantism's growth depended upon Catholic emancipation because only then would its adherents be free to see 'the light of truth . . . the power of reason'.[93] *The Scotsman*, a long-standing advocate of '*unqualified* religious liberty', praised the meeting as perhaps 'the most numerous and respectable meeting ever held under one roof in Scotland'.[94] On 10 April 1829 the Catholic Relief Bill passed through the House of Lords and it received royal assent on 13 April. While the majority of Scots were still not keen on the idea of emancipation, much of the violent aggression witnessed in previous years gave way to more liberal sentiments, particularly in the east, where the Irish were not as numerous. After 1829 Catholics in Scotland entered a new phase, officially declared equals under the law and entitled to the same rights and privileges as their Protestant brethren. On the other hand, the continued stream of Irish migrants, thought by many Lowland Scots to be causing the 'deterioration of the Scottish race',[95] would not permit an easy integration. The culture of the migrants was considered an impediment to Catholicism in Scotland and many of the bishops feared that the taint of 'Irishness' would not only reduce their status, but thwart their ability to participate as equals in Scottish society. Looking at it from this perspective, the 'isolate and alienate' approach many adopted towards the Irish in their district was simply a means of self-preservation. The campaigns of Daniel O'Connell, who exerted a tremendous influence upon Irish Catholics in the west of Scotland, and the Scottish reaction testify to the intensity of the anti-Irish and anti-Catholic animosity. A good example would be his 1835 tour, which drew a crowd of some 200,000 to Glasgow Green. Apart from *The Scotsman*, whose writers declared bigotry to be Scotland's 'master-failing' and asserted that O'Connell's visit represented the strong commitment to toleration and change, much of the published and associational reaction was negative.[96] The *Glasgow Courier*, for instance, warned that his safety could not be guaranteed in 'this Protestant and Covenanting city . . . [where] the ancient spirit of the land is not yet dead'.[97] The 'Great Protestant Meetings' that took place at Glasgow's Hope-Street Gaelic Church afford further proof, and although these meetings were staged to oppose the political activities of O'Connell, they often incorporated a more general condemnation of the Irish and Catholicism. Invoking covenanting rhetoric, J. C. Colquhoun, a Dunbartonshire Episcopalian MP strongly opposed to the disestablishment of the Church of Ireland, accused Irish priests of bullying helpless peasants into political agitation.[98] Another speaker argued passionately against Catholicism's destructive influence:

> Popery! Lies at the bottom of all Erin's woes and all Erin's wretchedness . . . what a striking contrast does the province of Ulster present when compared with that of Connaught! In Ulster where Protestantism preponderates, there is wealth, comfort, peace, freedom, knowledge, enlightened and real loyalty. In Connaught, where Popery preponderates, there is penury, misery, slavery. Barbarism and dissatisfaction.[99]

He thundered that these were the reasons why Daniel O'Connell was not welcome in 'this Protestant city – to this city of our fathers, which bore so much and braved so much for the faith which he now tramples upon – to their city, where the spirit of the Covenanters was so strong, where the arm of the Covenanters so firm'.[100] It was opinions like these that coloured how the Irish in Scotland were perceived. They fertilised cultural antagonism and enabled it to flourish in the heaving urban centres. Acutely aware of this, the Scots clergy hoped in vain that the Irish were simply a passing phase, labouring sojourners who would soon move on to richer pastures. Of course this did not happen.

By the turn of the nineteenth century, Catholics in Scotland were a small minority existing on the fringes of a society experiencing significant industrial and demographic change. Throughout the previous two centuries, the Catholic Church had lacked the organisation, financial resources and personnel needed to facilitate growth, and the Highlands suffered especial neglect. Irish migration had forced a reappraisal of Catholic identity in Scotland. The ethnic tension that would ensue between the Irish and Scottish Catholics would become the key factor shaping church development in the nineteenth century and, as we shall see, was closely linked to the broader issue of Scottish identity in Britain. The desire driving many of the old recusants and the leading Catholic clergy was, like the majority of Lowland Scots at this time, couched in the need to be regarded as British *and* Scottish. Scotland had been transformed by union and its access to empire had instigated unprecedented industrial growth and commercial prosperity. This translated into a new-found confidence in both its ability to cooperate as an effective imperial partner and to defend a Britishness that was predicated upon Protestantism and 'racial patriotisms'. Alongside this progressive Protestantism the indigenous Catholic population were eager to participate in the imagined British identity. The following chapter expands upon this theme, delving deeper into how the Catholic Church in Scotland worked to integrate itself more fully with Scottish and British society.

Notes

1 SCA SM15/2/7. Pastoral Letter, 12 July 1793.
2 Michael Lynch, 'Preaching to the converted? Perspectives on the Scottish Reformation', in A. A. MacDonald, Michael Lynch and Ian B. Cowan (eds), *The Renaissance in Scotland* (Leiden, E. J. Brill, 1994), pp. 301–43.
3 Mark Dilworth, 'Canons regular and the Reformation', in MacDonald et al. (eds), *The Renaissance in Scotland*, p. 182.
4 Lynch, 'Preaching to the converted?', p. 322.
5 Fiona MacDonald, *Missions to the Gaels: Reformation and Counter-Reformation in Ulster and the Highlands and Islands of Scotland, 1560–1760* (Edinburgh, John Donald, 2006), p. 232. A prefect apostolic was under the direct jurisdiction of the Pope and appointed to manage the Church in a mission territory.
6 Alasdair B. Roberts, 'The role of women in Scottish Catholic survival', in *Scottish Historical Review*, 70:190 (1991), p. 137.

7 MacDonald, *Missions to the Gaels*, p. 140. The Mission Oath was introduced in 1625 in an effort to move more priests into Scotland. Students who were maintained by mission funds had to promise that after their studies had finished, they would work as a secular priest in Scotland for a period of at least three years.

8 *Ibid.*, pp. 164, 176 and 225–6. Louis Innes, Principal of Scots College, Paris, wrote this in 1695.

9 Matthew Kilburn, 'Geddes, John (1735–1799)', *Oxford Dictionary of National Biography*, Oxford University Press, 2004. www.oxforddnb.com/view/article/10489 [accessed 9 August 2006].

10 These numbers are based on Geddes's notes.

11 SCA SM14/5. John Geddes's handwritten, hard-covered notebook entitled 'A catalogue of the Missionaries of the Secular Clergy in Scotland from the year 1653, when they first formed into a regular Body until the present year 1767'. According to this notebook, no fewer than fourteen did so.

12 *Ibid.* A vicar apostolic is a titular bishop who enjoys episcopal authority and has the power to ordain clergy. He is under the immediate jurisdiction of the Pope.

13 Roderick MacDonald, 'Bishop Scott and the West Highlands', *Innes Review*, 17:2 (1966), p. 116. Christine Johnson, *Developments in the Roman Catholic Church in Scotland, 1789–1829* (Edinburgh, John Donald, 1983), pp. 71–8. The seminaries were located at: Loch Morar (1732–38); Guidal, Arisaig (1738–46, abandoned between 1746 and 1768; Glenfinnan, Loch Shiel (1768–70); Bourblach, northwest corner of Loch Morar (1770–74 and 1776–79); Samalaman, Moidart (1783–1803); Lismore, Loch Linnhe (1803–23).

14 MacDonald, *Missions to the Gaels*, ch. 6. A handful of ex-Jesuits returned to Scotland and became seculars. The congregation was only fully restored by Pope Pius VII in 1814.

15 William Doyle, *Jansenism: Catholic Resistance to Authority from the Reformation to the French Revolution* (London, Macmillan, 2000), p. 2. J. F. McMillan, 'The root of all evil? Money and the Scottish Catholic Mission in the eighteenth century', in W. J. Sheils and Diana Wood (eds), *The Church and Wealth* (Oxford, Basil Blackwell, 1987), p. 274.

16 McMillan, 'The root of all evil?', p. 275.

17 Gallicanism was dominant in France and can be roughly explained as acknowledging the authority of the state, as opposed to the Pope, over the Catholic Church as it operated in a specific country.

18 Peter F. Anson, *Underground Catholicism in Scotland, 1622–1878* (Montrose, Standard Press, 1970), pp. 128–42.

19 SCA SM15/1/3. Pastoral Letter from Bishop James Gordon, Vicar Apostolic, 9 December 1740.

20 SCA. *An antidote against the infectious contagion of popery and tyranny*. Presbyterian Society in Edinburgh, 1745.

21 SCA SM14/5. Geddes, *Catalogue of the Missionaries of the Secular Clergy*. He

recorded the whereabouts of nine individuals in 1715 and it is known that four of them went to France, suggesting a desire to avoid capture.
22 William Clapperton, *Memoirs of Scotch Missionary Priests compiled from original letters, formerly preserved at Preshome, now at Blairs College* (Elgin, 1901), vol. 2, Part II (nos 45–9), pp. 1160–1288.
23 SCA SM14/5. Geddes, *Catalogue of the Missionaries of the Secular Clergy*. John Tyrie 'went along with the Highland Army to Culloden, & was there wounded'; Colin Campbell was at Culloden and 'was never heard from since' and was assumed to have been killed there; Allan MacDonald was with the army in England and then at Culloden. He was then imprisoned and banished; George Gordon is listed simply as having been 'involved at Culloden'.
24 Kilburn, 'Geddes, John', *ODNB*; F. Forbes and W. J. Anderson, 'Clergy lists of the Highland district, 1732–1828', *Innes Review*, 17:2 (1966), pp. 133–41.
25 Forbes and Anderson, 'Clergy lists', p. 141.
26 MacDonald, *Missions to the Gaels*, p. 170.
27 Martin Martin, *A Description of the Western Isles of Scotland*, reprinted (Edinburgh, J. Thin, 1976), pp. 92–9 and 277. Presumably Catherine of Alexandria, fourth century – although not mentioned as having a cult in Scotland, she was popular in England and was commemorated in stained glass windows at Oxford's Scottish college, Balliol. David Farmer, *Oxford Dictionary of Saints*, 5th edition (Oxford, Oxford University Press, 2004), pp. 95–6.
28 Lizanne Henderson and E. J. Cowan, *Scottish Fairy Belief: A History* (East Linton, Tuckwell Press, 2001), p. 27.
29 Neil Tranter, 'Demography', in Anthony Cooke et al. (eds), *Modern Scottish History: 1707 to the Present*, vol. 1: *Transformation of Scotland, 1707–1850* (East Linton, Tuckwell Press, 1998), p. 112.
30 Anson, *Underground Catholicism*, pp. 153–5.
31 *Ibid.*, pp. 151–2.
32 Alexander MacWilliam, 'Catholic Dundee: 1787 to 1836', *Innes Review*, 18:2 (1967), p. 75. William James Anderson, 'The autobiographical notes of Bishop John Geddes', *Innes Review*, 18:1 (1967), pp. 39, 56–7.
33 Noel MacDonald Wilby, 'The "Encreasce of Popery" in the Highlands, 1714–1747', *Innes Review*, 17:2 (1966), p. 93.
34 *Ibid.*, pp. 91–115. Reiterated throughout.
35 Forbes and Anderson, 'Clergy lists', pp. 133 and 143. In the eighteenth century, these included at least three priests: Colin Campbell of Lochnell, Angus MacDonald of Dallely and John MacDondald of Lochaber. The vicinity of Lochaber was highlighted as having had many conversions.
36 Colin Kidd, 'Constructing a civil religion: Scots Presbyterians and the eighteenth-century British state', in James Kirk (ed.), *The Scottish Churches and the Union Parliament, 1707–1999* (Edinburgh, Scottish Church History Society, 2001), p. 17.
37 SCA. *An antidote against the infectious contagion of popery and tyranny*, p. 10.

38 Wilby, 'The "Encreasce of Popery"', pp. 94–5 and 97 and MacDonald, *Missions to the Gaels*, p. 240.
39 Kidd, 'Constructing a civil religion', pp. 1 and 5.
40 John R. McIntosh, *Church and Theology in Enlightenment Scotland: The Popular Party, 1740–1800* (East Linton, Tuckwell Press, 1998), p. 100. Patronage was reintroduced in 1712, but was largely ignored until the 1730s.
41 Linda Colley, *Britons: Forging the Nation, 1707–1837*, 2nd edition (London, Pimlico, 2003), p. 18.
42 Thomas Bartlett, 'Ireland, Empire and Union, 1690–1801', in Kevin Kenny (ed.), *Ireland and the British Empire* (Oxford, Oxford University Press, 2004), p. 74.
43 Robert Kent Donovan, 'The military origins of the Roman Catholic Relief programme of 1778', *The Historical Journal*, 28:1 (1985), pp. 82 and 90. Donovoan, 'Sir John Dalrymple and the origins of Roman Catholic Relief', *Recusant History*, 17:2 (1984), pp. 188–96. Colley, *Britons*, p. 325.
44 Colley, *Britons*, p. 53.
45 Donovan, 'Sir John Dalrymple', pp. 188, 191–2. Scotland required separate legislation since the penal laws had been enacted before the parliamentary union in 1707. Nicholas Phillipson, 'Dalrymple, Sir John, of Cousland, fourth baronet (1726–1810)', *Oxford Dictionary of National Biography*, Oxford University Press, 2004. www.oxforddnb.com/view/article/7055 [accessed 26 March 2007].
46 Eugene Charlton Black, 'The tumultuous petitioners: the Protestant Association in Scotland', *Review of Politics*, 25:2 (1963), pp. 187–8, 191–2.
47 SCA SM4/47/1. *Sawney's Defence against the Beast Whore Pope and Devil*.
48 Colley, *Britons*, p. 31.
49 The Stamp Act was an effort to offset the war debt that had accrued between 1756 and 1763, but colonial outrage saw it repealed in 1766. http://avalon.law.yale.edu/18th_century/stamp_act_1765.asp [viewed 20 March 2007].
50 Ruth Bloch, *Visionary Republic: Millennial Themes in American Thought, 1756–1800* (Cambridge, Cambridge University Press, 1988), pp. 55–60. Passed on 16 August 1774, the Quebec Act permitted Catholics in Quebec the 'free exercise of their religion', thereby safeguarding Britain's interests in what would become Canada. Bernard Donoughue, *British Politics and the American Revolution: The Path to War, 1773–75* (London, Macmillan, 1964), pp. 105–26.
51 *Sawney's Defence*. Often depicted as vermin-like, impoverished and brutish. Christopher A. Whatley, *Scots and the Union* (Edinburgh, Edinburgh University Press, 2006), p. 1. Tamara L. Hunt refers to the plate as a rare example of a caricature of John Bull, identified as such before the 1790s: *Defining John Bull: Political Caricature and National Identity in Late Georgian England* (Aldershot, Ashgate, 2003), p. 146.
52 Black, 'The tumultuous petitioners', pp. 192–3.
53 Lord George Gordon (1751–93), born in London, died in Newgate prison. Interestingly, despite not voting against the first Roman Catholic Relief Bill for England in 1778, the 'unbalanced [and] irresponsible' Etonian became

an aggressive, 'obsessed' opponent, heading up the Protestant Association in England. Colin Haydon, 'Gordon, Lord George (1751–1793)'. *Oxford Dictionary of National Biography*, Oxford University Press, 2004 www.oxforddnb.com/view/article/11040 [accessed 4 March 2007].
54 Black, 'The tumultuous petitioners', pp. 194–5.
55 *A Narrative of the late riots at Edinburgh; and a vindication of its magistracy against the charges advanced in the memorial for the papists of Scotland* (London, 1779). Author unknown.
56 *Roman Catholic fidelity to Protestants ascertained or, an answer to Mr. W. A. D's letter to G. H. In which the conduct of government, in mitigating the penal laws against papists is justified*, 2nd edition (London, 1779). Sold by C. Elliot, Edinburgh.
57 George Hay, *A memorial to the public, in behalf of the Roman Catholics of Edinburgh and Glasgow; containing an account of the late riot against them on the second and following days of February, 1779*, 2nd edition (London, 1779).
58 Hay, *A memorial to the public*.
59 Colley, *Britons*, p. 332.
60 Michael Fry, 'Politics', in Cooke et al. (eds), *Modern Scottish History*, vol. 1, p. 58.
61 Bernard Aspinwall, 'Some aspects of Scotland and the Catholic revival in the early nineteenth century', *Innes Review*, 26 (1975), pp. 2–19.
62 Johnson, *Developments*, p. 91.
63 *Ibid.*, pp. 91–9.
64 *Ibid.*, p. 31.
65 National Library of Scotland. www.nls.uk/catalogues/resources/sbti/rae_reynolds.html [accessed 11 October 2007].
66 *Sawney and Bonaparte, a dialogue*. Printed in Stirling, 1807.
67 SCA SM15/2/7. Pastoral Letter, 12 July 1793.
68 *Ibid.*
69 SCA SM15/2/13. Pastoral Letter, 1798. SM15/2/14. Pastoral Letter, 7 May 1798.
70 Elaine MacFarland, *Ireland and Scotland in the Age of Revolution: Planting the Green Bough* (Edinburgh, Edinburgh University Press, 1994), p. viii.
71 *Ibid.* She notes, p. 69, that the radical connections between Ulster and the Scots Presbyterians are also largely unexplored.
72 Bernard Aspinwall, 'A long journey: the Irish in Scotland', in Patrick O'Sullivan (ed.), *The Irish World Wide: History, Heritage, Identity*, Volume 5: *Religion and Identity* (Leicester, Leicester University Press, 1996), p. 167.
73 John F. McCaffrey, 'Irish immigrants and radical movements in the west of Scotland in the early nineteenth century', *Innes Review*, 39:1 (1988), pp. 52–3.
74 SCA SM15/2/13. Pastoral Letter, 1798.
75 SCA SM15/3/2. Pastoral Address by George Hay, John Chisholm and Alexander Cameron, 1803.
76 *Ibid.*

77 SCA SM15/3/15. Pastoral Address by George Hay, John Chisholm and Alexander Cameron, 1813.
78 Ibid.
79 R. V. Comerford, 'O'Connell, Daniel (1775–1847)', *Oxford Dictionary of National Biography*, Oxford University Press, 2004. www.oxforddnb.com/view/article/20501 [accessed 23 April 2007].
80 SCA SM15/3/15. Pastoral Address, 1813.
81 Ibid.
82 Martin Mitchell, *The Irish in the West of Scotland, 1797–1848: Trade Unions, Strikes and Political Movements* (Edinburgh, John Donald, 1998).
83 *Account of Ceremonial, &c. at Laying the Foundation Stone of Knox's Monument, in the Merchant's Park* (Glasgow: Khull, Blackie, and Co., 1825), pp. 10 and 15.
84 Ibid., pp. 16–18. Other prominent participants included Thomas Chalmers, Henry Monteith, MP and James Cleland, Glasgow statistician.
85 *Declaration of the Catholic Bishops, the Vicars Apostolic and their coadjutors in Great Britain* (London, Keating and Brown, 1826), p. 6.
86 Ian A. Muirhead, 'Catholic Emancipation: Scottish reactions in 1829', *Innes Review*, 24:1 (1973), pp. 26–7. Stewart J. Brown, *Thomas Chalmers and the Godly Commonwealth in Scotland* (Oxford, Oxford University Press, 1982), p. 186. Begun by the Edinburgh printer, John Mennons, the *Glasgow Advertiser* was first published in 1783 and in 1802 changed its name to the *Glasgow Herald*. Irene Maver, *Glasgow* (Edinburgh, Edinburgh University Press, 2000), p. 32.
87 Muirhead, 'Catholic Emancipation', p. 30.
88 Colley, *Britons*, pp. 329–30.
89 Ian A. Muirhead, 'Catholic Emancipation in Scotland: the debate and aftermath', *Innes Review*, 24:1 (1973), pp. 104–6.
90 *The Scotsman*, 18 March 1829.
91 Brown, *Thomas Chalmers*, p. 188.
92 *Report (taken from the Caledonian Mercury) of the speeches of Sir James W. Moncrieff, Bart. Dean of Faculty, Dr. Chalmers, and other distinguished individuals at the meeting held at the Assembly Rooms on Saturday the 14th March 1820, in order to petition parliament for the removal of the disabilities affecting the Roman Catholics.*
93 Ibid.
94 *The Scotsman*, 9 July 1825, 7 February 1829 and 18 March 1829.
95 Colin Kidd, 'Race, Empire and the limits of nineteenth-century Scottish nationhood', *The Historical Journal*, 46:4 (2003), p. 884.
96 *The Scotsman*, 19 and 23 September 1835.
97 McCaffrey, 'Irish immigrants', pp. 49–50. Quoted in Mitchell, *The Irish*, p. 167.
98 J. C. Colquhoun, 'Great Protestant Meeting held at Hope-Street Gaelic Church, Glasgow, on Thursday, September 17th, 1835', in Mortimer O'Sullivan (ed.), *Romanism as it Rules in Ireland: A Full and Authentic Report of the meetings held in various parts of England and Scotland in which the Theology secretly taught, the commentary on the Bible clandestinely circulated, the law of the Papal States surreptitiously*

set up to govern Ireland, and the secret Diocesan Statutes of the Province of Leinster have been... detected and exposed, etc., vols 1 and 2 (London, R. B. Seeley, 1840), p. 292.
99 Nathaniel Patterson, 'Great Protestant Meeting held at Hope-Street Gaelic Church, Glasgow, on Tuesday, October 6th, 1835', in O'Sullivan, *Romanism*, p. 392.
100 Colquhoun, 'Great Protestant Meeting', p. 292.

2

Reinventing strategies: coping with change

As the previous chapter demonstrated, the tiny collections of Catholics that survived the Reformation relied upon their own initiative and secrecy to keep their church alive. Minimal support from Rome had allowed regional and national traditions to ferment, and this translated into a heterogeneous and disjointed catholicity. In 1827 the ecclesiastical boundaries of the old Highland and Lowland Districts were reorganised into the Eastern, Western and Northern Districts in an effort to improve church administration and to better accommodate the cultural and regional variation that had become more pronounced. Redrawing these boundaries enabled the three new Vicars Apostolic, those titular bishops appointed as delegates of Rome in lieu of an official church hierarchy, the freedom to manage their missions independently. This was particularly useful since needs in the east differed widely from those in the west, and the rural north, historically the epicentre of Scottish Catholicism, was fading into the background as the urban populations began to dominate. As a consequence of this structural change and in light of increasing levels of Irish migration, the period between 1830 and 1860 saw increased church development in Scotland's two main centres, Edinburgh and Glasgow.

This chapter will show how developments such as Catholic emancipation, reform, and the rise of evangelicalism and liberalism forced Catholic authorities and the state to reconsider Catholicism's position within society. This reappraisal would result in a complete transformation of the church's existing infrastructure and change the way in which it absorbed the influence of ultramontanism. Bourgeois enthusiasm was the driving force behind this new direction and the interests of the middle and upper classes would dictate church direction. The construction of an institutional infrastructure, the provision of new churches, schools, confraternities and clubs were vital, but equally important was the provision of an extended social welfare network that included poor relief, medical services (formal and informal), orphanages and employment training. The creation of these support networks, which were limited at first, was accomplished through the cooperative effort of male and female religious personnel and a committed and increasingly influential laity. Catholics embarked upon a campaign of religious voluntarism that mirrored the activities of their Presbyterian counterparts and established the roots of a social welfare network that would emphasise a commitment to the poor and guard Catholics against Protestant proselytism.[1] The moral agency of women was a key part of the process since it was believed that the transformation of society would be achieved by and through them. The period between 1830 and 1860 witnessed the gendering of church development as more and more women got involved with the active mission. This cooperative effort would translate into the reinvigorated Christian spirit that was necessary to uphold the authority of the church as it worked to integrate itself into the fabric of Scottish and British citizenry. Catholic authorities in Edinburgh turned out to be the most proactive and their efforts were not immediately matched by those in Glasgow, a consequence of the deeper problems plaguing the Western District.

When considering how the church operated in Scotland during the nineteenth century, it is important to recognise that for most of this period the Catholic community was in a state of flux and largely unsure of its own identity. Being 'neither purely Scottish nor purely Irish', the church was plagued by three competing agendas until the end of the 1870s.[2] Recusant elements, cocooned in isolated pockets, were averse to any kind of change and so adopted an isolationist stance in the hopes of guarding *their* church against outside interference. Between 1810 and 1843, John Menzies of Pitfodels, a wealthy recusant, had used much of his personal fortune to fund the Scottish mission and, driven by his contempt for the 'Irish demagogues', he worked to strengthen the native tradition and even gave over his massive estate at Blairs in Aberdeenshire for the creation of a seminary, the only one to exist in Scotland between 1829 and 1874.[3] The Irish, whose numbers had grown significantly since 1800, comprised the bulk of the Catholic population by 1850. It is estimated that in 1851 the number of Irish-born in Glasgow and Edinburgh was 59,801 (18.2 per cent) and 12,514 (6.5 per cent) respectively and that by 1871 the number in Glasgow had increased to 68,330 (14.3 per cent), whereas in Edinburgh the number had decreased to 8,031 (3.3 per cent). In Scotland as a whole, the number of Irish in 1851 was approximately 207,000 and 208,000 a decade later.[4] These figures do not count the children of the Irish migrants, nor do they reveal the number of Catholics, and there is no way to ascertain a precise figure, but scholars tend to assume that Catholics represented roughly three-quarters of the total Irish population.[5] Widely regarded as sojourning labourers, they were marginalised by the indigenous Catholics and were problematised as religious and political subversives. Many of the Irish felt that their needs were not being met and so began to press for a greater say in church affairs but they were consistently prevented from attaining positions of authority. Finally, there were the ultramontanes, who wanted a complete transformation of Catholicism in Scotland. This group would become more powerful as the century progressed and its strongest proponents were the wealthy middle- and upper-class converts who had been captivated by the Catholic revival. As newcomers to the church, indeed some recusants would call them outsiders, they had little or no understanding of Catholicism's historic experience or of the internal wrangling that had marred its post-Reformation existence. Detached from the cultural friction that dominated relations between the Irish and Scottish Catholics, ultramontanes were intent on creating a 'cohesive community' that was firmly committed to Britain and to a Roman-dominated church. In this respect, the campaign to restructure Catholic identity was not dissimilar to the campaign launched a century earlier by the Scottish kirk when it faced the daunting task of establishing itself as part of the newly created British state. It worked to reconstruct itself as a 'civil religion', one committed to the monarchy, hierarchy and social order.[6] This was a parallel to the situation for the Catholic Church in the nineteenth century as it struggled to gain acceptance in Scotland.

A new class of Catholics

Between 1830 and 1860 Catholicism experienced slow but steady growth. The legislative reforms introduced during the late 1820s and early 1830s, specifically Catholic emancipation and the first Reform Act, were important factors in helping to reduce anti-Catholic prejudice, though they did not, by any means, eradicate it. They lifted many of the remaining practical restrictions that had been imposed upon Catholics since the seventeenth century and made it legal for elected Catholics to take their seats in parliament. It was the election of Daniel O'Connell as an MP for County Clare in an 1829 by-election that effectively forced through this legislation. The Act made special reference to Scotland and repealed the old legislation that had been passed by William III in 1698. More generally the 1829 Act provided Catholics with the opportunity to hold civil and military offices.[7] The political enfranchisement of Catholics helped to focus more attention on the broader issue of reform despite the fact that regular calls for this had been happening since the last quarter of the eighteenth century. Support for change was strong in Scotland and in 1831 a demonstration at Glasgow Green attracted a crowd of approximately 80,000, though the majority of those in attendance would not benefit from the 1832 Reform Act, which only increased the electorate from 500,000 to approximately 800,000.[8] Nevertheless, all of this was a glaring sign of changing times and of the growing power of the middle classes.

Alongside legislative reform, social and moral improvement also topped the bourgeois agenda, and a key factor influencing church development in Scotland was what was happening in Europe. The rise of liberalism, an ideology that emphasised personal freedom, complemented the middle-class drive to create a more respectable, prosperous and moralistic society. Scholars suggest that regardless of religious denomination the middle classes across Europe tended to 'behave alike' and shared many of the same values and fears.[9] During the nineteenth century Scottish identity was re-invented as a testament to both liberalism and an enthusiastic imperialism. The principal protagonists were the bourgeoisie, whose growing political enfranchisement, philanthropic drive and 'committed Christianity' gave rise to a civil society that cemented Scottish autonomy in Britain and reaffirmed the dominance of Presbyterianism.[10] What is rarely appreciated in the Scottish context is that middle- and upper-class Catholics were mirroring the activities of their Protestant brethren in an effort to claim a role as active participants in the campaign for social and moral change. Initially, this liberalism could be accommodated by ultramontanism, but after 1850 it became increasingly difficult. It must be emphasised, however, that without liberalism, the rise of ultramontanism would have been impossible. Ultramontanism incorporated liberalism in as far as it worked to establish the machinery that was necessary to provide increased freedoms for Catholics that allowed them the liberty to construct and implement Catholic institutions. Once these were in place liberalism became nothing more than a competing ideology. The church infrastructure that liberalism helped to build effectively served to reassert the social hierarchy under the ultimate authority of the Pope. A scholar writing in the 1950s observed that while liberals were generally opposed to Romanticism, their rejection of the 'cold intellectualism of eighteenth-century reason' often meant that they adopted a romantic outlook. The liberalism of this group was conservative and was often criticised as a 'selfish creed' advocated by those who were really only interested in freedom for themselves.[11] This characterises exactly how the Scottish Catholic bourgeoisie, specifically the converts, operated. They, like their non-Catholic counterparts, believed that the improvement of society was paramount, but they were quick to oppose anything that would jeopardise their privileged position. They poured money into the foundation of churches, schools and convents and established Catholic societies based on European models in the hope that they would foster an allegiance to the church that would supersede national prejudices, particularly where the Irish were concerned. Considering the overwhelming cultural friction that existed between the Irish and Scottish Catholics, it is clear that the aim of the ultramontanes was to re-imagine the identity of Catholicism in Scotland so as to complement their own sympathies and preferences. First and foremost this group was *British* and so their loyalties to Rome had to be accommodated within that context. One of the most influential figures was Robert Monteith, the Oxbridge-educated director of the Caledonian Railway Company who is generously described by one scholar as the 'architect of modern Catholic social thought'.[12] Not only do his writings reveal a desire for 'patriotism and ultramontanism' but they show a man whose romantic and revivalist notion of Catholicism necessitated the re-invention of tradition:

> We shall have something independent alike of O'Connell and Lord Shrewsbery – and something to unite the poor cotton spinner of Glasgow with the chief and clansman of the north. We shall have a little Catholic government and parliament in the land without the folly of squabbling factions.[13]

Patrician interest in Catholicism had been reignited by the Catholic revival that swept across Europe from the end of the eighteenth century. The egregious events of the French Revolution had serious consequences for the elites, and many, still licking their wounds, sought refuge in an imagined past. The Old Church provided solace, as did events such as the 'discovery' of the Gaelic epic of Ossian, the hero son of Fionn Mac Cumhaill, an ancient Celtic warrior. Ironically, the epic was a fake, the invention of the well-educated Highland writer, James MacPherson. Nevertheless, it characterised an era where an interest in the Gothic spiralled and mystical places like Fingal's Cave on the tiny isle of Staffa, off the north-east coast of Iona, the sacred seat of St Columba, became a focal point for bourgeois Catholics across Europe.[14] Those who attached themselves to this ancient and unreal past were simply harnessing a means of reasserting the importance of a social hierarchy.[15] Individuals like Robert Monteith, who lived in a neo-Gothic mansion, and James Augustine Stothert, the 'distinguished' Edinburgh and Cambridge-educated poet-cum-priest (albeit temporarily), were just two of the many who had got caught up in the tail end of this frenzy. Their money and influence meant that they were able to indulge their own enthusiasm and wield tremendous influence over Catholicism in the process.[16] Monteith and Stothert were in the company of other influential figures such as J. R. Hope-Scott, the passionate supporter of the Jesuits and grandson-in-law of the poet and novelist Sir Walter Scott, and later James Grant, the romantic author who also happened to be Scott's second cousin. Grant is a particularly intriguing figure on account of his ideas about Scottish nationalism. He was joint-secretary of Scotland's pioneer unionist-nationalist organisation, the National Association for the Vindication of Scottish Rights, when it existed between 1853 and 1856.[17]

The relationship between Scottish nationalism and convert Catholicism is an area in desperate need of research, since the conversion of men like Grant suggests that the construction of modern Catholicism was more intimately connected with the imagining of Scottish nationhood than previously assumed. Catholicism existed on the fringes of society throughout the early modern period, and in this respect can be seen to parallel the Scottish position within Britain, and it is clear that from the 1830s this arrangement was no longer suitable for either. What must be discerned is how these converts to Catholicism defined their own identities and how far this influenced, or was influenced by, the construction of a Scottish national identity. There were important connections between what was happening to Catholic identity in Scotland and what was occurring south of the border. In England the Oxford Movement had forced a reappraisal of Catholic tradition within the Church of England and had subsequently sparked a number of high-profile conversions between 1840 and 1860. Men such as Henry Edward Manning, described as a 'fanatical convert' and 'ultramontane protagonist', and John Henry Newman would become aggressive modernisers in the Catholic Church in Britain and, for their efforts, they would be appointed cardinals, the highest ecclesiastical position under that of the Pope.[18] The Oxford Movement's blend of medieval romanticism and theology meant that a type of 'religious nationalist pride' had emerged which helped to bridge the gap between Catholicism and Protestantism. Sectarian tension persisted but theologically and ritually the two were brought closer. The Oxford Movement had a profound impact upon Anglicanism because it called for a deeper investigation of its Catholic connections and through this it was able to promote itself as the 'upholder of the historic Christian tradition of the British people'.[19]

In terms of Catholic Church development and transformation, the overall agenda was conservative and unionist and was strongly endorsed by individuals like Monteith who were unflinching in their loyalty to Britain and its empire. The majority of recusant Catholics, including Menzies of Pitfodels and the leading clergy in the Western District, shared these opinions and a general antipathy towards issues that threatened Britain's stability such as Ireland's incessant political crises and its repeated calls for Home Rule. The ultramontane enthusiasm to transform the character of Catholicism was an attempt to draw a line between the Catholic Church in Scotland and Ireland. This was no easy feat and Mary Hickman notes that the co-opting of anti-Catholic and anti-Irish sentiment served a range of political interests including the established Church of England's desire to prevent undenominational schooling, a point that will be discussed in greater detail in the fourth chapter.[20] Ultramontane enthusiasm also extended beyond this and characterised broader Catholic revivalist sentiments that were nothing short of extravagant, such as the activities of John Patrick Crichton-Stuart, the third marquess of Bute. Bute's Presbyterian background was rejected when, after taste-testing a range of religions at Christ Church, Oxford, he converted to Catholicism in 1868. He romanticised and re-invented an ancient past, wrote extensively about the history of Scotland and was so inspired by the Gothic revival that he rebuilt Cardiff Castle in that style.[21] The University of Glasgow's Bute Hall is another testimony to the man's love for all things Gothic. He was an intrepid inventor of tradition and while some of his activities bordered on the ridiculous, it is clear that without the efforts and patronage of individuals like him, the Catholic Church in Scotland would have remained isolated and disorganised. What is more, the upper-class status of many of these individuals, their political connections and their financial resources helped to bring about an increased tolerance of Catholics on some levels. This was aided by their sponsorship of institutions and initiatives designed to bring about the social and moral improvement of the working classes. Their paternalistic attitude was problematic for a number of recusants attached to Scottish Catholicism's insular traditions and for the poor, who resented their 'well-meaning' intrusion.

The rise of voluntarism in urban Scotland

The 1830s, 1840s and early 1850s witnessed an explosion in religious voluntarism. Events such as the Disruption, which was when the evangelical Free Church split away from the established Church of Scotland in May 1843, and the Irish Famine encouraged competition between dissenting groups and denominations.[22] The increasingly strained relationship between the state and the Church of Scotland heightened the anxiety of all church leaders and they were deeply unsettled by the events of May 1843, which seemed to provide clear evidence of the state's unapologetic intrusion into ecclesiastical affairs. Stewart J. Brown's definitive study of Thomas Chalmers emphasises the Disruption as the result of the state's growing authority. Patronage was the key issue: most simply defined, this was the right of a lay patron to select a parish minister with or without the local congregation's approval. This was highly contentious because it challenged the ecclesiastical independence of the church and made it subject to the state's agenda. Further evidence of the state's 'intrusion' was the introduction of the Poor Law (Scotland) Act, which brought poor relief, traditionally the responsibility of the established church, under state control. Not surprisingly, evangelicals were vehemently opposed and did everything in their power to circumvent this intrusion. One of their main objectives, and one that would be mirrored by Catholic authorities, was to get out and work with the people to cultivate a religiosity that was pure and impervious to state interference. The slums provided the perfect opportunity for this missionary enterprise and virtually every sect, apart from insular evangelicals like the Brethren, turned their attention in this direction in an effort to reverse social and moral decay and shore up their own positions. Soup kitchens, orphanages, magdalen homes, dispensaries and ragged schools for street children sprang up in the congested districts of Edinburgh's Cowgate, Canongate and High Street, and in the east end of Glasgow, specifically in Calton and in Bridgeton, towards the west in Anderston and on the south side of the River Clyde in the Gorbals.[23]

Thomas Chalmers, the influential evangelical whose life's goal was to implement a godly commonwealth, and his various grassroots initiatives, such as his St John's experiment in Glasgow which sought to reintroduce the notion of community to urban centres through regular house visits by church elders and deacons, were tremendously influential. A controversial though highly respected public figure, Chalmers had also delivered speeches in favour of emancipation in 1829 that had won him great esteem from many of the country's leading Catholics. However, when he made the mistake of suggesting that Catholics did not 'believe in the divinity of Jesus Christ', he was sharply criticised.[24] Nevertheless, Chalmers's initiatives had a profound impact upon the evolution of Catholicism and his stress on the values of 'thrift, sobriety, self-help and community' resonated with a middle-class liberal Catholic laity who sought widespread reform.[25] His emphasis on self-improvement and individual responsibility struck a particular chord with clerics like the young James Gillis, a Canadian-born priest who would emerge as one of the Eastern District's most influential bishops and who would assume a leading role in the transformation of the Catholic Church in Scotland.

One of the first things Gillis did, though it is unlikely that Chalmers inspired this idea, was to recruit a community of women religious to Edinburgh. When the Ursulines of Jesus, an upper-class French female congregation, arrived in 1834 they inaugurated a new era of church development by reintroducing convent life to Scotland. Crucially, their arrival installed an active female dimension in the Catholic Church and represented a radical departure from everything that Scottish Catholicism had previously known. The establishment of convents enabled the real work of church transformation to begin. In the late 1820s and early 1830s, when the idea of 'active' or apostolic

Figure 2.1. Etching of Bishop James Gillis, undated. Reproduced by permission of the Scottish Catholic Archives, Edinburgh.

communities of women religious was in its infancy, Gillis recognised the potential. His insatiable drive for church expansion was augmented by a desire to transcend national pretensions, which was a reflection of his Anglo-Catholic childhood in Quebec. Having been taught by the Sulpicians, a male order dedicated to preparing young men for the priesthood, Gillis learned the value of women religious. The Sulpicians had recruited the first congregation of nuns, the Daughters of Charity (better known as the Grey Nuns), to Montreal in 1745 and had later helped Elizabeth Ann Bayley Seton, a convert from Episcopalianism, to found the American Sisters in Charity in Maryland in 1809.[26] Gillis's exposure to these intrepid female missionaries acclimatised him to the concept of women religious and convinced him of their necessity in Edinburgh. One of his early patrons, the Jesuit-educated Menzies of Pitfodels, provided the funds necessary to establish the Ursulines in Edinburgh.[27] Such a move was characteristic of Gillis, who courted the indulgent enthusiasm of the elites and who was firmly convinced that the 'reconversion of Scotland' would be achieved through this group. A perusal of Agnes Trail's personal correspondence reveals an impressive array of letters and notes from influential European contacts and is indicative of a missionary drive beyond the capacity of most, but on another level this collection also testifies to the level of influence that the upper classes had.[28] Susan O'Brien, a pioneer researcher of women religious in Britain, makes a number of observations about the issue of class in religious communities that provide a better understanding of the complex social relationships that existed within and between communities. Although convents offered a unique opportunity to 'self-improving women' of the working class, O'Brien explains that they also served to preserve class distinctions, and the most obvious example was the difference between the choir and lay sisters. Dress and basic responsibilities were highly structured and the level of communication permitted between the two classes was also tightly controlled, and in some communities even recreation and meals were taken separately. It was also not uncommon for lay sisters, who were responsible for the domestic chores of the community, to be prohibited from speaking to the choir sisters.[29] Orders and congregations that catered for the needs of upper-class women included the Ursulines of Jesus and the Society of the Sacred Heart, but there were also a number of devotional organisations for girls and young women that fulfilled the same function, for example the Congregation of the Children of Mary, which was dedicated to the 'formation of the spiritual cadre' of young ladies.[30]

Overall, the establishment of Scotland's first post-Reformation convent was a clear signal that the church was changing, but naturally not everyone shared this enthusiasm. Many, including a collection of clerics from the Enzie in Banffshire, who oversaw affairs in the Western District, were less convinced and viewed the decision to introduce women religious to Scotland as rash and premature. This reluctance reveals Catholicism's inherent divisions and reflects, to some extent, the more cautious approach taken by many indigenous Catholics. The incorporation of women religious into the public mission of the church also reveals how certain elements were assimilating ideas about women's potential as missionaries. Any reluctance to recognise the utility and necessity of collective female agency was dismissed by women like Agnes Trail, Scotland's first post-Reformation nun. The daughter of a Church of Scotland minister, Trail had converted to Catholicism in June 1828, joined the Ursulines of Jesus in 1833 and, like many converts, was a zealous missionary who had little time for 'timid Catholics'. She believed that it was the opportune moment to re-introduce convent life to Scotland since she felt that Protestant opposition towards them was in decline.[31] Contemporaries such as Henry Cockburn, the Whig and former Solicitor-General for Scotland, agreed, and he observed in his memoirs that the toleration of Catholics was 'one of the striking changes of [his] time' and that nothing 'shocked some people in Edinburgh, or entertained others, more than the reappearance of a regular Catholic nunnery with its small chambers, its chapel and its Sisters of Charity' (Sisters of Charity became a generic term for all women religious).[32] Neither Trail nor Cockburn, however, experienced life at the working-class level and so neither appreciated the depth of Scottish anti-Catholicism, particularly in the west.

Not only was the arrival of the Ursulines of Jesus in Edinburgh a significant achievement for the Catholic Church in Scotland, but it represented a unique response to Protestant voluntarism. After 1840 Catholic associations and societies began to emerge as a consequence of this developing culture of religious voluntarism. Edinburgh became the hub and it was no coincidence that Scotland's capital, which was also the seat of the General Assembly of the Church of Scotland, witnessed the founding of the first Catholic voluntary organisations. It was easier to initiate these activities there because it had a smaller Catholic population with fewer Irish and because the clergy settled there were more receptive to input from wealthy patrons who envisioned a 'compassionate cohesive order'.[33] According to Simon Gunn, who writes on the public culture of the Victorian middle class, voluntary societies provided a 'distinct urban milieu for middle-class men, and a platform from which a succession of cultural projects were launched, aimed variously at improving, disciplining and reforming' those who might be classed as the 'improvident and immoral poor'.[34] Two of the earliest examples were the Holy Gild of St Joseph, a home-grown friendly society founded in 1843, and the Saint Vincent de Paul Society (SVP), a French organisation brought to the capital in 1845. While both had humanitarian mandates, they were also meant to show that Scotland's Catholics were loyal and respectable citizens committed to building a better society. Another initiative was the Association of St Margaret: its wide purview ranged from orphan care and grants to teachers in training to emigration assistance and the provision of cheap Catholic literature. It was an ultramontane initiative designed to promote Catholic harmony and unity, and it was thought that by offering support in these areas the association would foster an increased loyalty to 'priests and papacy'.[35] Included within the Association's mandate was the development of educational opportunities, and the *Glasgow Free Press* challenged it to bring about more efficiency in the schools so that more might qualify for grants. The newspaper took the position that if Catholics did not start taking care of their own poor, others would, and that Catholics 'now numerous and poor will remain poor and become few indeed'.[36]

Much of the activity going on was in response to the growing number of Irish in Scotland, which acted as an impetus for Catholic and Protestant social reformers. Accounting for a disproportionate percentage of the poor, the Irish inspired the establishment of groups such as the Edinburgh Irish Mission and Protestant Institute. This Free Church initiative was set up to convert Irish Catholics after its fiery evangelical director, James Begg, who also edited *Bulwark*, had become convinced that the city was 'swarming with emissaries of Rome'.[37] His plan was to establish an army of Irish-speaking scripture teachers, visiting agents and pupil-teachers to run day schools, prayer meetings, Protestant inquiry classes and Bible study groups. Crucially, his enthusiasm does more than simply highlight the priority of securing conversions; it reveals deeper insecurities about Presbyterianism in Scotland:

> She establishes hosts of agents in every direction. Unlike Protestant ministers working single-handed, and overborne generally in large cities by innumerable engagements, Popery appoints two, three, and sometimes four priests who require no study to repeat the weekly pantomime of which their service consists, have their whole time devoted to the great work of watching their own adherents and breaking in upon the struggling and unguarded front of weak and divided Protestants.[38]

Although these fears were certainly inflated, it is clear that Catholicism was experiencing solid growth, and the period between 1830 and 1860 saw significant progress made in both cities despite the paucity of financial and human resources. The Catholic Church introduced initiatives that mirrored Protestant ones in terms of access to spiritual guidance, social services and education. Educational reform was deemed crucial to the forging of appropriate social relations and, as Mary Hickman argues, it was intimately tied to the construction of the state.[39] The progress made with education, albeit limited during this period, demonstrates the willingness of Catholic authorities to engage with Scotland's national tradition of education and with the ambitions of the British state. Although this point will be discussed in more depth in the fourth chapter, it is important to highlight the early educational developments as a reflection of the growing influence of voluntarism.

The *Catholic Directory for Scotland* was first published in 1831, and although the volumes contain a number of errors and omissions, they provide invaluable information about church expansion not found elsewhere. According to the 1833 volume, Edinburgh had five resident priests and two chapels, one in the Old Town and another in the New Town. In addition to their responsibilities in the capital, the clergy assigned to Edinburgh made regular trips to the outlying towns of Dunfermline, Kirkliston and Roslin in an attempt to meet the needs of the growing collections of Catholics living there. In the city itself, there were a number of adventure or private schools up and running in the Cowgate, on South Bridge and on Scotland Street. These entrepreneurial initiatives fed upon the middle-class desire for respectability. They were unregulated, denominational and fee-charging, and have been described by one scholar as 'hopelessly inadequate'.[40] More was also being made available to the children of the lower classes, with congregational subscriptions and weekly fees generating enough of an income to support the establishment of poor schools in Blackfriars Wynd, in High Street at the Old Stamp Office, in West Port and in Leith, where the bulk of the Irish migrants were congregating.[41] Fifteen years later, in 1848, the number of priests had risen to ten and there were two permanent chapels, two temporary chapels and a convent. Both St Mary's, Broughton Street, founded in 1814, and St Patrick's in the Cowgate, founded in 1834, offered two masses on Sundays as well as weekday morning masses. The temporary chapels in Leith and in Creighton Moss provided Sunday services and the Ursuline nuns and privileged guests also received a daily mass in the chapel of St Margaret's. The number of schools had grown by this point with new ones having been opened in St Patrick's and on Market Street to serve roughly 200 pupils each, though this is likely to be a high estimate since truancy was endemic.[42] Edinburgh had been the first place in Scotland where Catholic schools opened themselves to government inspection in an effort to qualify for Privy Council grants. In 1849 the first two schools had been registered for the scheme and by 1854 the number had risen to four. The reports indicate that the schools' performance was linked to the class of children, and a number of concerns, such as inadequate schoolrooms and offices and poor playground facilities, were raised for St Catherine's, a poor school on the High Street. Inspectors observed that the poverty and truancy of the children meant that it was virtually 'impossible to extend instruction'.[43] St Mary's, on the other hand, was a school for middle-class children and as a result received much more favourable reports, with one inspector writing that it 'fully maintains its high reputation' and that the liberal spirit of clergymen like the Kirkcudbrightshire native, George Rigg, was a real asset for Catholic education in Edinburgh.[44]

In the west, a similar growth pattern can be seen. In 1833 there were two permanent priests who delivered four weekly masses at St Andrew's Cathedral on the Clyde (1816) and at a smaller chapel in Calton in the city's east end. There were also six schools and eleven Sunday schools in addition to the orphanage in Marshall's Lane in the Gallowgate. The orphanage, which opened in January 1833, had been established to care for the children left parentless by the 1832 cholera epidemic and to ensure that Catholic children were not swept away into Protestant institutions.[45] Much of the initial impetus made for Catholic education in Glasgow had come from the Catholic Schools Society, an organisation that had been founded in 1817 by a group of businessmen who employed large numbers of Irish migrants and children. The schools funded by the society focused on reading, writing and arithmetic, and the Protestant version of the Bible 'without note or comment' was to be used. In 1818 schools were established in Boar Head Lane in the Gallowgate and in the Gorbals, in 1819 one was set up in Bridgeton, and in 1821 another was started in Anderston. They offered day and night classes and it is estimated that between 1818 and 1838 approximately 20,000 pupils, mostly mill workers, had passed through their doors.[46] This educational initiative was in fact an attempt to thwart the introduction of child labour laws by demonstrating that children and young people were being sufficiently looked after, since they could work during the day and attend school at night. The board of this society included fifteen Catholics and fifteen Protestants and was chaired by Kirkman Finlay, the hugely successful textile merchant and MP who had a reputation for opposing any legislation that targeted child labour.[47] The schools established and funded by the society were eventually absorbed into the newly founded parish schools. By 1848, the Catholic population of the city had exploded on account of the Irish Famine, and this translated into the number of chapels rising to four and the number of priests increasing to fourteen. The existing chapels provided a total of nine masses per week with three Sunday masses being said at both St Andrew's and St Mary's, Abercromby Street (1842), two at St Alphonsus Liguori's, Great Hamilton Street (1846), and one at St John's, Portugal Street (1846). A few additional poor parish schools had also been established and Sunday schools were running in every parish. The city's more affluent Catholics could also boast a new convent boarding and day school run by the Franciscan Sisters of the Immaculate Conception, who arrived from France in 1847, and who will be discussed in greater depth in the following chapter.[48]

Although these developments in Glasgow may appear to be significant at first glance, what actually existed was grossly inadequate and was indicative of the indigenous clergy's reluctance to accept the Irish migrants as permanent additions to Scotland's Catholic community. Nevertheless, when taken together with the developments in the east, what emerges is a picture of a church that was organising and expanding. This was augmented by the rise of a Catholic publishing industry that provided a growing range of popular and religious literature. Even though the only Catholic newspaper to exist at this time was the *Glasgow Free Press*, which served to divide rather than unite the Catholic community on account of its overt political and pro-Irish slant, the fact that it existed at all, running sporadically during the 1820s, 1830s, 1850s and 1860s, is significant. Aside from the political commentaries, it also reported on educational matters such as school openings and pupil learning progress.[49] Scotland's other Catholic newspaper, the *Glasgow Observer*, later the *Observer*,

Figure 2.2. Etching of St Mary's Chapel, Edinburgh, c.1830s. Reproduced by permission of the Scottish Catholic Archives, Edinburgh.

Figure 2.3. Etching of Gorbals Chapel, c.1840. Reproduced by permission of the Scottish Catholic Archives, Edinburgh.

only emerged in 1885. Thus for much of the nineteenth century, the *Catholic Directory for Scotland* was the only Catholic publication consistently available, and although there is no way to determine just how many people read it, its main audience would have been the literate middle and upper classes, those who wanted to see what kind of church their money was building. In addition to the religious calendar and information on the movement of clerics, notable obituaries, new churches and new schools, from 1845 the details of the leading clergy in England and in Ireland were also included. An increase in Catholic literature was followed in the early 1850s by an increase in devotional activities such as Corpus Christi processions and the singing of the Litany of Loretto, a Marian devotion dating back to the sixteenth century that was introduced by James Gillis and the Ursuline nuns.[50] Anxious to shake off the impression of Scotland as an isolated mission territory, a new class of Catholics, led largely by ultramontanes, were working for greater integration with the nation, the state and the international, Romanising church.

As already noted, two of the most prominent societies to emerge in Scotland were the Gild of St Joseph, founded in Edinburgh in 1843, and the Society of St Vincent de Paul (SVP), introduced to Edinburgh in May of 1845. These organisations were a response to evangelical fervour, but their establishment in Scotland offers important insight into how far broader European developments such as liberalism and ultramontanism were beginning to influence Catholicism in Scotland. Both organisations were directed by senior priests, received substantial support from recusant and ultramontane corners, and exerted a patriotic and paternal influence over a vulnerable and distressed population. In the long run, these organisations helped to implement the wider ultramontane strategy of consolidation. The SVP enabled Catholicism in Scotland to become more integrated with an emerging international devotional culture and eventually it absorbed the Gild of St Joseph, which had a strong recusant presence. The SVP had been founded by six students at the Université Sorbonne in France in 1833 and fifteen years later a branch was established in Edinburgh by Bishops Andrew Carruthers and James Gillis. Heralded as the 'only successful national body for the defence of Catholic interests', the SVP was a lay male organisation that was dedicated to the moral and social improvement of the poor through visitations.[51] In many respects the SVP embodied principles advocated by Thomas Chalmers: work in and with the community. James Augustine Stothert, also previously introduced, had been its first president, and when it began there were just four members. Growth was rapid and within a year it had eighty-five families officially under its care, fifteen active members, twenty-two honorary members and more than 300 contributors, benefactors and benefactresses. In addition to the

Figure 2.4. Etching of St Andrew's Chapel, Dundee, 1836. Reproduced by permission of the Scottish Catholic Archives, Edinburgh.

private donations it received, it was also allocated a portion of the money collected during the morning masses. Its membership, which excluded women, reinforced the idea of men providing for the family. The Victorian cult of respectability had seen the relationship between women and domesticity strengthened and so women were not eligible for SVP membership, but they were encouraged to offer financial support. The notion of women operating in the public domain as social welfare providers was alien, especially before the 1860s, on account of Catholicism's and society's patriarchal traditions. Indeed, the concept of active communities of women religious was still new. Women's exclusion from the SVP was influenced by ideas about respectability and domesticity, since the middle class emphasised that a respectable society depended upon women being in the home and men being in paid employment. The roots of a moral society began in the home and women were responsible for ensuring that their children grew up to be good social citizens and good Christians.[52] The domesticity of Catholic women was prioritised in an effort to ensure the transmission of the faith to their children. Victorian commentators made great distinctions between work and home, and because voluntary organisations such as the SVP relied upon its middle-class members to teach Christianity and respectability to the labouring poor, many felt that only men were suited for public, active roles. Even women religious, whose work took them into the community, followed strict rules about public conduct and visibility. The success of the SVP in Edinburgh meant that by 1848 another branch of this middle-class male outreach society was founded in Glasgow by Peter Forbes, the 'indefatigable' senior priest of St Mary's Parish.[53] Members in both cities preached Christianity to the poor and working classes, they visited the dying in the hospitals and they distributed clothing, food, straw bedding and medicines. From the beginning it had a special focus on the spiritual and temporal needs of orphaned and poor children, and the report of the Edinburgh branch's first general meeting emphasised the importance of proselytising vulnerable children.[54]

Similarly, the Gild of St Joseph operated as a friendly society and focused its energy on the labouring classes by providing orphan care and by arranging apprenticeships for young men. It had been proposed by Menzies of Pitfodels, who was perhaps the 'wealthiest and most influential Catholic' in the early-to-mid nineteenth century.[55] Members paid monthly subscriptions that entitled them to assistance when sick and to a type of pension when over the age of sixty-five but, in the early 1850s, this organisation was absorbed into the SVP. What is particularly interesting is that it was a home-grown initiative with a significant recusant presence, and the kinds of activities that the Gild sponsored highlighted the deeper Catholic desire to participate in the success of Britain and empire. The perpetuation of an image that was overtly British was a consequence of the broader desire by its patrons to align Catholicism with mainstream Scottish and British society. In Scotland there existed a 'plurality of identities' that was felt by all Scots, regardless of denomination. In her study of female education in Scotland Jane McDermid emphasises the importance of understanding Scottish nationalism in the nineteenth century and of appreciating that its unionist character did not 'preclude a distinct sense of national identity'.[56] Scottish Catholics were deeply committed to the Scottish nation but they, particularly the recusants, also recognised the precariousness of their position. Scholars such as Linda Colley and Mary Hickman have argued that national unity in Britain relied upon the existence of a 'neighbouring "popish"' Irish and an internal 'papist enemy', which drove the indigenous Catholic population to transform itself into an 'ultra-loyal minority'.[57] According to Steven Fielding, after 1850 the Catholic hierarchy in England took every opportunity to show off its 'patriotic English character'.[58] Aware that antipathy towards Catholicism had been enhanced by the presence of the Irish, the Scottish clergy worked with an influential laity to forge a loyal identity and minimise the degree to which Irish Catholic culture could influence Catholicism in Scotland. This was accomplished by a combination of integration, assimilation and ostracising strategies that included the development of an associational and societal culture, Sunday schools, the establishment of a Catholic elementary education system, and the unofficial prohibition of Irish clerics from leadership positions within the church.

The sheer size of the Irish population in the Western District meant that negative opinions were more common and persistent in places like Glasgow than they were in the east. An illuminating example of this comes from John Gray, the Vicar Apostolic of the Western District, when he commented upon the state of his mission in 1866 and observed, without apology, that Catholicism in his district was 'seen to be professed by congregations almost exclusively belonging to a race which is regarded with distrust if not aversion'.[59] Organisations like the SVP and the Holy Gild of St Joseph were intended to improve the social and moral condition of working-class Catholics while demonstrating a deep loyalty to the state. In other words, their job was to circumvent or at least dilute Irish Catholic culture in Scotland. (See Appendix.)

Other organisations dedicated to expanding Catholicism's presence and influence were also launched at this time and some, like the Western District Fund and the St Andrew's Society, had no purpose other than the extension of Catholicism in Scotland. Founded in Edinburgh in 1850, the St Andrew's Society aimed to help Catholics maintain their faith in areas where the population was too small to support a full-time priest. It collected money for the establishment of missions, and in 1851, after having managed to raise £171 over and above its expenses, it identified Linlithgow, Kirkcaldy and Kirkcudbright as new mission towns.[60] In 1858 collections and donations were still pouring in, but senior clerics complained that they could not do everything they intended because of a shortage of religious personnel. It was hoped that with the proper support it would not be long before the Society would succeed in rekindling in every portion of this interesting vicariate the light of the ancient faith, which once burned so brightly in this northern division of the Island of Saints.[61]

The St Andrew's Society is particularly interesting because rather than calling itself the Eastern District Fund like its counterpart in the west, it took the name of Scotland's patron saint and thus claimed a space for Catholics in the Scottish national consciousness. This revivalist need to appropriate an ancient past characterised the ultramontane convert mindset that was best expressed by a number of the society's patrons. Invoking the authority of a past age, wealthy and influential laymen such as the Earl of Traquair, Sir William D. Stewart, Marmaduke and William Constable Maxwell and Robert Monteith grafted Catholicism to a national spirit. In addition to these figures, the Society's committee of management included a number of competent Eastern District clergy, including George Rigg, the proactive liberal educationalist; James Stothert, the convert past president of the SVP; and James Gillis. Importantly, and in contrast to anything that would have been seen in the Western District, this committee also included Stephen Keenan, an Irishman who was a leading priest in Dundee.[62] In the west, the church authorities were notorious for their overt exclusion of the Irish.

While a shortage of priests would continue to plague the Catholic Church in Scotland throughout the century, it was around this time that the number of female religious congregations recruited to Scotland began to increase rapidly. Although the first community was recruited relatively early on in 1834, the next one did not arrive until 1847. Between 1834 and 1858, eight new communities were established, but apart from the Ursulines of Jesus and the Sisters of Mercy in Edinburgh, who had been founded in 1834 and 1858 respectively, the rest were concentrated in and around Glasgow, where the bulk of the Irish were settling. In the decade after 1858 fourteen new communities had been founded, and rather than being confined to the west, the bulk of these new foundations were in Leith, Dundee and Aberdeen. The Marist Brothers were the first male religious to arrive in Scotland, coming in 1858, and over the next decade eleven additional male communities were established; five of these were Jesuit and they were equally distributed between the Eastern and Western Districts.[63] The role played by women, both lay and religious, in the expansion and transformation of the Catholic Church was pivotal, but this was a role played by women across the denominational spectrum. According to Lesley Orr, an authority on women and Presbyterianism in Scotland, the home was promoted as *the* 'place of order, private virtue and spiritual reinforcement' and because of this women came to be regarded as *the* 'custodians of Christian values'.[64] Callum Brown also links piety to the feminine by stressing the centrality of women to the 'aggressive home mission' that emerged with modern evangelicalism.[65] The Holy Gild of St Joseph, like many of its non-Catholic, male-directed social welfare counterparts, placed significant emphasis upon the moral and domestic responsibilities of women and organised events such as prize-giving galas for the cleanest houses. The purpose of such events was twofold. Firstly, they were a platform from which to showcase Catholic respectability, loyalty and Britishness, and secondly, they celebrated domesticity by rewarding women who set good examples. These events began with a toast to the Queen and a singing of the national anthem, which was then followed by a few keynote speeches by members of the clergy. The festivities were concluded with a distribution of prizes, including beds, tables, chests of drawers, crockery, blankets and kitchen utensils, to those women who excelled in their domestic chores.[66] Gild members firmly believed that this would have a direct impact upon the overall improvement of society because it was directed at working-class women, the group whose perceived failings were believed to be the cause of urban decay, intemperance and vice. Following on from this, the published reports stressed the responsibility that women had for the morality of their husbands and families. They were warned that those who kept clean homes, provided 'frugal' yet nourishing meals and greeted their husband with 'bright eyes and sunny smiles' would produce happy and healthy families, whereas those who failed in this would end up miserable and expose their families to a life of drunkenness, poverty and crime.[67]

Women religious, in Britain and elsewhere, occupied a more public role by working to transform the religiosity of grassroots Catholics through a range of social welfare activities, and in this they were joined by a number of Anglican women who embraced a similar life-path. After 1845, as a consequence of the Oxford Movement, Anglican sisterhoods began to emerge, and by 1900 some ninety Anglican communities with at least 4,000 members were operating in Britain and abroad. What is more, the Wesleyan Methodists also established their own female religious community, the Sisters of the Poor, in 1887.[68] Anglican sisterhoods, in contrast to the male ones, were a tremendous success and were dedicated to social welfare work of all kinds. They had been inspired by the Roman Catholic congregations, but, as Susan Mumm points out, Anglican sisterhoods were the private enterprises of aristocratic and professional ladies and so were 'not answerable to any ecclesiastical authority'.[69] This annoyed most clergymen and meant that these sisters faced stiff and sustained opposition from those who viewed female authority and autonomy as deeply offensive to Anglo-Catholic theology. Women religious of both denominations faced a barrage of negative publicity and were regularly and falsely accused of criminal and immoral activity that ranged from financial mismanagement to the kidnapping and imprisonment of innocent young women.[70] Ironically, however, it was these women who provided the most capable and dedicated care to those classed as 'fallen women': the prostitutes and drunks. By considering the experience of Anglican sisters, it is clear to see how gender boundaries cut across denominational lines and were a source of tension. Regardless of the negative publicity, women religious were crucial to church transformation and, as the century progressed, they continued to expand and redefine their role in the construction of religious culture. The prevalence of female religious agency demonstrates that significant numbers of women constructed their own interpretation of the female ideal that did not include marriage or motherhood. Through the religious life they found a way to create their own alternatives and successfully carved out their own niche based on religious conviction and the desire to undertake meaningful work. In Roman Catholic circles this had to be done within the boundaries of the church. After it had relegated it to the sidelines for centuries by various papal decrees, the church finally began to tap into this female agency after 1749 when *Quamvis Iusto* reversed *pericluso*, the papal bull that had made the enclosure of all nuns mandatory. By the middle decades of the nineteenth century, though still tightly controlled, sisters and nuns had embraced an active apostolate and had moved swiftly to the heart of the church's mission. Their identity, however, continued to be informed by ideas about femininity and morality. The nineteenth century saw the churches converge in the belief that the reform of society would ultimately be accomplished through the pious influence of women and that this group required 'proper' instruction. In Catholic circles the reform of women fell largely to women religious, those engaged in social welfare work with women and girls.

Across Europe and North America, women religious successfully navigated the patriarchal terrain to achieve a level of autonomy that was unavailable to most women, let alone Catholic ones. They created their own religious spaces and were part of international and influential female congregations whose membership increased exponentially during the second half of the nineteenth century. Although subject to the authority of the Pope and the local bishop, women religious learned how to work within church boundaries, testing and expanding them as they went. Scotland, though isolated and culturally distinct from the rest of European Catholicism, was pulled closer to Rome by women religious. They came to wield tremendous influence over church development, since their congregational ethos gave them an official social and religious mandate to establish an institutional infrastructure of schools, hospitals, care homes and asylums. They also worked with their male counterparts to bring the Catholic Church in Scotland closer to the nation and the state. During the 1842 visit to Edinburgh by Queen Victoria and Prince Albert, the Ursulines of Jesus organised a Catholic show of loyalty to the royals:

> The cortege proceeded up the Canongate, and here, we may be sure, the bishop had not forgotten the little orphans of Milton House. The Sisters had managed to provide the children with white frocks and neat blue bonnets. Each child was provided with a basket of choice flowers and all were placed on a platform the height of the garden wall. As the royal carriage passed, they rendered their homage to the Queen by showering down their bouquets on her and the prince.[71]

Where the male orders tended to be concentrated in the field of education, the female congregations would, during the second half of the nineteenth century, expand their focus to include not only education, orphanages and nursing work, but also asylums, organised poor relief, care for the elderly and prison visitations. In the process of these works, they transformed the religious culture and devotional attitudes of countless Catholics. On one level sisters were absolutely necessary for the provision of practical relief services, and it is a fact that the church could not have coped without them, whereas on another level women religious would emerge, and not necessarily intentionally, as the embodiment of an ultramontane church. On account of their sheer number, by the end of the nineteenth century they acquired the reputation as foot soldiers whose works of charity put them in touch with every class of Catholics, from the devout to those whose adherence was nominal. The next chapter focuses entirely upon the recruitment and establishment of women religious in Edinburgh and Glasgow and will demonstrate that rather than being isolated as female 'others', they were incorporated as pivotal and cooperative protagonists in a changing church.

Notes

1 Bernard Aspinwall, 'The welfare state within the state: the Saint Vincent de Paul Society in Glasgow, 1848–1920', in W. J. Sheils and Diana Wood (eds), *Voluntary Religion* (Oxford, Basil Blackwell, 1986), p. 452.
2 John McCaffrey, 'Roman Catholics in Scotland in the 19th and 20th centuries', *Records of the Scottish Church History Society*, 21 (1983), p. 288.
3 Philip Carter, 'Menzies, John, of Pitfodels (1756–1843)', *Oxford Dictionary of National Biography*, Oxford University Press, 2004. www.oxforddnb.com/view/article/18566 [accessed 23 August 2007].
4 Roger Swift, *Irish Migrants in Britain, 1815–1914: A Documentary History* (Cork, Cork University Press, 2002), pp. 31 and 35.
5 Charles Withers, 'The demographic history of the city, 1831–1911', in W. Hamish Fraser and Irene Maver (eds), *Glasgow*, vol. 2 (Manchester, Manchester University Press, 1996), pp. 141–3.

6   Colin Kidd, 'Constructing a civil religion: Scots Presbyterians and the eighteenth-century British State', in James Kirk (ed.), *The Scottish Churches and the Union Parliament, 1707–1999* (Edinburgh, Scottish Church History Society, 1999), pp. 5–6 and 13.
7   A Bill for the Relief of His Majesty's Roman Catholic Subjects, Hansard (24 March 1829).
8   George Woodbridge, *The Reform Bill of 1832* (New York, Thomas Y. Crowell Company, 1970), pp. 23–4 and 72. This translated into the following ratios: 1 in 8 men could vote in Scotland; 1 in 5 in England and Wales; 1 in 20 in Ireland.
9   Thomas Megel, 'Ultramontanism, liberalism, moderation: political mentalities and political behaviour of the German Catholic Bürgertum, 1848–1914', *Central European History*, 29:2 (2001), pp. 160–1.
10 Lindsay Paterson, *The Autonomy of Modern Scotland* (Edinburgh, Edinburgh University Press, 1994), p. 47.
11 Irene Collins, *Liberalism in Nineteenth-Century Europe* (London, The Historical Association, 1957), pp. 12–13.
12 Bernard Aspinwall, 'The welfare state', p. 448.
13 *Ibid.*, p. 454.
14 See Bernard Aspinwall, 'Some aspects of Scotland and the Catholic revival in the early nineteenth century', *Innes Review*, 26 (1975), pp. 3–19.
15 *Ibid.*
16 Aspinwall, 'The welfare state', p. 446.
17 Graeme Morton, *Unionist Nationalism: Governing Urban Scotland, 1830–1860* (East Linton, Tuckwell Press, 1999), p. 135.
18 Nigel Yates, *The Oxford Movement and Anglican Ritualism* (London, The Historical Association, 1983), pp. 19 and 40.
19 *Ibid.*, p. 41.
20 Mary Hickman, *Religion, Class and Identity: The State, the Catholic Church and the Education of the Irish in Britain* (Aldershot, Avebury, 1995), pp. 45–6.
21 K. D. Reynolds, 'Stuart, John Patrick Crichton, third marquess of Bute (1847–1900)', *Oxford Dictionary of National Biography*, Oxford University Press, 2004. www.oxforddnb.com/view/article/26722 [accessed October 2006].
22 Morton, *Unionist Nationalism*, p. 69.
23 R. D. Anderson, *Scottish Education since the Reformation* (Stirling, Economic and Social History Society for Scotland, 1997), p. 22.
24 Agnes Trail, *Revival of conventual life in Scotland. History of St. Margaret's Convent, Edinburgh, the first religious house founded in Scotland since the so-called Reformation; and the autobiography of the first religious Sister Agnes Xavier Trail* (Edinburgh, 1886), pp. 26–7.
25 Aspinwall, 'The welfare state', p. 448.
26 Setonian tradition (American) and Vincentian tradition (French). The Daughters of Charity were founded in France in 1633 by Vincent de Paul and Louise de Marillac and marked a significant turning point for the apostolic life. David Farmer,

Oxford Dictionary of Saints, 5th edition (Oxford, Oxford University Press, 2004), pp. 525–6. www.sisters-of-charity.org/history.htm [accessed 22 May 2007].
27 SCA MC3/3. Memorandum with reference to Properties of St. Margaret's Convent, Edinburgh.
28 SCA MC4. General correspondence.
29 Susan O'Brien, 'Lay sisters and good mothers: working-class women in English convents, 1840–1910', in W. J. Sheils and Diana Wood (eds), *Women in the Church* (Oxford, Basil Blackwell, 1990), p. 459.
30 Ibid., pp. 456–7.
31 Trail, *Revival of conventual life*, p. 24.
32 Henry Cockburn, *Journal of Henry Cockburn being a continuation of the memorials of his time, 1831–1854*, vols 1 and 2 (Edinburgh, 1874), pp. 83.
33 Aspinwall, 'The welfare state', pp. 452–3.
34 Simon Gunn, *The Public Culture of the Victorian Middle Class: Ritual and Authority and the English Industrial City* (Manchester, Manchester University Press, 2000), p. 27.
35 Aspinwall, 'The welfare state', p. 453.
36 *Glasgow Free Press*, 5 February 1851 and 11 June 1860.
37 *The true way of dealing successfully with Popery; being the report of the Edinburgh Irish Mission with the list of subscriptions* (Edinburgh, 1851).
38 *Appeal in reference to the extension of the Edinburgh Irish Mission and Protestant Institute, addressed to the friends of Protestantism* (Edinburgh, early 1850s).
39 Hickman, *Religion, Class and Identity*, p. 40.
40 Anderson, *Scottish Education*, p. 22. Helen Corr, 'An exploration into Scottish education', in W. Hamish Fraser and R. J. Morris (eds), *People and Society in Scotland*, vol. 2: *1830–1914* (Edinburgh, John Donald, 1990), p. 292.
41 *Catholic Directory for Scotland* (CDS), 1833, pp. 59–60.
42 CDS, 1848, pp. 60–2.
43 Ian Stewart, 'Teacher careers and the early Catholic schools of Edinburgh', *Innes Review*, 46:1 (1995), pp. 54–5.
44 Ibid.
45 CDS, 1833, p. 64.
46 Thomas A. Fitzpatrick, 'Catholic education in Glasgow, Lanarkshire and South-West Scotland before 1872', *Innes Review*, 36:2 (1985), p. 87.
47 Monica Clough, 'Finlay, Kirkman (1773–1842)', *Oxford Dictionary of National Biography*, Oxford University Press, 2004. www.oxforddnb.com/view/article/9467 [accessed 21 December 2007].
48 CDS, 1848, pp. 69–71.
49 The opening of St Mungo's School was reported in the *Glasgow Free Press* on 15 February 1851 and the internal inspection of St Lawrence's School in Greenock was recounted for readers in the paper's 7 July 1860 issue.
50 Trail, *Revival of conventual life*, pp. 136–8.
51 Bernard Aspinwall, 'The formation of a British identity within Scottish Catholicism,

1830–1914', in Robert Pope (ed.), *Religion and National Identity: Wales and Scotland, c.1700–2000* (Cardiff, University of Wales Press, 2001), p. 278.
52 Paul O'Leary, 'Networking respectability: class, gender and ethnicity among the Irish in South Wales, 1845–1914', *Immigrants and Minorities*, 23:2–3 (2005), p. 262.
53 *Brotherhood of Saint Vincent of Paul; Conference of Edinburgh. Report of the first general meeting, held in Saint Marie's school, April 30, 1846*; Bernard Aspinwall, 'A Glasgow pastoral plan 1855–1860: social and spiritual renewal', *Innes Review*, 35:1 (1984), p. 33.
54 *Brotherhood of Saint Vincent of Paul, Conference Report, 1846*.
55 Christine Johnson, *Developments in the Roman Catholic Church in Scotland, 1789–1829* (Edinburgh, John Donald, 1983), p. 209.
56 Jane McDermid, *The Schooling of Working-Class Girls in Victorian Scotland: Gender, Education and Identity* (London, Routledge, 2005), p. 14.
57 Mary Hickman, 'Incorporating and denationalizing the Irish in England: the role of the Catholic Church', in Patrick O'Sullivan (ed.), *The Irish World Wide: History, Heritage, Identity*, Volume 5: *Religion and Identity* (London, Leicester University Press, 1996), p. 197. Linda Colley, *Britons: Forging the Nation, 1707–1837*, 2nd edition (London, Pimlico, 2003), p. 18.
58 Steven Fielding, *Class and Ethnicity: Irish Catholics in England, 1880–1939* (Buckingham, The Open University Press, 1993), p. 40.
59 GAA, WD12/43. *Report on the State of Religion in the Western District*. Handwritten by John Gray, 1866.
60 *CDS*, 1852, pp. 65–7.
61 *CDS*, 1858, p. 147.
62 *CDS*, 1852, p. 65.
63 Mark Dilworth, 'Religious orders in Scotland, 1878–1978', *Innes Review*, 29:1 (1978), pp. 92–107.
64 Lesley Orr MacDonald, *A Unique and Glorious Mission: Women and Presbyterianism in Scotland, 1830–1930* (Edinburgh, John Donald, 2000), pp. 30–1.
65 Callum G. Brown, *The Death of Christian Britain: Understanding Secularisation 1800–2000* (London, Routledge, 2001), p. 9 and MacDonald, *A Unique and Glorious Mission*, pp. 43–4 and 52–4.
66 *A report, &c. with an account of the speeches delivered, and of the gild premiums awarded for the cleanest and tidiest kept houses. Edinburgh, 21st October 1842*.
67 *A report, &c. with an account of the speeches delivered, and of the gild premiums awarded for the encouragement of domestic comfort. Edinburgh, 31st January 1845*.
68 Susan Mumm, *Stolen Daughters, Virgin Mothers: Anglican Sisterhoods in Victorian Britain* (London, Leicester University Press, 1999), p. 1.
69 *Ibid.*, pp. 137–8.
70 Susan Mumm (ed.), *All Saints Sisters of the Poor: An Anglican Sisterhood in the 19th Century* (Woodbridge, The Boydell Press, 2001), pp. xi–xiii.
71 Trail, *Revival of conventual life*, pp. 102–3.

3

The recruitment of women religious

Women religious were at the centre of the ultramontane campaign to transform Catholicism and bring the national churches under the authority of Rome, and yet many were not ultramontanes. The professional skills they offered, the institutions they founded and the religious authority they possessed enabled them to build a more unified Catholic culture. The sisters who founded the pioneer communities in Scotland were intrepid missionaries dedicated to rebuilding and extending the Catholic Church in a nation dominated by Presbyterianism. The first communities to arrive were primarily involved with teaching but it was not long before they were joined by others offering different services such as care for the elderly and assistance to single or deserted mothers. By the end of the century, women religious were providing assistance to women at every stage of their lives, from cradle to grave, and this directly enhanced the standing and authority of the church. Their ability to carve out such an extensive niche testifies to their enthusiasm and resourcefulness, but more specifically to emphasise the agency of female collective action.

The establishment of convents was the first major step towards the widespread overhaul of Catholicity in Scotland and the purpose of this chapter is to provide an introduction to the women religious who spearheaded this cultural change. It would be impossible to see how women religious worked to transform Catholic culture through education, for example, without first seeing how they were established in Scotland and how convent culture was manipulated to ensure that the religiosity being transmitted by them was suitable for Scottish needs and preferences. The first part of this chapter charts the recruitment of four teaching communities of women religious to Scotland's two main cities: the Ursulines of Jesus and the Sisters of Mercy in Edinburgh and the Franciscan Sisters of the Immaculate Conception and the Sisters of Mercy in Glasgow. According to Canon Law, there were three types of religious institutes: contemplative, active and mixed. In contemplative institutes nuns were enclosed and took solemn, lifelong vows; active institutes were 'chiefly devoted to works of charity' and their members, referred to as sisters, took simple vows; mixed institutes combined the contemplative and active life but tended to be more devoted to one than the other depending on local circumstances.[1] The Ursulines of Jesus and the Franciscan Sisters of the Immaculate Conception were mixed communities, whereas the Sisters of Mercy were active. Convincing women religious to come to Scotland was only the first step in establishing them as part of its religious landscape, and so the second section of this chapter investigates how gender and ethnicity influenced the development of these communities. Women with religious authority who demonstrated a willingness to use what independence they had to further their mission provoked intense anxiety among clerics. The sisters who lived and worked in Scotland were predominantly Scottish and Irish, but a number also came from France and England, and some from as far afield as the West Indies, Jamaica, Gibraltar, Bavaria and even the United States. Ethnicity thus became integral and defining features of the Catholic Church in nineteenth-century Scotland. As members of religious congregations with diverse international memberships, sisters were expected to leave their national attachments behind them, but local circumstances and personal attachments often meant that this was difficult in reality.

Europe and North America witnessed an explosion in the number of women religious during the nineteenth century and this was the result of sustained economic growth, legislative reform and ultramontanism. The pioneer institutes had inspired countless women to either join existing communities or to found new ones. This migration to the religious life represents the radicalisation of women who turned their backs on marriage and motherhood, opting instead for a life that gave them a professional status. In Scotland the recruitment of new congregations like the Good Shepherds and the Little Sisters of the Poor, both of which were established in France in 1829 and 1839 respectively, and the seventeenth-century Daughters of Charity, also from France, in the 1850s and early 1860s, shows how the Catholic Church was consolidating. Much of the change was being prompted by legislative reform such as the Poor Law (Scotland) Act that saw the state become more involved with the provision of social welfare and the churches scramble to secure their positions by expanding the range of services that they could provide. Communities of women religious fulfilled specific functions that included the running of reformatories for children and homes for the elderly, extending support and shelter networks for the destitute, and providing specialised health care for the sick and the dying. These services offered practical support to some of society's most vulnerable members, but they also gave the church a bigger presence in people's everyday lives. As these female-directed communities spread throughout Europe, North

America and Britain, the Catholic Church acquired a stronger national and international presence. In the United States, for example, the 106 new foundations that were made between 1830 and 1900 provided a 'collective workforce' of approximately 50,000, and in New York City alone the number of sisters jumped from eighty-two in 1848 to approximately 2,846 by the end of the century, triple the number of priests and brothers, and the majority were Irish.[2] Irish sisters also predominated in Canada, and statistics for two congregations in Toronto, the Sisters of St Joseph and the Institute of the Blessed Virgin Mary, show that between 1847 and 1900 well over 300 Irish-born or first generation Irish-descended women had entered these communities.[3] In Scotland it was not long before the pioneer communities expanded beyond Glasgow and Edinburgh to Aberdeen, Perth, Dundee, Roswell, Lanark, Bishopbriggs, Oban and Dumfries.[4] Additionally, many of the new congregations did not have lay sisters, thus illustrating the growing success of ultramontanism and its desire to incorporate as many people as possible into the machinery of the church. Both the Little Sisters of the Poor and the Daughters of Charity drew their membership chiefly from the lower middle class, and it was these women who took responsibility for the less desirable work, the tasks that 'women from wealthy backgrounds [were] unable and even unwilling to do', such as caring for the poor and 'washing and medicating diseased bodies'.[5] A community that falls into this category was the Ursulines of Jesus, the first community to return to Scotland after the Reformation.

Ursulines of Jesus

The Ursulines of Jesus had been founded in Chavagnes-en-Paillers in La Vendée, France in 1802 by Charlotte Gabrielle Ranfray, in religion Mère St Benoit, and Louis-Marie Baudouin, the local bishop. Their Rule was derived from that of St Augustine and they operated as a diocesan institute wherein individual communities were autonomous and subject to the jurisdiction of the local bishop. They specialised in education and because they drew their membership chiefly from elite circles their activities were prioritised accordingly – they were devoted first to the 'young ladies of the upper and middle classes, then the poor and lastly, women of every condition'.[6] Groundwork for the Scottish foundation was prepared in the late 1820s when James Gillis was on a fundraising tour of the Continent. In France the Bishop of Luçon put him in touch with Baudouin and Ranfray to discuss the possibility of establishing a convent in Edinburgh. It was only after the death of Bishop Alexander Patterson in 1831 and the consecration of Bishop Andrew Carruthers as the new Vicar Apostolic of the Eastern District in 1833 that everything began to fall into place. Financial support was promised by John Menzies, and two Scotswomen were found to lead the foundation. Sr Agnes Xavier Trail, a Forfarshire native who was introduced in the previous chapter, and Sr Margaret Teresa Clapperton of Fochabers, Morayshire, entered the French novitiate in 1833 to begin their religious training. On 27 July 1834 they were the first women religious to return to Scotland since the Reformation and they were accompanied by nine other French nuns: Mother St Hildaire; Mother St Paula; Sr St Damian; Sr Alexis; Sr John Chrysostom; Sr Mary Emily; Sr Angelina; Sr Stephen and Sr Eustelle. Their diocesan structure meant that the Edinburgh community would be independent of the French mother house and subject to the jurisdiction of the Vicar Apostolic of the Eastern District, but it is clear that the two communities remained close throughout the century. As a diocesan institute, their overall membership remained relatively small, but as their boarding school grew, so did the number of nuns. Beginning with eleven in 1834, the community numbered fourteen religious, nine pupil boarders and two servants by 1841. Twenty years later there were sixteen choir sisters, ten lay sisters and eighteen pupil boarders, who came from England, Ireland, Scotland and the West Indies. There was also one general servant and a gardener, an Irishman by the name of Bernard McManus.[7] In 1871 the number of choir sisters had increased by three, the number of lay sisters was unchanged, there were twenty-five pupil boarders, four servants, the gardener and a chaplain.[8] In 1891 the membership was largely unchanged with eighteen choir sisters and fourteen lay sisters, but a new German governess had been hired for the nineteen pupil boarders.[9] This levelling off was a consequence of the new foundation they had made in Perth in 1865 and of the other communities that had established themselves in Scotland; by 1900 there were twenty-three female religious communities.

Their convent was Whitehouse, a mansion house on two acres of land in the south of Edinburgh that dated back to the early sixteenth century.[10] The property had been purchased for £3,000 and the sale was handled by Gillis, but the money came from Menzies of Pitfodels through a 'Bond of Relief'. He stipulated that this money was for the advancement of religious education through the establishment of a 'Roman Catholic Seminary for the education of the daughters of the higher class of Roman Catholics in Scotland and for other religious purposes'.[11] Substantial support also came from the sisters themselves and many of the choir sisters entered with large dowries of £1,000. Agnes Dunn, in religion Sr M. Aloisia, a young woman from Newcastle upon Tyne, made her first profession in 1855 and in addition to the £1,000 dowry, she also brought with her an additional £3,000 that was to be used for new

Figure 3.1. A group of pupil boarders at St Margaret's Convent, Edinburgh, 1864. This photograph includes Elizabeth Gray, Mary Alice Parkinson, Kate Robertson and Annie Telford. The other girls are unidentified. Reproduced by permission of the Scottish Catholic Archives, Edinburgh.

property and convent maintenance.[12] Overall, the community was well supported by the upper classes, and the financial contributions they received in the early years enabled the nuns to commission their own chapel, which further enhanced their image as genteel and cultured women. Designed by the Dunblane-born James Gillespie Graham, Scotland's most prolific nineteenth-century architect,[13] the Chapel of St Margaret's was completed in the summer of 1835 and the dedication service was held in June:

> There were bishops, odours, flowers, robes, good music, etc., etc. The most striking part of the ceremony, however, was the entry of three British (but all English) ladies of good birth and education as novitiates, by taking the white veil ... Scotland had not seen the like for a long while.[14]

St Margaret's and its chapel became a focal point for many of the Catholic elite, and influential individuals such as Menzies, the Hope-Scotts and, for a time at least, Canada's first Bishop of Kingston, Alexander MacDonell, were buried in its crypt. The property itself was ideal for an upper-class convent. Not only was it exclusive and opulent, but its history was so well

The recruitment of women religious 79

Figure 3.2. An unidentified religious novice before her profession with the Ursulines of Jesus. Reproduced by permission of the Scottish Catholic Archives, Edinburgh.

known to the locals that no one could claim, according to Agnes Trail, that 'it contain[ed] prisons, dungeons, or any of those horrors related to monasteries'.[15] Nevertheless, one contemporary observed that some of the workmen hired to improve the property felt uneasy, a symptom of a ubiquitous anxiety towards nuns and convents.[16] Public paranoia had been roused by unscrupulous publishers who made a fortune from selling convent tales, and in the mid-1830s two books, *Six Months in a Convent, or, the Narrative of Rebecca Theresa Reed* and *The Awful Disclosures of Maria Monk*, brought anxiety to a new high. The former was the story of a young woman who had allegedly attempted to escape from an Ursuline convent in Charlestown, Massachusetts, and believing the tale to be true, an angry mob torched the building in 1835. The second book was a tale of sexual exploitation, infanticide, imprisonment and murder in a Montreal convent. It was a complete fabrication and despite the revelation of Maria Monk's true identity as a prostitute soon after the book's publication, it remained a sensation, with multiple editions being printed by countless publishers in North America and Britain; in Scotland editions were published in Edinburgh, Glasgow and Paisley.[17] Magazines such as *Blackwood's* also cashed in by printing their own versions of life behind the grille, sacrificed daughters, imprisoned virgins and separated lovers being the most frequent storylines.[18] In 1851 it was alleged by a Free Churchman that a young woman had been 'dragged from a carriage, and, despite her efforts and her shrieks, forcibly taken into, and pitilessly immured within, the walls of St Margaret's'.[19] The story, which was printed in *The Scotsman*, corresponded with intense anti-Catholic sentiment heightened by the restoration of England's Catholic hierarchy. James Gillis, like many of the nuns' supporters, publicly condemned the accusation as a 'wicked and deliberate falsehood'.[20] Attacking convents was an easy way to provoke anti-Catholicism and so anti-convent literature remained in the public domain throughout the century.

When compared to some of the other communities, however, the Ursulines of Jesus did not experience a lot of bigotry since their upper-class status shielded them from most of it.[21] Highly connected and adequately supported, the Ursulines of Jesus became a tremendously influential community that assumed a matriarchal role for all women religious from various congregations across Scotland. They forged particularly strong connections with the Sisters of Mercy, whom they helped support when their communities were being established in Glasgow and Edinburgh. In fact, one of the letters they received congratulating them on their Golden Jubilee in 1884 was from Sr M. Bernard Garden, a woman who had briefly led the Mercy community in Glasgow and who went on to found five other Mercy houses in the north-east of Scotland. She had first visited St Margaret's at the age of eleven.[22] Similarly, the Grant sisters, Jane and Helen, had been pupil boarders at St Margaret's in the 1840s before joining the Mercy novitiate in Limerick in preparation to lead the Edinburgh foundation.[23] Their social status placed them at the heart of the church's efforts to transform Catholic culture in Scotland, but in many respects the Ursulines of Jesus operated on a completely different level than the other communities in this study. Situated in the heart of the Eastern District and drawing their members mainly from the daughters of the Scottish and English elite, the Ursulines of Jesus remained largely detached from the masses of the Irish poor in the city's slums. In Glasgow a culture war was under way between the Irish Catholics, whose numbers were increasing with unprecedented speed, and the Scottish Catholics, who felt invaded. The Ursulines did not confront this issue to any great extent, but rather they existed on another level, one in which useful connections were forged with the politicians, the businessmen and the aristocrats – those who could help to elevate the status of Catholicism in Scotland.

Franciscan Sisters of the Immaculate Conception

Glasgow, the second city of the Empire, was an industrial centre situated in the west of Scotland on the River Clyde. A lucrative eighteenth-century tobacco trade paved the way for a nineteenth century dominated by labour-intensive industries such as textiles and shipbuilding. Slums and squalor confounded the city's ability to cope with the influx of migrant labourers, and while poor relief had traditionally been the responsibility of the Church of Scotland, its inability to meet existing needs led to the introduction of the Poor Law (Scotland) Act in 1845. In addition to installing a Board of Supervision and parochial boards, it extended the poor rates and brought in poorhouses. The legislation also imposed a five-year residency requirement, which served to exclude the Irish Famine victims from relief. Viewing this legislation as nothing less than the state-sanctioned extension of Protestantism, Catholic authorities weighed their options and, realising that they had neither the money nor the personnel to cope with the suffering or to fend off Protestant proselytism, they turned to women religious. In 1847, as upwards of 1,000 impoverished Irish were landing in Glasgow each week, the first two nuns arrived and like so many other foundresses they initially divided their time between teaching and impromptu nursing work in an effort to alleviate the misery caused by typhus, cholera and consumption.[24]

Mother M. Adelaide Vaast, Mother M. Veronica Cordier and Constance Marchand, their benefactress, arrived in Glasgow on 18 June. A skilled teacher, Vaast had come from Merville in northern France and had entered the religious life in 1834. Cordier was the daughter of a prosperous farmer in France's Saint-Armand district, and Marchand was a young woman of independent means who wished to help establish schools. The trio had been recruited by Peter Forbes, a pragmatic priest from the newly constructed St Mary's Parish, Abercromby Street. While on a collecting tour of the Continent he visited the Franciscan Convent of Notre Dame des Anges in Tourcoing, a textile town in the north of France, and caught the attention of Vaast and Cordier, who were desperate to work as missionaries abroad. Their prioress was initially reluctant to part with them, but a bigger concern was that they belonged to a pontifical institute, and since the Glasgow clerics had stipulated that the nuns would have to found a new and completely independent congregation, this prevented an easy departure. The crux of problem was that rather than being members of an autonomous diocesan community under the authority of a local bishop, their order was governed by a superior general and by Rome directly, which meant that before they could go to Scotland they had to formally withdraw as nuns from the Tourcoing community. Their decision to do this was tremendously

Figure 3.3. Veronica Cordier, co-foundress of the Franciscan Sisters of the Immaculate Conception, Glasgow. Reproduced by permission of the Franciscan Sisters of the Immaculate Conception, Glasgow.

brave, for not only had they taken a significant risk by stepping out of the security of their order to build a new one, but they had volunteered to live and work in a country where the language, culture and climate were very different from what they were used to. On the other hand they recognised similarities, since Tourcoing, like Glasgow, was a town that had experienced rapid industrialisation and relied heavily upon female and child labour. Their work with women and children there, although primarily in a convent setting, gave them crucial experience and empathy for the urban Scottish mission.[25]

Severing ties with France took about a year. During that time communication between Tourcoing and Glasgow was poor and there is conflicting evidence as to whether the Scottish clergy actually knew they were coming, since nothing had been prepared for them when they arrived. Ironically, their lack of English turned out to be an advantage, since it meant that for the first three months they could board with a local woman who provided language lessons. Mrs MacDonald's Boarding School for Young Ladies at 25 Monteith Row was their first residence until they had gained proficiency in English. Afterwards, a small house overlooking Glasgow Green at 11 Monteith Row was rented for them for £50. This was their base until 1849, when they moved temporarily to

Bellgrove Street and then permanently, later that year, to 76 Charlotte Street, a property that also overlooked the Green. They survived on the money they had taken with them from France (roughly 500 francs), on funds provided by Marchand and, like the Ursulines of Jesus, on what they received from some of the city's more affluent Catholics such as Robert Monteith. According to the community's obituary records, some of the clergy, specifically Alexander Smith and John Gray, also provided financial assistance and bequeathed a portion of their estates to the sisters upon their deaths.[26] This outside support was a lifeline until they were more established with postulants, boarding school pupils and paid teaching posts. The private school that they opened soon after their arrival was an invaluable source of income that helped to sustain them and subsidise their other less profitable activities. Creating a sound financial foundation was crucial, and as the community expanded so too did their financial management skills. Women religious are generally credited with being competent and clever businesswomen, but this remains an under-researched area since most communities have tended to judge their financial records as either 'strictly confidential' or too unimportant to bother saving.[27]

Soon after they were established in their own residence Vaast and Cordier began to accept parlour borders: essentially these were women of independent means who paid to live there. The ability to attract parlour borders could make or break a foundation because of the extra income they provided. Margaret and Mary Gatherer, a pair of sisters from Banffshire, were the community's first parlour boarders and with their 'ample means' and willingness to assist the nuns with their teaching they set the community on a more sturdy financial footing. Incidentally, on 15 August 1852 Margaret was professed as a Franciscan Sister at the age of forty-two.[28] Another boarder was Eliza Russell, an Irish woman from County Kerry whose hopes of becoming a sister were dashed by ill health, and when she died in 1852 she left a considerable sum to the community.[29] Mary Margaret Brewster was a young convert who also boarded with the community, but rather than contributing financially she taught English and music in their early convent school.[30] These examples demonstrate that lay and religious women in Glasgow were proactive in the organisation of social welfare activities, and this corresponds with what Mary Peckham Magray suggests when she claims that for every woman receiving charity, another was dispensing it.[31] Women were believed to be predisposed to such works and because of this they 'came to claim a certain moral authority in the nineteenth century'.[32] Parlour boarding was important because it linked wealthy Catholic lay women to the broader Victorian philanthropic drive by permitting them to become involved with works of charity. In Catholic circles it was women religious who exercised the 'greatest power and control over philanthropic endeavours', and so very few Catholic charities were operated by lay women. It was also the case that women were excluded from membership of organisations such as the SVP, and so had to create their own avenues by which to become directly involved in good and meaningful works of charity. In becoming parlour boarders, bourgeois women were given the opportunity to assist with the financial survival of a religious community and to participate in its apostolic works as unpaid assistants. On another level, for women like Margaret Gatherer, the Franciscan Sister, and Agnes Trail, foundress of the Ursulines of Jesus in Edinburgh, it was also a route into the religious life.[33]

The Franciscan Sisters confronted serious obstacles that posed a threat to their survival almost immediately. The most serious was the death of Adelaide Vaast from cholera in 1849, and at the time some of the clergy suggested that Cordier should return to France because they felt that she could not cope on her own in Scotland. She refused and with the support of Bishop Smith, she received her first postulants in the winter of 1850.[34] Constance Marchand became Sr Mary Francis and was joined by two Irish women from County Cork, Sr M. Hyacintha (Julia) Condon and Sr M. Joseph (Joanna) Fitzgerald. From 1851 forward there was a rich supply of entrants and between that year and 1900 approximately 168 women joined the congregation (Table 3.1 below shows the number of annual professions between 1851 and 1900). Interestingly, there was a surge of entrants in the 1850s that was almost three times the number of any other decade. From the 1860s, having finally become firmly established with a sufficient membership, the community could afford to be selective, but the lower entry rates after this point were also a consequence of more choice. As the century progressed, the number of religious communities in Scotland grew and in the 1850s and 1860s alone seven other congregations established ten communities: Good Shepherds at Dalbeth in Glasgow (1850); Daughters of Charity in Lanark (1860) and Coatbridge (1867); Little Sisters of the Poor in Glasgow (1862), Edinburgh (1863) and Dundee (1863); Poor Sisters of Nazareth in Aberdeen (1862); Institute of the Blessed Virgin Mary in Leith (1863–69); Apostolines of the Immaculate Conception in Aberdeen (1866–76); Holy Family in Leith (1869).[35]

Not everyone who entered chose to stay and the reception and profession books reveal the names of twenty-two women who did not persevere. Some left for unknown reasons, others were declared unfit for the religious life by the community, and some were compelled to leave on account of poor health. Those rejected for health reasons were seen as a potential drain on the community since it was likely that they would be incapable of work and therefore an unnecessary tax on its limited resources. The majority of women rejected during the community's formative stage, between 1850 and 1867, for having no vocation were Irish and this leads to speculation about whether this had anything to do with the heightened tension between the Irish and Scottish Catholics in this district. What this might also indicate is that some of the unsuitable entrants had viewed convent life as an improvement on their present condition or as a source of security that was unavailable to them otherwise. Despite these rejections, membership grew and with it so too did their geographic range: in addition to their motherhouse at Charlotte Street in Glasgow, they spread to Inverness (1854), Aberdeen (1855), Glasgow, Abercromby Street (1861), Innellan (1872–74), Greenock (1878), Bothwell (1878), Edinburgh (1880–93), Glasgow, Crosshill (1894), Girvan (1898) and Bishopbriggs (1898).[36] While the sisters claimed that they had a 'vocation' for the religious life, this must be placed within the context of their expectations for convent life.[37] A family's wealth, the number of siblings a woman had, her relationship with those siblings, marriage prospects and fears of childbirth were all factors influencing a woman's decision to enter a religious community. Young women were attracted to the Franciscan Sisters because of the stability offered after 1850 and because the particular works of charity appealed to them. Although teaching was their primary focus, they undertook informal nursing work during outbreaks of disease, provided general poor relief and, later on, undertook prison visitations. Beginning in 1885 at Duke Street Prison and later at the Greenock Women's Prison, the Franciscan Sisters offered consolation to female inmates such as Susan Newall, the Coatbridge woman convicted of murder. In 1923 Newall was accompanied to the scaffold by Sr M. Philippa Gilhooly for Glasgow's last female hanging.[38]

Sisters of Mercy in Glasgow

The organisational structure of the Sisters of Mercy differed significantly from both the Ursulines of Jesus and the Franciscan Sisters of the Immaculate Conception. The founding Franciscan nuns and, to a lesser extent, the Ursulines of Jesus, had come from religious orders as opposed to religious congregations, and it was only after arriving in Scotland that they developed into mixed communities with a more active apostolate. Originally founded as a religious congregation whose members took simple, as opposed to solemn, vows and who were apostolic and unenclosed rather than contemplative and enclosed, the Sisters of Mercy were, from the very beginning, sisters as opposed to nuns. Founded in Dublin in 1832 by Catherine McAuley, their mandate was to work directly with the poor outwith their convent. As an active institute the Sisters of Mercy were predisposed to the type of work that was required of them in Glasgow. The Glasgow foundation was made from

Limerick by Mother M. Elizabeth Moore, the superior of St Mary's convent. Initially criticised as a 'faint-hearted soldier' by McAuley, Moore emerged as a formidable and intimidating missionary force who founded twelve houses during her tenure.[39] The Glasgow foundation was formally established on 25 August 1849 by five sisters from Limerick: Mother Moore, Sr M. Clare (Mary) McNamara, Sr M. Catherine (Anne) McNamara, Sr M. Joseph (Margaret) Butler and Sr M. Clare (Helen) Kerrin. The group had steamed across the Irish Sea to Port Glasgow and from there they were accompanied to Glasgow by Fr Cody, a Tipperary-born priest who had been working in Dumbarton. They resided first at Charlotte Street but soon afterwards moved to Abercromby Street and lived above the orphanage.

Very little is known about how the Sisters funded themselves upon arrival, but it is likely that they received some support from the clergy and wealthy members of the laity, though what they got was not enough to prevent extreme financial hardship. The Glasgow Sisters of Mercy were the poorest of the communities discussed here and this was partly because their diocesan structure prevented them from expanding like the Franciscan Sisters and thus limited their membership and the number of dowries they could invest. Small communities also had fewer sisters engaged in paid employment and this directly affected convent coffers. Poverty was a primary vow of all women religious but the degree to which it was experienced varied significantly between communities and was a reflection of structure, membership, income, assets, property and dowries. The level of poverty communities actually experienced can usually be gauged from their financial records, but where these are difficult to obtain, as in the case of this community, statistics on sickness and death become useful indicators. The Sisters of Mercy undertook nursing work in addition to their teaching responsibilities and as a result they were hit hard by sickness and death. Records show that between 1849 and 1877, twenty-one sisters were lost to typhus, consumption and cholera, and four of these deaths occurred before profession. This was a remarkably high figure considering that only forty-two women had joined the community between 1849 and 1900. To put this into perspective, the Franciscan Sisters lost sixteen sisters between 1849 and 1866 but because they received 171 sisters between 1849 and 1900 the overall impact of this loss was not as great.[40]

The diocesan structure of the Mercy community, their poverty and the aversion that some of the clerics had towards their Irishness were obstacles impeding recruitment and growth. Between 1849 and 1900, forty-two women from Scotland, England, Ireland and France joined the Mercy community in Glasgow, but as noted above, half of them died of disease. In addition, during the first two decades of the community's existence an astonishing thirty-eight women chose not to persevere with the religious life; the bulk of the departures corresponded with leadership vacuums, conflicts with clerics and illness peaks. Schism in the early 1850s saw seven Irish sisters return to Ireland because they and their superiors were unwilling to accept the anti-Irish bigotry and excessive workload. To make matters worse, the return of cholera in 1853 reignited fears about the health and welfare of those sisters who worked with the sick poor; the stress proved too much for sixteen young postulants, who deserted the community between 1850 and 1855. The effect that death and disease had upon community stability should not be overlooked, since the process of having to watch fellow sisters wither away, and in many cases die, was extremely difficult and, understandably, caused many to fear for their own safety. Some of the more austere religious were annoyed by this and one even complained that 'You would imagine from the excessive care they take to preserve life that in entering religion their sole object was to avoid dying.'[41] Fear and anxiety were natural responses and showed the reality of the religious life to those young women who had perhaps rushed in without properly considering the consequences.

Financial instability and sickness conspired to undermine the stability of the Mercy foundation in Glasgow, but the conflicts that erupted between this community, male clerics and the Franciscan Sisters proved equally devastating. Early in her career Elizabeth Moore was identified as someone who needed to learn how to 'respect local needs and preferences' and her abrasive character offended many of Glasgow's leading clerics.[42] Tension began during the negotiation stage when, prior to the sisters being sent to Glasgow, Moore had forwarded a list of conditions to the clergymen with the addendum that unless her terms were agreed to by their signatures, sisters would be withheld.[43] Incensed, but struggling to support the Famine migrants, Bishop Murdoch was compelled to satisfy her request, but his coadjutor, Alexander Smith, refused his signature in protest and according to him was, from that point, labelled an 'enemy of the Convent of Mercy'.[44] There was little improvement in the way Moore dealt with the Franciscan Sisters, though part of the problem was that both of these communities had been recruited to the same parish by Peter Forbes and were thus in direct competition for entrants and scarce resources. Initially, Cordier proved no match for the Mercy community and according to a statement written by her some years later, their early relationship was fraught with tension:

> At first I continued to take fee-paying pupils but when they took them from us, I took up classes at the orphanage again. I lived at a good distance from the orphanage and they wished me to be nearer. But where could I go? . . . they wished me to go and live in a block of buildings consisting of working men's

houses. I did not accept... I did not despise the poor locality but being in a Protestant country, I wished to uphold the dignity of my vocation... I continued to go to my classes at the orphanage and the Sisters of Mercy began to do their work... But a short time after, they took a dislike to the house. They asked for and obtained the orphanage to make a convent of it. I was then obliged to withdraw...[45]

This account was corroborated by Alexander Smith in a document he titled 'A Statement of the Convent of Mercy', which he wrote in an attempt to clear the air.[46] It is clear that the terms under which the Sisters of Mercy had come to Glasgow were poorly considered, but this was symptomatic of the clergy's lack of experience in dealing with women religious. The whole concept of active female communities was still new and so the boundaries of authority were somewhat obscure, but as the century progressed the clergy consolidated their authority over the religious communities. This was by no means easily accomplished. The Ursulines of Jesus were in the habit of receiving so many visitors and holding so many breakfasts with high-profile guests that their house resembled more of a sorority than a convent. In fact, James Gillis had become so frustrated with their socialising that he attempted to reprimand them on New Year's Day 1844:

[A] great deal too much gossip goes on, both within the communities and with persons from without – the parlour is a great deal too much frequented and as I have often grieved to see, too willingly – there is a great deal too much anxiety to know all that is going on.[47]

His words appeared to have fallen on deaf ears and the annals reveal that this kind of activity lasted well into the 1850s. Class was obviously an important factor, and upper-class communities generally exercised greater autonomy over their social calendars than the others. The Glasgow communities did not enjoy the same social atmosphere as the Ursulines, but they did experience struggles with clerics, though these tended to revolve more around issues of ethnicity, as will be discussed in more depth below. Although the clergy could not have accomplished any widespread church transformation without women religious, the vast majority resented and resisted the independence and agency that these women continually demonstrated.

Sisters of Mercy in Edinburgh

One of the most common problems facing researchers of women religious concerns archive access and while many congregations and communities are extremely helpful and willing to accommodate researchers, some are not.

First-hand access to this community's archives proved impossible and so much of the material presented here has been compiled from other Mercy archives in Glasgow, Limerick, Bermondsey and Dublin and from other repositories in Edinburgh, specifically the Scottish Catholic Archives, the National Library of Scotland and National Register House. Enough material has been gathered to sketch a picture of the Edinburgh Mercy community and to show that for those sisters who settled in the Scottish capital it was an experience that differed significantly from that of their Glasgow counterparts. The Edinburgh community had been established in 1858, was a diocesan institute under the authority of the local bishop and, like Glasgow, was founded from Limerick by Elizabeth Moore and Clare McNamara. This community was originally proposed for 1850 but it is suspected that the troubles experienced in Glasgow during that year and the early 1850s delayed Edinburgh's foundation until 1858. This foundation got off to a much smoother start, and the ease with which they were settled was largely due to the influence of Gillis and to the supportive relationship that had been forged between the Mercy congregation and the Ursulines of Jesus at St Margaret's. Not only had a number of the women who would go on to become Sisters of Mercy been pupils at the Ursulines' convent boarding school, but whenever a contingent of Mercies from England or Ireland visited Scotland, St Margaret's was their first port of call. This was a highly supportive relationship and one that clearly made all the difference.

On 24 July Sr Clare McNamara, an original member of the Glasgow Mercy community, Sr M. Julia (Helen) Grant, an Edinburgh native and former St Margaret's pupil, and Sr M. Gertrude (Catherine) Hynes, a woman from County Clare, arrived to make the necessary arrangements for the Edinburgh convent. Their first job was to improve the house that had been taken for them at Lauriston Lane, a dwelling described in their annals as 'very inadequate to carry out to advantage the objects of the Institute'.[48] They came to teach and soon after their arrival opened a convent boarding school, took charge of the local parish school at St Mary's, and opened an evening Sunday school for the young women who could not attend the day school during the week.[49] Like the others they received support from the local clergy and laity, and in fact the land on which their convent was situated and the house that later became their orphanage and House of Mercy was gifted to them by Isabella Cunningham Hutchison, the convert widow of the East India Company's Lieutenant Colonel George Hutchison. Their convent and the renovations, some of which were covered by Cunningham Hutchison, cost somewhere between £5,000 and £6,000.[50] Their convent school provided them with an immediate source of income and although the size of the community grew steadily, they did not take in large numbers of entrants until the 1880s, when additional sisters were needed to run their new foundations made at Dalkeith in 1875 and at Linlithgow in 1893.[51]

Table 3.2 below provides statistics gleaned from a list compiled by the congregation's archivist and shows that the 1880s and 1890s were the decades when the community received the most entrants: twenty-two and seventeen respectively, when compared to seven in the 1860s and six in the 1870s. Overall, thirty of the sixty-eight sisters were Scottish-born, approximately 44 per cent, eighteen were English-born, equalling 26 per cent, and twelve, or 18 per cent, were Irish. The table also reveals that there were members from as far away as Jamaica and India, which hints at Scottish Catholics' participation in Britain's imperial activities.[52] The censuses are useful for determining the actual size of the community at a particular juncture and the details available for 1871 show that it numbered twenty-one religious, one school mistress, four pupil-teachers, nineteen pupil boarders and three servants. This indicates a healthy membership and a prosperous boarding school wherein the vast majority of the pupil boarders were Scottish and English.[53] Entries also exist for the 1891 census, but the enumerators did not specify who was religious and who was not, thus making it difficult to ascertain who was a sister and who was a servant employed by the convent.[54] However, it does reveal that the number of pupil boarders was nineteen and that the majority (twelve) were Scottish with two coming from Orkney. What is also interesting to note is that one of the pupil boarders was from Demerara, revealing that the old connections between Scotland and South America's sugar capital were still intact and that Catholics were commercially active in this corner of the empire.[55]

Although the Edinburgh foundation was much more stable than the one in Glasgow, it was not without its problems. In 1867, less than a decade after it was first begun, McNamara returned to Edinburgh to check on the progress of the community and reported that although there were nineteen or twenty sisters, only four or five of them were professed. While this showed strong growth potential, with many new members coming up through the ranks, the lack of professed sisters was a serious concern, since it would be difficult to provide proper religious training for the new recruits. McNamara hinted that the troubles facing the community surrounded the issue of leadership and that the appointment of the superior, Sr M. Teresa MacPherson, by Bishop John Menzies Strain was controversial. She noted that 'Sr. M. Teresa is anything but desirous of the office – for it is hard to come as a perfect stranger among so many.'[56] This problem seems to have been rectified by 1871 because the census shows that a new convent leadership team had been installed: Elizabeth

Bolster from County Cork was superior, Gertrude Day from London was the assistant superior, and Agnes Snow, a Birmingham native, was the bursar.[57]

Gender and ethnicity in religious communities

It was between 1850 and 1860 that the Glasgow communities experienced their highest level of growth, but this was also when the overall number of religious congregations and convents in Scotland was small. The pontifical status of the Franciscan Sisters meant that they rapidly overtook the Sisters of Mercy in terms of size, soon expanding beyond Glasgow to Inverness and Aberdeen. These new communities had the benefit of support and guidance from the Glasgow mother house, and the congregation in general achieved greater exposure and gained access to more resources. This growth was part of a much more general trend of expansion, and during the 1850s seven new congregations were established in Scotland. This influx increased competition, which partly explains why the number of entrants levelled off in the Franciscan and Mercy communities after 1860, but it was also the case that both were settled with a solid membership that allowed them to be more selective about the women who entered.

The expansion of female institutes did not mean that their male colleagues accepted them. Clerics regularly interfered with convent affairs because they were uncomfortable with women who crossed traditional boundaries and 'modified' gender limitations to acquire moral authority.[58] One of the most obvious ways women religious did this was with their names or with titles such as superior. Most religious names contained the prefix Sister Mary, but this was often followed by male or gender-neutral names such as Vincent, Stephen, Francis, Joseph, Benedict, Dominic, Of Mercy, Of the Cross, Of Lourdes or Of the Visitation. Similarly, the title mother superior has a dual meaning since 'mother' was feminine, denoting care-giver and nurturer, and 'superior', in the nineteenth century, was masculine, implying leader.[59] Names and titles like these gave sisters more assertive identities and so misogyny was a common feature of the religious life. In the mid-1870s, for example, Michael Condon, a priest working in the Western District, wrote of a fellow priest defining a nun as a 'woman who puts on her head a yard of dirty linen and defies the Pope'.[60] This type of reaction was symptomatic of a church whose custom, tradition and governance had been founded upon patriarchy and gender inequality. The anxiety towards women religious was also prevalent in Protestant quarters because it was believed that convent life challenged the ideal of marriage and motherhood. One pamphlet, published in London in 1850, argued that the conventual system deceived 'a woman's heart, that unconquerable maternal instinct, the basis of a woman's character'.[61] The concept of chaste, single women existing beyond the reach of most men seemed to disgust the anonymous pamphleteer, who viewed women religious as the epitome of 'sterile widowhood, a state of emptiness [whose lifestyle represented] an intellectual and moral fast'.[62]

One way that clerics tried to gain control over women religious was through the manipulation of their rules and constitutions and, where possible, bishops and priests often co-authored these important documents. The process of creating a new rule for the Franciscan Sisters was begun as a joint project between Alexander Smith and Veronica Cordier, but constant disagreements destroyed their working relationship. It has been speculated that Cordier's French ways may have been too abrasive since she was a 'typical French woman... brought up in the strict and even narrow traditions of French spirituality'.[63] Her wish to preserve a strict convent hierarchy wherein the superior had absolute authority was not something that Smith could endorse.[64] The rule that was eventually approved by Rome still allowed for practices such as the Chapter of Faults, which required sisters to accuse themselves of 'infractions' in front senior members thus fostering humility, but Smith felt it necessary to work in the need for young and old sisters to be understanding of each other and to keep themselves healthy by avoiding 'excessive mortification' such as extreme fasting or self-flagellation.[65] The preservation of the older European traditions, principally the strict division between choir and lay sisters and that between old and young religious, were obstacles that confronted countless communities around the world. New sisters, culturally distanced and often much younger, had expectations of convent life that were radically different from their predecessors and this often provoked antagonism. The gradual abandonment of class distinctions in the religious life in the twentieth century and the phasing out of the heavy, woollen full-length habit and veil, are two examples of change that were not easily achieved.

In Scotland, as in other mission territories like Canada and the United States, cultural identity and ethnicity also became central preoccupations because it was believed that these characteristics could be transformed to suit local needs. The previous chapters made reference to the fact that the development of Catholicism in Scotland was affected by the anti-Irish sentiments that were expressed by some of the clergy and that this was more pronounced in the west than in the east. The tension that existed between the Irish and Scottish Catholics had a tremendous impact upon the development of Catholicism in Scotland. Impressions of the Irish as racially, culturally and religiously inferior had convinced many Scottish clerics of the need to transform the migrants into respectable, loyal and obedient Scottish citizens and British subjects. These feelings were especially acute in the Western District, where the leading clergy invested tremendous energy in minimising the degree to which Irish Catholics were able to influence Catholic culture and identity. At least two-thirds of the migrants who arrived in Scotland settled in and around Glasgow and the antagonism they faced upon arrival made it virtually impossible for them to become part of Scottish society.[66] Although the Irish far outnumbered Scots in the total Catholic population, they were prevented from assuming positions of authority within the church because the indigenous clergy, particularly those in the Western District, and influential laymen worked diligently to assert their cultural authority. Women religious were an integral part of this process since it was believed that they had the potential to transform Catholic culture. Their particular focus on children and young women meant that they were uniquely positioned to reshape people's devotional attitudes by instilling a strong sense of loyalty and obedience to the church and, because of this, the class and ethnicity of the sisters was closely monitored. In the Eastern District, where the number of Irish was comparably smaller, class appears to have been the predominant concern, whereas in the Western District, where the Irish population was larger and where confrontations between Scots clerics and a number of politically active Irish occurred more frequently, ethnicity was more important. What is clear is that Western District bishops and their coadjutors linked the presence of Scottish-born convent superiors to the creation of a suitable Catholic identity.

In 1851 Glasgow's population was 329,097 whereas Edinburgh's was 193,929.[67] Glasgow's Irish population was approximately 59,801 (18.17 per cent) and it is assumed that roughly three-quarters were Catholic. There are no comparable statistics for Edinburgh, but in 1841, on the eve of the Famine, the *Statistical Account* lists 7,100 Irish in the county of Midlothian, where Edinburgh was located, and it is likely that the majority were Catholic and living in Edinburgh and Leith.[68] Even without specific population figures for 1851, it is obvious that the number of Irish in Glasgow was much higher, and this was reflected in the membership of the religious communities. Of the 165 Franciscan Sisters and the 35 Sisters of Mercy who were professed in Glasgow between 1850 and 1900, the number of Irish-born was 61 and 9 respectively.[69] The majority came from the provinces of Munster and Leinster and were members of Ireland's emerging and increasingly influential Catholic middle class. In Ireland, this sector drove the modernisation of Catholicism, and the resurrection of conventual life was an integral part of the process.[70] Conversely, in Edinburgh the majority of the Ursulines of Jesus were Scottish and English, with comparatively fewer Irish-born sisters joining the community between 1834 and 1900. The Sisters of Mercy there also had a low Irish

Table 3.1. Glasgow professions, Franciscan Sisters of the Immaculate Conception and the Sisters of Mercy

Decade	Franciscan Sisters of the Immaculate Conception		Sisters of Mercy	
	Professions	Place of birth	Professions	Place of birth
1850s	29	Scotland	8	Scotland
	25	Ireland	5	Ireland
	2	England	2	England
	3	France		
	2	Jamaica		
	1	Belgium		
	1	Gibraltar		
	1	Guernsey		
Total	64		15	
1860s	15	Scotland	1	Scotland
	9	Ireland	3	Ireland
	2	England	2	England
Total	26		6	
1870s	16	Scotland	4	Scotland
	6	Ireland	1	France
	1	England		
	1	Bavaria		
Total	24		5	
1880s	15	Scotland	3	Scotland
	8	Ireland	2	England
	1	England		
Total	24		5	
1890s	11	Scotland	3	Scotland
	13	Ireland	1	Ireland
	2	England	1	England
	1	United States		
Total	27		5	

Source: FSICA. Sister Professions & Receptions, Vols. 1 and 2. SMA, Glasgow. Names of Sisters who entered in Glasgow.

membership between 1858 and 1900, with just 18 per cent of the community's sixty-eight sisters being Irish-born, while 44 per cent were Scottish-born and 26 per cent were born in England. More detailed breakdowns are shown in Tables 3.1 and 3.2.

Table 3.2. Edinburgh professions, Ursulines of Jesus and the Sisters of Mercy

Decade	Ursulines of Jesus		Sisters of Mercy	
	Professions	Place of Birth	Professions	Place of Birth
1830s	0	N/A	N/A	N/A
1840s	9	Scotland	N/A	N/A
	4	England		
Total	13			
1850s	2	Scotland	1	Scotland
	2	England		
Total	4		1	
1860s	4	Scotland	2	Scotland
	6	England	3	Ireland
	4	Ireland	2	England
Total	14		7	
1870s	6	Scotland	4	Scotland
	1	England	1	Ireland
	4	Ireland	1	England
	1	India		
	1	Canada		
	1	At sea, near St Helena		
Total	14		6	
1880s	5	Scotland	8	Scotland
	1	England	4	Ireland
	6	Ireland	5	England
			1	India
			1	Jamaica
			1	Spain
			2	Unknown
Total	12		22	
1890s	4	Scotland	7	Scotland
	2	England	4	England
	4	Ireland	1	Italy
	1	Switzerland	1	Spain
			4	Unknown
Total	11		17	

Sources: SCA. Ursulines of Jesus Profession book. These numbers only count those women who made their final profession, not simply those who entered but left. SMA, Birmingham. List of the Edinburgh Sisters of Mercy.

Although both the Edinburgh and Glasgow Mercy communities were founded from Limerick, it is important to explain that Limerick had not been the intended founding community. It was the Mercy community in Liverpool that was supposed to have established these Scottish foundations and young Scots had been sent down to England in preparation, but when a wave of illness and death swept through the Liverpool community the Scottish clerics were directed to Dublin to find an alternative solution.[71] It made practical sense to turn to the Irish communities, since their numbers were so much higher than anywhere outside France. France had witnessed an unparalleled rise in the number of women entering the religious life, and between 1800 and 1880 roughly 200,000 women had joined over 400 congregations.[72] Ireland also experienced a dramatic rise and although the number of women religious there was nowhere near the number in France, the growth was still considerable and jumped from 120 in 1800 to over 1,500 by the middle of the century. In England it was a completely different story, with one estimate suggesting that before 1830 there were only twenty-four contemplative convents in England and none in Scotland. Between 1830 and 1850 ten active congregations and six contemplative orders had settled in England, while just three had been founded in Scotland.[73] Establishing religious communities was a labour-intensive process that required the experience of professed religious whose familiarity with convent structure, rules and constitutions could guide new foundations. Many had come from abroad and so trained the new entrants in the traditions of their congregations and while this served to unify the sisters, it also transferred cultural norms. In Protestant countries like Scotland and England, where the indigenous Catholic population was small, clerics were compelled to recruit from abroad. Irish Catholic culture was not something the Scottish clergy wished to promote and so where possible they turned to France despite Ireland's close geographic proximity. During the nineteenth century twelve of the twenty-two congregations that had communities in Scotland originated in France, whereas five came from England and three from Belgium. Only two came from Ireland.[74]

In Glasgow there was tension over the status and position of Irish sisters within the convents and much of the trouble surrounded the two most powerful posts: the superior and the novice mistress. Superiors were 'good shepherds', the leaders of religious communities who ensured that vows were fulfilled and the rules were observed.[75] They were confirmed by a male ecclesiastical superior after their election by secret ballot, but in diocesan institutes, they could also be appointed by the local bishop and, in very special circumstances, selected by postulation.[76] They directed the community's day-to-day affairs and oversaw the spiritual development of the community, and through practices like the Examination of Conscience (a private conference between a sister and the superior) they exercised unrivalled influence over the community. Although Canon Law forbade women from having ecclesiastical jurisdiction (the power to 'govern the faithful'), superiors were charged with reshaping people's values and beliefs, arguably one of the most important positions within the church.[77] Equally important was the post of novice mistress, because the sister who held this office took sole responsibility for the care and training of novices, the young women preparing to become professed sisters and nuns. The superior was not allowed to interfere with how the novitiate was governed and this afforded the novice mistress significant autonomy in shaping the hearts and minds of the new sisters.[78] Leadership was a key component in the establishment of a successful community that promoted an 'appropriate' Catholic culture and in Scotland this often meant the exclusion of Irish sisters.

In Edinburgh, between 1834 and the turn of the century, the Ursulines had held eighteen elections and had been governed by nine different superiors, all of whom had been French, Scottish or English. This is not too unusual considering that this reflected the majority of its membership. The 1841 census lists fourteen women religious at St Margaret's, seven French, five Scots and two English. In 1861 the number of religious had increased to twenty-six, and although the birthplaces of five are illegible, eleven were English, six were Scottish and four were Irish. A decade later the total number of religious was thirty and in addition to the twelve Scots, eight English and seven Irish, two had been born in India, though one of these ended up leaving the community, and one young woman, Mary Jane Eyre, in religion Sr M. Agatha, a lay sister, had been born 'at sea, near St Helena'.[79] Interestingly, while there were a few Irish women who entered as choir sisters with dowries, the vast majority were lay sisters (three out of four in 1861 and four out of seven in 1871) who had no input in community affairs.[80] The majority of the Irish in Scotland did not come from affluent backgrounds, but the pattern of assigning Irish women lowly positions was repeated in numerous communities throughout Britain, even in those that did not have a two-tier choir/lay system. In her study of women religious in England and Wales, Barbara Walsh points out that in congregations like the Sisters of Notre Dame de Namur, where there was no such stratification, Irish sisters were commonly relegated to 'humble roles' and very few held leadership posts.[81] A community of this congregation was established in Glasgow in 1894 and here too there is evidence of anti-Irishness, with the superior, on one occasion, exclaiming that 'some Irish girls are perfectly useless'.[82]

Statistics for the Sisters of Mercy in Edinburgh are less complete but the

Table 3.3. Superiors, Ursulines of Jesus, Edinburgh

Name in religion	Name	Place of birth	Dates in post
Sr M. Hilaire	Unknown	France	1834–37
Sr M. Emily	Unknown	France	1837–47, 1850–55
Sr M. St Damian	Unknown	France	1847–50
Sr M. Angela	Elizabeth Witham	England	1855–67, 1873–76
Sr M. Teresa	Margaret Clapperton	Scotland	1867–73
Sr M. Ursula	Ann Clapperton	Scotland	1876–82, 1891–1901
Sr M. Bernard	Mary Margaret Leslie	England	1882–91

Table 3.4. Superiors, Sisters of Mercy, Edinburgh

Name in religion	Name	Place of birth	Dates in post
Sr M. Gertrude	Catherine Hynes	Co. Clare, Ireland	1858–61
Sr M. Juliana	Helen Grant	Banffshire, Scotland	1861–64
Sr M. Aloysius	Susan Grady	Edinburgh, Scotland	1864–67
Sr M. Ignatius	Elizabeth Bolster	Cork, Ireland	c.1867–71
Sr M. Stanislaus	Mary Snow	London, England	c.1871–86
Sr M. Evangelist	Theresa MacPherson	Edinburgh, Scotland	c.1886–92
Sr M. Baptist	Teresa Henderson	Edinburgh, Scotland	c.1892–1901

censuses for 1871, 1891 and 1901 reveal that there were two Scottish-born superiors and one Irish-born superior. Elizabeth Bolster was born in Cork and is thought to have led the community for approximately three years.

In Glasgow the cultural antagonism was most acute between the late 1840s and the late 1860s when community identity was especially pliable. During this time the positions of superior and novice mistress in both communities were subjected to intense clerical scrutiny and the ethnicity of the candidates was usually the underlying factor. The bishops wanted to instil within the communities an identity that was distinctively Scottish, but the predominance of Irish-born members made this difficult. To minimise the degree of Irish Catholic influence the bishops took an active role in community elections and appointments, and a glimpse at the ethnicity of the superiors reveals the dominance of Scottish-born women. The Sisters of Mercy had just one Irish-born superior between 1849 and 1870 and she was Sr M. Catherine McNamara, the woman installed by Elizabeth Moore when the community was first founded. The five women who succeeded her were of Scottish and English birth. It was

Table 3.5. Superiors, Sisters of Mercy, Glasgow

Name in religion	Name	Place of birth	Dates in post
Sr M. Clare	Mary McNamara	Limerick, Ireland	1849–51
Sr M. Bernard	Margaret Garden	Aberdeenshire, Scotland	1851–52
Sr M. Aloysius	Mary Anne Consitt	Durham, England	1852–54
Sr M. Aloysius	Teresa Mary Rigg	Kirkcudbrightshire, Scotland	1854–64
Sr M. de Sales	Elizabeth Dend	Edinburgh, Scotland	1864–70
Sr M. Ignatius	Jane Anne Hope-Johnston	Moffat, Scotland	1870–71
Sr M. of Mercy	Ellen Strachan	Dublin, Ireland	1871–77 and 1883–96

Source: SMA, Glasgow. Names of Sisters who entered in Glasgow.

only in 1871 that the next Irish woman was installed as superior. Sr M. Of Mercy (Ellen) Strachan gave the community great stability and was highly respected by her fellow religious, but it is important to emphasise that her approved election only came after the English ultramontane, Charles Eyre, was appointed Vicar Apostolic of the Western District. It is unlikely that she would have held the post had this change in diocesan leadership not occurred; in 1868 the tension between the Irish and the Scots Catholics had become so pronounced and poisonous that Rome intervened and appointed Eyre. Over time, and with the ultramontane strategy becoming more firmly embedded, the 'ethno-cultural distances' became less pronounced.[83]

The installation of a Scottish superior had been on the agenda before the community was even founded. In 1845 Bishop Murdoch had sent Margaret Garden, a young woman from Aberdeenshire, to the Liverpool Mercy community for her novitiate and it was assumed that when ready, she would lead the Glasgow community. This was not an uncommon practice and it will be recalled that a similar plan had been carried out with the Ursulines of Jesus. The Scotticisation of these communities was a priority and in this particular case Garden was deemed the perfect candidate: from recusant stock, she would safeguard the Scottish Catholic tradition. A devastating blow to this plan was dealt when she was transferred first to Dublin and then to Limerick by her Mercy superiors, who then refused to send her back to Glasgow because they felt that she needed to make a stronger connection with the Mercy ethos.[84] Angered by this assertion of female authority, an incensed Murdoch travelled to Ireland to personally retrieve her. This blatant disregard for the authority structure of a female community and his anti-Irish attitude, diplomatically described by his coadjutor, Alexander Smith, as 'national feelings', damaged his relations with the Mercy congregation beyond repair.[85] In 1851 Murdoch's persistence to have Garden installed as superior resulted in the Mercy leadership taking the decision to transfer the original Irish sisters back to Limerick.[86] Soon afterwards McNamara, the Irish superior, also left and this had a catastrophic effect on the fledgling community, which had to cope with the loss of five professed sisters, two novices and four postulants.[87] This was followed by the desertion of six more postulants, and so when Garden did finally become superior, the community was in tatters and numbered just two professed sisters, three novices and two postulants.[88] This episode reflected both cultural antagonism and the clergy's uncompromising attitude towards the status of women religious.

There was deep resentment towards the Irish women who attempted to assert their autonomy and circumvent clerical authority. The bishops regarded the events at the Mercy convent as yet another example of Irish Catholic culture attempting to displace Scottish traditions, and in a letter to James Kyle, who served as bishop of the Northern District between 1827 and 1869, Murdoch complained that

> those who opposed MMB's coming to Glasgow were quite in the wrong... They might have thought that she was not ripe to become superior. In this I and you too would have joined them. It would have been highly desirable that she had some years before of religious profession over her head before she got that charge. It was I understand necessity... But to seek to prevent a Scotch woman from giving & her own poor country women who stood so much in need of religious instruction which they judged she was called by God to impart was I think unreasonable and contrary to all due order.[89]

The community only stabilised after 1854 when Sr M. Aloysius Rigg, a Scot from Kirkcudbrightshire, began her decade-long tenure as superior. Like Garden, Rigg came from a recusant family but she received crucial emotional support from her two sisters and five cousins, who also joined the community in the 1850s. This family essentially saved the Glasgow Mercy foundation when it was in complete disarray following the Irish exodus.[90] Although much of the evidence relating to anti-Irishness in the Western District comes from the clergy, it is important to emphasise that women religious also actively participated in the relegation of Irish sisters. The dilution of the Mercy community with Riggs is just one example. Garden herself exhibited similar tendencies while superior, and on one occasion, when asking Smith to send along any interested aspirants, she wrote that Scottish women, as opposed to Irish women, were preferred.⁹¹ What makes this example so poignant is the influence and religious authority that she would acquire as she put into practice the church's grassroots expansion policy by founding five other convents in northeast Scotland between 1870 and 1880.⁹²

The turmoil that confronted the Franciscan Sisters was not dissimilar to what the Mercies experienced, but their pontifical status and French roots provided more of a buffer against clerical interference and gave them more freedom over the selection of superiors. As congregational foundress, Cordier held the post of prioress until 1857, when she left Glasgow after a series of rows with Alexander Smith. In 1857 Cordier, along with Sr M. Philomena (Julie Victoire) Dalle and Sr M. Paula (Laureute) Charlet, both from France, and Sr M. de Sales (Catherine) O'Neil from Aberdeenshire, quit Glasgow entirely to found a new congregation in Jamaica. Cordier was succeeded by Sr Angela McSwinney, an Irish woman, whose tenure was embroiled in controversy. The inaugural General Chapter on 23 July 1854 saw all religious, as opposed to just those who were professed, invited to participate in the election of the offices and, as ecclesiastical superior, Smith was also present. Cordier was unanimously elected prioress and Sr M. Aloysius Mackintosh, a young Jamaican-born woman of Scottish Catholic parentage, was elected sub-prioress. As prioress, Cordier had the authority to appoint the novice mistress, but when she selected McSwinney, Smith vetoed her. His right to do this had been enshrined within the congregation's constitutions that he himself had written:

> The Religious convinced that their Bishop or any of his deputies to them is the representative of God, and that whatever commands they receive from him are issued in the name and with the sanction of his divine master, will submit with alacrity to whatever he orders or direction he may be pleased to communicate to them.⁹³

Clauses like this were designed to establish a gender hierarchy within communities and to ensure that Rome and its representative bishops had ultimate jurisdiction over women religious. Boiled down, this meant that Rome feared 'nuns on the loose'.⁹⁴ What it also did was enable the clergy to implement changes according to their own specific needs, and because mistress of the novices was not an elected post, Cordier was obliged to accept Smith's decision. In 1856, unable to stand Mackintosh's 'negligence', she accused the woman of being unfit for the post. Mackintosh took the matter to Smith, who contemplated forcing Cordier to make a public apology to the community. Frustrated and humiliated, Cordier resigned, but during the next set of elections, the community showed tremendous solidarity by electing McSwinney

Table 3.6. Superiors, Franciscan Sisters of the Immaculate Conception, Glasgow

Name in religion	Name	Place of birth	Dates in post
Sr M. Veronica	Veronica Cordier	Saint-Armand, France	1849–57
Sr M. Angela	Hannah McSwinney	Co. Cork, Ireland	1857–60 and 1866–69
Sr M. Vincent	Mary Dolan	Dublin, Ireland	1860–63
Sr M. Aloysius	Barbie Mackintosh	Jamaica	1863–66
Sr M. Gonzaga	Mary Simm	Morayshire, Scotland	1870–84
Sr M. Of the Cross	Cecilia Black	Glasgow, Scotland	1884–96
Sr M. Athanasius	Joanne Maclean	Moidart, Scotland	1896–1909

Source: FSICA. Sister Professions and Receptions, vols 1 and 2.

Figure 3.4. Mother Mary of the Cross (Cecilia) Black, superior of the Franciscan Sisters between 1884 and 1896. Reproduced by permission of the Franciscan Sisters of the Immaculate Conception, Glasgow.

prioress and her younger sister, Sr M. Catherine (Mary) McSwinney, sub-prioress. This was a clear act of defiance since Smith had no ability to interfere with elected posts and, what is more, Mackintosh was completely ostracised and forced to retreat to Italy on account of mental distress.[95] Thus between

1856 and 1863 the Franciscan Sisters were governed by Irish women, first by McSwinney and then by Sr M. Vincent (Mary) Dolan, which frustrated a powerless clergy to no end. Smith, who had once criticised Murdoch for his anti-Irishness, displayed a similar attitude in his report on the state of the Western District in the late 1850s:

> The Franciscans – don't please me at all. There is nothing very far amiss – but the Prioress is intensely Irish – Irish in her feelings & prejudices, associations, want to order, want of cleanliness – manifesting her sympathies – this in respect to priests, nuns & people and children.[96]

Nor did this contempt disappear after the deaths of Murdoch and Smith in the early-to-mid 1860s. Battles continued to rage between the clergy and the community over the issue of superiors until the late 1860s, a symptom of the culture war that had gripped the Glasgow clergy.[97] Murdoch's successor was John Gray, but for the first time an Irish coadjutor, James Lynch, was assigned and this had explosive consequences that finally made way for the installation of an ultramontane bishop. In 1867 the Archbishop of Westminster, Henry Manning, was sent to Scotland by his superiors in Rome to investigate and report on what was going on. He spent five dreary October days meeting with various Irish and Scottish clerics and influential laymen, and in his report he highlighted 'racial antipathy' and 'mutual prejudices' as the main problems afflicting the Western District.[98] What Manning also discovered was that rather than there being a Vicar Apostolic and a coadjutor, there were two men operating as 'quasi independent' bishops having virtually no communication with each other. The clergy had polarised into camps and the whole ugly situation was seriously threatening church stability. He reported that a number of second- or third-generation Irish clergy were 'anti-Scotch' and accused the fiery *Free Press* of 'ecclesiastical sedition', strongly criticising the Irish clerics who published in it.[99] He highlighted the 'national arrogance' of the Scots, called them aloof and said that they were in want of fraternal charity. Manning believed that both Gray and Lynch needed to be replaced, but admitted that the situation had been 'out of control' well before Lynch had been appointed.[100] The man who replaced them in 1868 was Charles Eyre, a wealthy recusant and ultramontane from York, who had been identified early in his priestly career as bishop material. When Angela McSwinney's term as superior of the Francsican Sisters ended in 1870, however, all of her successors, at least until 1908, were Scottish-born and had long tenures. This appeared to stabilise the entire congregation and did much to ensure their success in the field of female elementary education.

To put the experience of the two Glasgow communities into context, one need look no further than the Sisters of Mercy in Dundee. Recruited from Derry in 1859 by Stephen Keenan, the Irish priest in St Andrew's Parish, the founders of the community were Mother M. Catherine Locke, Sr M. Joseph Mehan, Sr M. Francis Locke, Sr M. Vincent Docherty and Sr M. Xavier White. This community had an all Irish-membership until 1870 when Sr M. Francis de Sales (Marianne) Driscoll, a woman of English birth but of Irish descent, entered. The first Scottish-born sister joined in 1888, but like Driscoll, Sr M. Aloysius (Rosanne) McDaniel was also of Irish descent. It was only in 1901 that the first indigenous Scot, Sr M. Aquin (Emma) Hunter, entered the community.[101] Crucially, Keenan had supported the Irish identity of the community and had even used the town's Irish population to his advantage when approaching the Derry superior with his proposal for a convent: 'we have lots of the best hearted Irish lasses that you could meet anywhere, if they were all educated you might have a convent of 500 nuns'.[102] Dundee had shown, much better than either Glasgow or Edinburgh, the ability to incorporate Irish Catholic culture and in this respect reflected more closely than elsewhere in Scotland what was happening abroad in countries like the United States and Canada. Across the Atlantic, Irish communities were known for retaining their 'homogeneous ethnic identity' and for many it was a source of pride and accomplishment.[103]

The movement of Irish and French sisters to countries like Scotland, England, Australia, Canada and the United States was a common feature of nineteenth-century religious life, but some sisters adapted to life abroad better than others. In every case the success of the foundation rested upon the ability of superiors to make cultural adjustments, and scholars who have published on women religious in the United States show that the communities that succeeded in Americanising were the ones most likely to thrive.[104] In Scotland, the establishment of communities of women religious that were 'Scotticised' was a priority, especially in the Western District, where the bulk of the Irish migrants had congregated. This was to correspond with moves to create a Catholic system of education across Scotland that would offset proselytisation and improve the overall status of Catholicism. As the communities grew more established with a stronger and more experienced membership, their educational work expanded and they were in a better position to effect real religious and cultural change. Women religious offered night and day schools, private boarding schools, poor parish schools and Sunday schools, and although their efforts were directed mainly at infants, girls and young women, they also ran boys' schools when there was no one else to do it. The following chapter expands upon the role played by women religious in the transformation of Catholic culture in Scotland by investigating their involvement with the establishment of a Catholic elementary education system.

Notes

1 Fintan Geser, *The Canon Law Governing Communities of Sisters* (London, B. Herder Book Co., 1950), p. 32.
2 Maureen Fitzgerald, *Habits of Compassion: Irish Catholic Nuns and the Origins of New York's Welfare System, 1830–1920* (Urbana, University of Illinois Press, 2006), pp. 3–4.
3 S. Karly Kehoe, 'Special Daughters of Rome: Glasgow and its Roman Catholic Sisters, 1847–1913'. Unpublished PhD thesis, Faculty of Arts, University of Glasgow, 2005, p. 174.
4 Mark Dilworth, 'Religious orders in Scotland, 1878–1978', *Innes Review*, 29:1 (1978), pp. 103–4.
5 Silvia Evangelisti, *Nuns: A History of Convent Life* (Oxford, Oxford University Press, 2007), p. 228. Fitzgerald, *Habits of Compassion*, p. 3.
6 Agnes Trail, *Revival of conventual life in Scotland. History of St. Margaret's Convent, Edinburgh, the first religious house founded in Scotland since the so-called Reformation; and the autobiography of the first religious Sister Agnes Xavier Trail* (Edinburgh, 1886), p. 36.
7 Registrar General for Scotland (RGS) 1841 Census, RD:685/02 ED:163/000 and 1861 Census, RD:685/05 ED:100/000.
8 RGS 1871 Census, RD:685/05 ED:113/000.
9 RGS 1891 Census, RD:685/05 ED:110/000. Dilworth, 'Religious orders', pp. 103–4.
10 Charles J. Smith, *Historic South Edinburgh* (Edinburgh, John Donald, 1978), p. 47.
11 SCA MC3/3. Memorandum with reference to Properties of St. Margaret's Convent, Edinburgh.
12 SCA. Dowry Book for St. Margaret's Convent.
13 Charles McKean, 'Graham, James Gillespie (1776–1855)', *Oxford Dictionary of National Biography*, Oxford University Press, 2004. www.oxforddnb.com/view/article/11203 [accessed 6 August 2007].
14 Henry Cockburn, *Journal of Henry Cockburn being a continuation of the memorials of his time, 1831–1854*, vols 1 and 2 (Edinburgh, 1874), p. 98.
15 Trail, *Revival of conventual life*, p. 31.
16 Cockburn, *Journal*, p. 85.
17 Nancy Lusignan Schiltz (ed.), *Veil of Fear: Nineteenth-Century Convent Tales by Rebecca Reed and Maria Monk* (West Lafayette, IN, Notabell Books, 1999), p. xvii.
18 *Blackwood's Edinburgh Magazine*, 71:436 (February 1852), p. 222. Miriam Elizabeth Burnstein briefly discusses how convents were featured in nineteenth-century literature in *Narrating Women's History in Britain, 1770–1902* (Aldershot, Ashgate, 2004), pp. 137–9.
19 *The Scotsman*, 26 March 1851.

20 *Ibid.* SCA. St. Margaret's Convent, *Annals*, 6 March 1851 and 25 March 1851.
21 Bernard Aspinwall, 'Trail, Ann Agnes (1798-1872)', *Oxford Dictionary of National Biography*. Oxford University Press, 2004. www.oxforddnb.com/view/article/45566 [accessed 9 August 2006].
22 SCA MC4/50/13. Letter to Rev. Mother from M. M. Bernard Garden, 8 June 1886.
23 SCA St. Margaret's Convent, *Annals*, 24 June 1849.
24 Charles Withers, 'The demographic history of the city, 1831-1911', in W. Hamish Fraser and Irene Maver (eds), *Glasgow*, vol. 2 (Manchester, Manchester University Press, 1996), pp. 149-50. Carol K. Coburn and Martha Smith, *Spirited Lives: How Nuns Shaped Catholic Culture and American Life, 1836-1920* (Chapel Hill, University of North Carolina Press, 1999), pp. 190-1.
25 Béatrice Craig, 'La structure de l'emploi féminin dans une ville en voie d'industrialisation: Tourcoing au XIX siècle', *Canadian Journal of History*, 27:2 (August 1992), pp. 299-330.
26 FSICA, The Franciscan Sisters of the Immaculate Conception Obituary Book. Kept with the Superior.
27 Barbara Walsh, *Roman Catholic Nuns in England and Wales, 1800-1937: A Social History* (Dublin, Irish Academic Press, 2002), p. 91.
28 FSICA, Obituary Book.
29 *Ibid.*
30 Letter from Mary Margaret Brewster to Mrs Kyle (Bishop Kyle's sister-in-law), 13 October 1849. Thank you to Hannah McCarthy for providing me with copies of these letters.
31 Mary Peckham Magray, *The Transforming Power of the Nuns: Women, Religion and Cultural Change in Ireland, 1750-1900* (Oxford, Oxford University Press, 1998), p. 34.
32 *Ibid.*, p. 35.
33 Trail lived in the Benedictine Convent at Hammersmith in England after her conversion to Catholicism in 1829. Trail, *Revival of conventual life*, p. 350.
34 Private Collection. Letter from Brewster to Kyle, 29 December 1849.
35 Dilworth, 'Religious orders', pp. 103-4.
36 John Watts, *A Canticle of Love: The Story of the Franciscan Sisters of the Immaculate Conception* (Edinburgh, John Donald, 2006), p. 258.
37 Maria Luddy, *Women and Philanthropy in Nineteenth-Century Ireland* (Cambridge, Cambridge University Press, 1995), p. 27.
38 *The Franciscan Sisters of the Immaculate Conception: Celebrating 150 years in Glasgow.* Produced by the community, 1997, pp. 100-1.
39 MICA, Dublin. Record Group 100-3.2. Xeroxed copies of Letters, set 2 of 2. Letter from Catherine McAuley to Sister Mary Francis Ward, St. Leo Convent, Carlow.
40 FSICA Obituary Book; Sister Professions and Receptions, vols 1 and 2. SMA, Glasgow. Names of the Sisters who entered in Glasgow. Held in green plastic

folder marked 'Brief History of Glasgow Foundation' and 'Hand-written account of Foundation'.
41 SMA, Glasgow. Anonymous, handwritten chapter entitled 'On the necessity of dying to self and not taking too much care of our health'. 'Instructions of St. Theresa' on the cover of a soft-back jotter, c.mid-nineteenth century.
42 McAuley offered Moore advice in the form of a poem which was meant to remind her to be patient, affectionate and encouraging. MICA Record Group 100–3.2. Letter from Catherine McAuley to Elizabeth Moore, 9 December 1838.
43 MICA Record Group 300–2.5 England/G. B. Glasgow. Statement of the Convent of Mercy. Written by Bishop Alexander Smith, Glasgow 1857.
44 *Ibid.*
45 FSICA. Box marked Mother Adelaide and Mother Veronica, ref. #011. Copy of manuscript sent from Tourcoing in 1930, pp. 55–7. Medium-sized red notebook, Mother Adelaide and Mother Veronica 1936.
46 MICA Statement of the Convent of Mercy.
47 SCA MC 4/2/7. Letter to the Ursuline Sisters from James Gillis, 1 January 1844.
48 SMA, Limerick. Annals of the Sisters of Mercy, Limerick, vol. 1, 1838–58, p. 215.
49 James Gillis, *Objects of St. Catherine's Institute of our Lady of Mercy, Lauriston Gardens, Edinburgh* (1861).
50 Imelda King, *Sisters of Mercy of Great Britain: Brief Historical Sketches* (Glasgow, John S. Burns, 1978), p. 89.
51 Dilworth, 'Religious orders', pp. 103–4.
52 SMA, Birmingham. List of the Edinburgh Sisters compiled by the archivist.
53 RGS 1871 Census, RD:685/04 ED:094/000.
54 RGS 1891 Census, RD:685/04 ED:074/000 and 1901 Census, RD:685/04 ED:060/000.
55 RGS 1891Census, RD:685/04 ED:074/000.
56 SMA, Bermondsey. 400/2/19. Letter from Sr. M. Clare McNamara to the sisters of St. Mary's Convent, Limerick. 12 September 1867.
57 RGS 1871Census, RD:685/04 ED:094/000.
58 Coburn and Smith, *Spirited Lives*, p. 83.
59 *Ibid.*, p. 82.
60 GAA WD5. Condon Memoirs. Note for 19 May 1874.
61 *Hints to Romanizers: No. 1. The Confessional, and the Conventual System.* Extracted from Michelet's 'Priests, Women and Families' (London, Seeleys, 1850), p. 25.
62 *Ibid.*, pp. 21–2 and 25.
63 FSICA. Unpublished Manuscript. Sr. M. Dolores Cochrane, Franciscan Sisters of the Immaculate Conception. In the Beginning. Part One (1986), p. 40.
64 Watts, *A Canticle of Love*, p. 34.
65 *Ibid.*, p. 35. Suzanne Campbell-Jones, *In Habit: An Anthropological Study of Working Nuns* (London, Faber & Faber, 1979), p. 87.

66 John McCaffrey, 'Roman Catholics in Scotland in the 19th and 20th centuries', *Records of the Church History Society*, 21 (1983), pp. 275–300.
67 Withers, 'The demographic history of the city', p. 142. Census of Great Britain, 1851, Population tables, I. Number of the inhabitants in 1801, 1811, 1821, 1831, 1841 and 1851. II BPP 1852–53 LXXXVI, p. 30.
68 http://stat-acc-scot.edina.ac.uk/link/1834–45/Edinburgh/Edinburgh/ [accessed 10 August 2006].
69 Kehoe, 'Special Daughters of Rome', ch. 2.
70 Magray, *The Transforming Power*, pp. 5 and 33.
71 SMA, Limerick. Annals, vol. 1. Entry for 1849.
72 Susan O'Brien, 'French nuns in nineteenth-century England', *Past & Present*, 54:1 (1997), p. 144 and Magray, *The Transforming Power*, pp. 8 and 26.
73 Carmen Mangion, *Contested Identities: Catholic Women Religious in Nineteenth-Century England and Wales* (Manchester, Manchester University Press, 2008), pp. 34–8.
74 Dilworth, 'Religious orders', pp. 103–5.
75 Geser, *The Canon Law*, p. 115.
76 *Ibid.*, pp. 84 and 111.
77 *Ibid.*, pp. 69–70.
78 *Ibid.*, pp. 226–7.
79 RGS 1841 Census, RD:685/02 ED:163/000, 1861 Census, RD:685/05 ED:100/000 and 1871 Census, RD:685/05 ED:113/000.
80 SCA Dowry Book for St Margaret's Convent. RGS. 1861 Census, RD:685/05 ED:100/000 and 1871 Census, RD:685/05 ED:113/000.
81 Walsh, *Roman Catholic Nuns*, p. 143.
82 *Ibid.*
83 O'Brien, 'French nuns', p. 164.
84 SMA, Bermondsey, Mother Mary Bernard Garden. Manuscript of paper produced for a congregational meeting, 15 November 2003.
85 MICA Statement of the Convent of Mercy.
86 *Ibid.*
87 SMA, Glasgow. History of the Sisters of Mercy, pp. 9–10.
88 SMA, Limerick. Annals. Book I, entry for 1851, p. 137. MICA Statement of the Convent of Mercy.
89 SCA OL2/83/5. Letter from Kyle to Murdoch, 3 May 1852.
90 SMA, Glasgow. Names of the Sisters who entered in Glasgow.
91 SCA BL6/625/1. Letter from Garden to Smith, 2 October 1851.
92 SMA, Bermondsey, Mother Mary Bernard Garden.
93 FSICA *Rule of the Community of the Immaculate Conception of the Third Order of St. Francis, Glasgow; as Revised and Modified by the Sacred Congregation of Bishops and Regulars at Rome and Approved by his Holiness, Pius IX A.D.* 1853.
94 Watts, *A Canticle of Love*, p. 35.

95 FSICA Obituary Book. Unpublished Manuscript, pp. 42–3. Watts, *A Canticle of Love*, p. 49.
96 SCA OL4/6/1. Alexander Smith: Report on 'clergy and convent', in his mission, c.1858–60.
97 Watts, *A Canticle of Love*, p. 55.
98 James Walsh, 'Archbishop Manning's visitation of the Western District of Scotland in 1867', *Innes Review*, 18:1 (1967), p. 12.
99 David McRoberts, 'The restoration of the Scottish Catholic hierarchy in 1878', *Innes Review*, 24:1 (1978), p. 11.
100 Walsh, 'Archbishop Manning's visitation', pp. 13–17.
101 SMA, Dundee. List of the names of the sisters who entered the Dundee foundation. Provided by the community.
102 SMA, Dundee. Letter from Stephen Keenan to M. Francis Locke, 30 March 1859.
103 Coburn and Smith, *Spirited Lives*, p. 86. Kehoe, 'Special Daughters of Rome', p. 157.
104 Coburn and Smith, *Spirited Lives*, p. 86.

4

Constructing a system of education

> From the home of her sires she has wandered alone
> To the land of the Celt and the Saxon she's gone
> The olive branch waves in her white gentle hand
> And her accents of peace greet the cold frozen land
>
> Midst the foe, and the stranger she seeks not renown
> She courts not their smiles, and she heeds not their frowns
> Could she only impart unto childhood and youth
> The science of God, of religion, and truth ...
>
> See her stand in the midst of the listening young
> While they hear the blessed words in a sweet foreign tongue
> How they gaze with delight on the form that imparts
> Their duties to God, to their innocent hearts
>
> The black cloud of ignorance now disappears
> Where darkly it brooded for numberless years
> Blind heresy weakened will also decay
> As the light of instruction illumines the way.[1]

This poem was written by Bishop Alexander Smith as a tribute to Veronica Cordier, co-foundress of Glasgow's Franciscan Sisters. Initially he, like many others, feared that the city was 'not yet prepared for the good sisters' but by the mid-1850s he was singing a very different tune, as the number of Irish kept growing and the state was becoming increasingly concerned with expanding its authority over education.[2] The publication of Pope Pius IX's *Quanta Cura* in 1864 represented an official attack on liberalism and one of its key points was the necessity of providing a religious-run Catholic education system.[3] It denounced the concept of 'liberty of conscience and worship [as] each man's personal right' and argued against 'absolute liberty ... restrained by no authority whether ecclesiastical or civil'.[4] It was an attempt to thwart the secularising effect that liberal elements were thought to be having on society and private families.[5] Church authorities in Scotland realised that securing Catholicism in Scotland would require the establishment of a viable system of education and that those best able to handle the responsibility were the religious communities whose members were equipped to undertake the practical work associated with running schools. The sisters, nuns, priests and brothers would pave the way for widespread religious change by exposing children to an obedient, loyal and respectable Catholic culture.

Education is held up as one of the defining symbols of Scottish identity but until the middle of the nineteenth century Catholics were excluded from this *national* 'tradition'. Given this background it is paradoxical that it was education that would ultimately safeguard Catholicism's position in Scotland. The construction of a Catholic elementary education system achieved two important goals: firstly, it cemented the church's authority by ensuring that children of all classes were exposed to institutionalised Catholicism. As the state cracked down on truancy, more and more children started going to school and were exposed to church-prescribed rules, customs and beliefs. Secondly, education enabled the church to participate in and enhance the civic life of the nation. Although Catholic education would stand out for its insular character, it did succeed in making the myth of a democratic tradition more of a reality since it ensured the inclusion of two previously excluded populations, Catholics and women. Traditionally, Scottish women experienced education on a level that was inferior and unequal to men in a system that was intensely masculine in character.[6] This was most marked in urban areas where Protestant schoolmistresses were restricted to infant schools or female industrial departments because they were thought to be too delicate for the urban environment. In contrast, Catholic sisters and nuns delivered a female-centred programme to the urban mission.[7] Motivated by a desire to do good work, they assumed levels of professionalism that were well beyond the reach of the vast majority of women, whose domestic responsibilities prevented them from dedicating themselves to teaching.

This chapter shows how women religious took female elementary education and catholicity in Scotland to a new level, and it is divided into two. It considers the role that women religious played in the development of Catholic education and examines how this was interlinked with the state's ambition to reduce working-class radicalism and with Scotland's emerging national identity. The first section outlines educational provision at mid-century and compares it to what existed on the eve of the Education (Scotland) Act of 1872. The second section considers the impact that state funding and the Catholic Poor Schools Committee, a body largely governed by English interests, had upon the direction of Catholic education in Scotland. The 1840s was the decade when the Catholic Church became intertwined with the educational agenda of a liberalising state in an effort to reclaim marginal Catholics, increase its authority over the masses and transform the Irish Catholics into respectable and loyal citizens. This section also highlights the growing influence of ultramontanism and the pivotal role that the religious communities' educational work played in this. Anglicisation and the gendering of Catholic identity through education occurred at this time, and while some women religious had an anglicising influence, particularly the Sisters of Notre Dame de Namur who ran Scotland's first Catholic teacher training college, others worked to ensure the continuation of a distinctively *Scottish* identity.

Schools and teachers before 1872

Before the late 1850s provision was inconsistent and in most places completely absent. The twenty years between 1851 and 1871 were a period of crucial change for Catholicism in Scotland. Not only were new parishes established but the arrival of women religious and, after 1858, male religious, sparked unprecedented institutional expansion. While some of the statistics provided by CDS were out of date, sometimes by a few years, they nevertheless give an idea of what was happening on the ground. In 1851 the Western District had approximately fifty-nine clergymen serving forty-two churches, chapels and stations. In the East there were thirty-one clergy serving twenty-three churches and chapels, and in the Northern District it is estimated that there were twenty-nine priests and thirty-one church buildings.[8] This was impressive growth, particularly when one recalls the scarcity of clergy that typically characterised the Scottish mission since the Reformation, but the clergy still struggled to provide even minimal contact to those people identifying themselves as Catholics.

In the Western District, in places like Balfron, Strathblane, Kilsyth and Kirkintilloch, for example, where the number of Catholics averaged around 300 per community, masses were delivered once a month by a travelling priest. It was a similar situation for towns, villages and districts such as Fort William, Lochaber, Arisaig, Badenoch, Moidart, North Morar, Knoydart and Fort Augustus and for the isles of Eigg, Canna, Barra and South Uist.[9] This shortage was less a reflection of a widespread opposition to schooling, though poorer families did prefer the wages that children earned, than it was of an inherent lack of financial and human resources. That education of any kind was available to children in these remote regions was due to efforts of the Scottish Society for the Propagation of Christian Knowledge and the Free Church.[10]

In the central towns of the Western District there was a more dramatic improvement in provision but standards were low. In the densely populated textile town of Paisley, there was just one parish day school, St Mirin's, in 1851, and a handful of other private institutions.[11] Other areas such as Coatbridge and Barrhead also had day and evening schools, whereas Hamilton and Airdrie had no schools until 1852 and 1857 respectively.[12] In Greenock, at the mouth of the Clyde, the Irish represented 11.6 per cent of the town's population in 1841 and worked mainly in the textile and paper mills.[13] By 1851 the town had seven Catholic schools: one attached to St Mary's chapel founded by a local priest who sought to prevent children from turning to Protestantism and becoming 'soupers', one ragged school and five other privately administered institutions.[14] Unskilled Irish workers were also pivotal to the expansion of Ayrshire's manufacturing sector and did most of the hard labour such as stone breaking, digging and wagon filling.[15] Despite the region having a Catholic population of approximately 5,000 or 6,000 in the 1830s, a permanent school was not established in Ayr until 1856 or in Kilmarnock, a few miles away, until 1857. Catholic education in the region suffered from a lack of money and from endemic truancy until the end of the century. It is likely that the situation remained so dismal for so long because no teaching congregations were ever established there. In fact, the only communities to be founded in the area during the nineteenth century were the Poor Sisters of Nazareth, who opened a convent in Kilmarnock in 1891 and ran a home for girls, and the Servants of the Sacred Heart (later the Sisters of the Sacred Heart of Jesus and Mary), who had a convent in Ayr between 1894 and 1904, but neither were teaching communities.[16] In the Eastern District, outside Edinburgh in Leith, where a significant number of Irish Catholics had settled, there was a day and evening school. There were also schools in Dumfries (day and evening) and in Arbroath (evening) but in the Borders, in places like Hawick, Peebles and Galashiels, Catholic children attended Protestant schools. Provision in the Northern District was generally sparse but an orphanage and two schools (one for boys and one for girls) were attached to St Peter's parish in Aberdeen and another mixed school existed just outside the town in Woodside. Braemar, Huntly and Inverness all had mixed day schools, while St Mary's in Glenlivet had a separate day school for boys and girls. Surprisingly, or perhaps not, considering that these were recusant strongholds, Preshome, Buckie, Achinalrig, Portsoy, Banff, Keith, Dufftown, Tomintoul and Fochabers had no schools.[17]

Given the population density, growth was more marked in Glasgow and Edinburgh, where the number of Catholics had ballooned on account of Famine migration. In 1851 there were approximately seven parish schools up and running in Glasgow, and women religious, despite their recent arrival in the city, had already assumed the bulk of the responsibility for this embryonic system.

Figure 4.1. A group of the early teaching sisters from the Charlotte Street Convent. Reproduced by permission of the Franciscan Sisters of the Immaculate Conception, Glasgow.

Table 4.1 shows the Catholic schools that existed in Glasgow in 1851, but it was estimated that an additional 200 children were enrolled in other Catholic-run adventure schools and 300 more were attending Protestant-run schools.

Table 4.2 shows the Edinburgh Catholic schools in 1851 and what is particularly revealing is the dependency upon pupil-teachers. This is a point that is revisited below but it is important to emphasise just how vital these individuals were to the basic operation of Catholic schools. When the pupil-teacher scheme was formally introduced by James Kay-Shuttleworth in 1847, it was intended to be a mentoring programme where the ratio was to be one pupil-teacher to every twenty-five children and where the trainees would receive one and a half hours of instruction from the head teacher per day.[18] Catholic schools were not in a position to offer this level of mentorship to their pupil-teachers because they were relied upon as de facto teachers; many were poorly trained and responsible for groups of thirty-five to forty children.

Class played a pivotal role in the type of education that children would receive, and educational authorities prioritised subjects like sewing for working-class children because it would provide them with an employable skill for the industrial or service sector. As a consequence most children did

Table 4.1. Educational provision in Glasgow, 1851

School	Facility	Type*	Teachers
St Mary's (Abercromby Street)	Day and evening	Girls (400) Boys (300)	Sisters of Mercy Lay master
St A. Liguori's (Great Hamilton Street)	Day and evening	Mixed (400)	Lay mistress Lay master
St Andrew's (Great Clyde Street)	Day and evening	Girls (250) Boys (250)	Franciscan sisters Lay master
St Mungo's (Parson Street)	Day and evening	Girls (350) Boys (350)	Sisters of Mercy Lay master
St Patrick's (Hill Street)	Day and evening	Mixed (200)	Lay mistress Lay master
St Joseph's (North Woodside Road)	Day and evening	Girls (220) Boys (204)	Franciscan Sisters Lay master
St John's (Portugal Street)	Day and evening	Girls (250) Boys (150)	Franciscan Sisters Lay master
Charlotte Street Convent School	Boarding and day	Girls (70)	Franciscan Sisters 2 lay assistants

Source: CDS, 1851.
* The numbers in this column are averages and are likely to represent a higher-than-average figure.

Table 4.2. Educational provision in Edinburgh, 1851

School	Type	Teachers
St Patrick's (Lothian Street)	Boys (200)	Lay master 6 pupil-teachers
Holy Cross School (Carfrae's Close)	Boys (150)	Lay master
St Mary's (Broughton Street)	Girls (200) Infants (unknown)	Lay mistress 11 pupil-teachers
St Catherine's (High Street)	Girls (100)	Lay mistress 3 pupil-teachers
Edinburgh United Industrial School (South Gray's Close, High Street)	Mixed (140 total, 100 of whom were Catholic)	1 Catholic teacher 1 Protestant teacher
George Square	Girls (boarding school) (35)	Ursulines of Jesus 1 pupil-teacher
St Margaret's Convent	Girls (13)[19]	Ursulines of Jesus

Source: CDS, 1851.

not advance beyond a low elementary level.[20] The most vulnerable were likely to attend a ragged or industrial school and according to one contemporary, a typical day looked like this:

> The children come in the morning at eight o'clock, and get a good breakfast of porridge and milk. They then get lessons and work until one o'clock, when they receive a bowl of broth and a slice of bread for dinner, after which they have a little play, and then lessons and work till six, when they get their supper, consisting of a scone, or porridge and milk again, and about seven go home (if many of their houses can be called *homes*).[21]

In the poor parish schools children were taught the basics of reading, writing, arithmetic and plain sewing, whereas children attending the Franciscan Sisters' convent school learned geography, history, grammar and ornamental sewing as standard in addition to the three Rs and also had the option of taking French, Italian, drawing and music lessons for extra fees.[22] In Edinburgh, the Ursulines of Jesus also provided for the educational needs of middle- and upper-class girls at their convent boarding school and at their school in St George's Square. Annals entries for the period between 1847 and 1853 are preoccupied with notes about their pupils and describe retreats, sightseeing trips and picnics to places like Craigmillar Castle. At times the middle-class children from the St George's Square School would mingle with the upper-class convent pupils at events such as Corpus Christi processions, masses in the convent chapel and awards days.[23] The teaching sisters were tremendously effective in giving the girls' schools stability and structure, but unfortunately many of the boys' schools did not have access to this level of teaching competency. In Glasgow, for example, the first female community arrived in 1847, whereas the first male community came over a decade later in 1858.[24] In Edinburgh women religious with an emphasis on teaching were represented by the Ursulines of Jesus as early as 1834 but there was really no progress with the poor parish schools until 1858, when the Sisters of Mercy arrived. Again, like Glasgow, the male communities were slower to arrive with the Jesuits settling in 1860 and the Marist Brothers following almost two decades later in 1877, though their foundation only survived eleven years.[25]

A shortage of trained teachers meant that standards in the schools, particularly in boys' ones, were poor but this was exacerbated by poverty, the nature of working-class life and a lack of consistency. St Patrick's in Edinburgh, for example, was a school that changed location three times in 1858 alone, setting up for a time in Lothian Street, Blackfriars Wynd and Buccleuch Street. The mobility of this school concerned education officials, but in response to an unnamed report in 1860, a teacher at the school complained that because attendance was volatile and in many ways immeasurable it was inaccurate for authorities to say that 325 boys had been admitted to the school while 500 had left.[26] He described four main factors affecting attendance and emphasised that each was specific to the particular class of children being served by the school. Firstly, the parents of most of the children survived at a subsistence level and so sent children to work when the family needed money. Secondly, since it was common practice for boys to pass back and forth between the city's two Catholic boys' schools and the United Industrial School, perhaps a consequence of parental mobility, it was difficult to know who was in school and who was not. It was pointed out that if authorities tried to stop this flow, they ran the risk of seeing children leave the system entirely. Thirdly, many boys tried out early apprenticeships and when they did not work out many returned to school, at least for a time. Fourthly, the changing locations meant that attendance levels varied from place to place and this could not be helped until more money could be found to provide a stable facility.[27] Efforts to improve school standards were driven by the need to access government funding, and because they were better organised, those administered by women religious tended to receive much more favourable reports from government inspectors. For example, in 1851 St Mary's in Glasgow became one of the first Catholic schools to submit to government inspection and receive a grant for school books. St Mary's Girls' School, under the direction of the Franciscan Sisters in 1852, was praised by inspectors, who observed that the school demonstrated 'active progress and [was] organised with judgement and assiduity'. Conversely, the boys' school, which was governed by a lay master, was described as 'feeble'.[28] The Committee of Council on Education found that girls' schools were outperforming those for boys across Britain, and in the Catholic system it was the result of the work being done by the women religious, who specialised in female education and who tended to arrive on the scene well before their male counterparts.

By 1871, the eve of the Education (Scotland) Act, the number of Catholic schools in Scotland had grown significantly. In the Eastern District, excluding Edinburgh, much of the expansion that had taken place was the result of the work of the St Andrew's Society, which had been founded in Edinburgh in 1850 to extend religious provision. In the space of two decades the number of churches and chapels had increased to eighty-one and there were forty-five schools.[29] Schools had been established in Dalkeith, Pathhead, Dunfermline, Haddington, Bathgate, Broxburn, Bo'ness, Blairgowrie, Stirling, Falkirk, Kilsyth, Denny and Milngavie. Another was under construction in Castle Douglas in the south-west and more had been set up in Jedburgh, Kelso, Peebles and Galashiels. In Perth, where the population was more affluent, and in Dundee, where a large Catholic population existed, schools were also up and running under the direction of religious communities. In Perth the Ursulines had taken over the girls' school at St Joseph's and were also visiting Catholic inmates in the local prison. In Dundee, the Sisters of Mercy worked in the female schools 'in the west end of the town' and the Marist Brothers taught in the parishes of St Andrew's and St Mary's.[30]

In the Northern District there were a total of seventeen parish schools, thirty-four clergy, forty churches, chapels or stations and four convents by 1871. Provision was still insufficient, but new schools had been established in places like Keith, Tomintoul, Campbelltown, Dufftown, Eskadale and Buckie.[31] Apart from Fort Augustus, which was opened in 1876 and run by Benedictine monks, male religious had virtually no presence in these schools. The Franciscan Sisters ran parish and convent boarding schools in Aberdeen and Inverness and the Sisters of Mercy, under the direction of the Aberdeenshire native Sr M. Bernard Garden, were teaching in Dornie and Elgin and were poised to make three more foundations in the under-served villages of Keith, Tomintoul and Fort Augustus before 1888.

In many of the places with small or relatively poor populations parents and children relied upon non-Catholic alternatives. Although religious communities drastically reduced the cost of providing separate Catholic schools, they needed the support and donations of a town's wealthier classes as well as prospective pupils for their private convent schools. Most areas had neither the population nor the money to support them, so that is why the religious communities established foundations in places like Perthshire and Aberdeenshire as opposed to the Western Isles or in Dumfries and Galloway. The most prominent male teaching congregations were the Marist Brothers and the Jesuits, whose first Scottish bases were in Glasgow in 1858 and 1859 respectively, but neither had the geographic reach that the female communities had, as shown in the map (p. 119) which shows the locations of teaching communities before 1870.

The Franciscan Sisters opened houses in Inverness in 1854 and in Aberdeen in 1855. In the latter they taught at St Joseph's, and despite Inverness being described by Cordier as a poor town, the sisters were able to run a convent school for fee-paying day pupils alongside their parish school at St Mary's.[32] In 1865 the Ursulines of Jesus established another convent in Perth, opened a private boarding school and took responsibility for the girls' school in St Joseph's parish. The Sisters of Mercy had founded communities in Dornie (1870), Elgin (1871), Keith (1872), Tomintoul (1880) and Fort Augustus (1888) and ran the parish schools there.[33] This congregation was also instrumental in getting Catholic education up and running in Dundee. Located on

Constructing a system of education 119

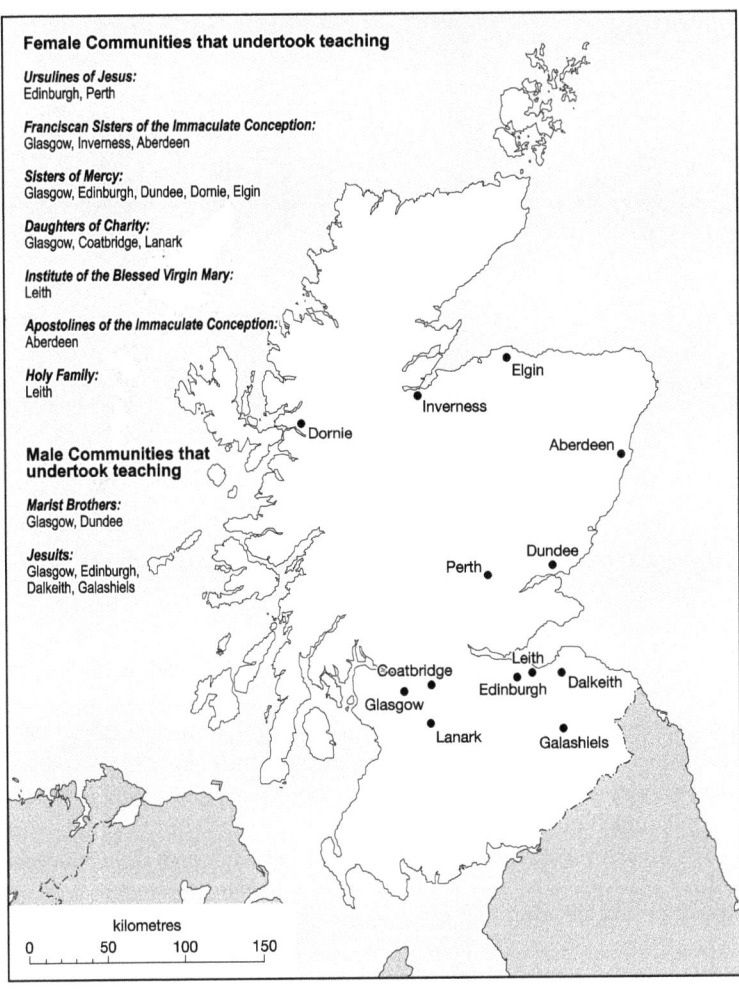

the east coast between Edinburgh and Aberdeen, Dundee was a booming textile town that relied heavily upon Irish female labour. When Stephen Keenan, an Irish priest working in St Andrew's parish, wrote to the Sisters of Mercy in Derry in 1859, he asked for five or six sisters who would be willing to establish a convent in the 'dark and bigoted protestant town'.[34] Keenan wanted the sisters to run evening schools for the factory girls aged between twelve and twenty-five and a convent boarding school but he also hoped that they would eventually take charge of three or four of the other parish schools

Figure 4.2. Secondary pupils in an art class at the Convent of Mercy's Secondary School, Lawside, Dundee, c.1900–10.

once they were established. Money, he warned them, would be tight, since Dundee's Catholic community had 'few rich people' and those who were there were 'not the most liberal'.[35] He also explained that they would have to attend mass with the public since there were not enough priests to give them a private convent mass. As an added incentive he offered the 'prettiest and best Irish cow that could be found in Scotland.'[36]

The Western District had also grown significantly and again much of it was concentrated in and around Glasgow. In the surrounding areas of Partick, Govan, Maryhill, Springburn and Pollokshaws new schools had been established but communities such as Johnstone and Linwood, and Wishaw and Carfin, shared schools. Further out there were new schools in Carluke, Carstairs, Chapel Hall, Mossend, Eastmuir, Rutherglen, Dalry, Kilwinning, Kilbirnie, Saltcoats, Rothesay, Alexandria, Dumbarton, Helensburgh, Fort Augustus, Arisaig, Busby, Neilston, Pollokshaws and Port Glasgow. By this time, those not also being used as chapels would have been under government inspections so as to access the grant money that would help with building costs, books and teachers' salaries. In Coatbridge and Lanark, the boys' and girls' schools were being run by the Daughters of Charity, who had first arrived in Lanark in 1860 and then Coatbridge seven years later. Although women religious did not normally teach boys, they often made exceptions in mission territories like Scotland when there was no alternative. The Sisters of Charity also ran an undenominational poor hospital and orphanage in Lanark, with the latter housing up to 250 boys and girls whom authorities hoped would become 'useful members of society' by being 'trained to labour before and after school hours'.[37] The Sisters and their orphanage at Lanark cooperated with the Poor-Law Guardians to find suitable places for the children and utilised lay female networks to access additional financial support. A Ladies' Association was established to fundraise for the orphanage; members were required to raise at least one pound per year and those who raised or donated nine pounds or more had the right to place a child in the institution, since space was at a premium. How the children were selected, from where and from whom is not known, nor is it known how many children this scheme affected. The Association's members were instructed 'for the sake of the Catholic perishing orphans in Scotland … [to] use their influence in every way'.[38] This cooperation between lay and religious women was crucial to the survival of the convents and to the authority that women learned to exercise over the social welfare initiatives that would preserve and extend Catholicism.

Growth in Glasgow itself was significant and Table 4.3 provides a list of the schools and head teachers and reveals that in addition to its parish school, St Mary's housed an industrial school. Destitute and vulnerable children were always a concern for benevolent Victorians desperate to clean up and reform society. The children housed in this facility were aged between five and fourteen, came from all across Scotland and had been placed in the school if they had been caught begging or if they were deemed destitute and to be without a suitable guardian. The school felt more like a factory, as the boys did work ranging from tailoring, slipper making, shoemaking, stocking making and paper bag making to woodcutting, wright work, carving and painting. The girls did housekeeping, washing, knitting, sewing (shirt making and dressmaking) and shoe binding.[39] Although these practical skills were meant to make the children more employable, the work they did paid for their upkeep in the institution. The two Catholic Reformatories, one for boys at Parkhead and another for girls under the direction of the Good Shepherd Sisters at Dalbeth, were the same and many of the girls became servants. The Good Shepherds arrived in 1851 and ran a Magdalen Asylum that housed approximately 120 women, and like the reformatories and industrial schools, the women in this facility paid for themselves with their labour, which included needlework and making altar linens.[40]

While education was clearly divided along sectarian lines, the Edinburgh United Industrial School (EUI) was something of a special case on account of its interdenominational status. It provided industrial training to some of urban Scotland's most vulnerable children between the ages of seven and thirteen.

Protestant and Catholic children from very poor families, those requiring protection from abusive parents and those classed as vagrants or on warrant from the courts attended this facility. Usually Catholic authorities rejected the idea of interdenominational education on the grounds that it threatened the church's authority, but there was a firm commitment to this school because it helped to provide for the most destitute of Catholic children and because the clergy had free access to them for religious instruction.[41] In other institutions problems arose when parochial boards ordered Catholic children to live with Protestant families or to attend Protestant schools. At the EUI, between 1847 and 1874 approximately 866 Protestant children and 1,277 Catholic children had been admitted and were given clothing, three daily meals and basic lessons and trades skills.[42] The school provided shelter but it was a difficult life and illness and disease outbreaks were frequent; in 1865 a typhus outbreak almost forced its closure.[43] Children were not intended to stay in the schools for more than a couple of years, but there were cases of children spending as many as eight years in the facility and the chance of them de-institutionalising was slim.[44] Those outwith the industrial schools were not necessarily better off and required organised support. In Edinburgh, organisations such as the Association for Improving the Condition of the Poor existed to ensure that support was given to destitute children not in the industrial schools, whereas in Glasgow, the Catholic industrial schools and some of the others received subsidies under the provision of a local act that permitted a rate of a penny per pound to aid those schools caring for the poorest children.[45] The minutes of the Edinburgh School Board reveal that in 1877 twelve schools (six Catholic and six non-Catholic) were provided with daily food donations. Many children preferred paid work, and the minutes identified twenty-six Catholic and thirty-five Protestant school-age newspaper sellers and noted that although most of them attended school at least some of the time, four had very irregular attendance and seven were not in school at all. Of the Catholic children, ten had competent parents, nine lived with drunks, two had a parent in prison, one lived with an invalid and one had been deserted by his father. No details were provided for the parents of two of the boys.[46] Poverty plagued almost every school, and in 1885, in an appeal for subscribers, the Committee for Feeding and Clothing Destitute Children reported that it had assisted 342 Protestant families with 771 children and 115 Catholic families with 230 children over the past seven years because it was 'not only useless, but cruel to try to teach little children who are cold and hungry'.[47]

By the late 1860s the Sisters of Mercy had begun to emerge as *the* formidable educational force in Edinburgh but, as Tables 4.3 and 4.4 show, the schools in both Edinburgh and Glasgow were dominated by women religious. From

Table 4.3. Educational provision in Glasgow, 1871

School	Facility	Type (d = day; n = night)	Teachers
St Mary's (Abercromby Street)	Day and evening	Girls (220 d/180 n) Boys (320d/110n)	Franciscan Sisters Marist Brothers
	Industrial school	Girls (150) Boys (180)	
St Alphonsus' (Great Hamilton Street)	Day	Girls (unknown) Boys (unknown)	Franciscan Sisters Marist Brothers
St Andrew's (Great Clyde Street)	Day and evening	Girls (350d/150n) Boys (400d/100n)	Franciscan Sisters Marist Brothers
St Mungo's (Parson Street)	Day and evening	Girls (280d/180n) Boys (280d/160n)	Sisters of Mercy Marist Brothers
St Patrick's (Hill Street)	Day and evening	Girls (180d/100n) Boys (150d/50n)	Lay mistress Lay master
St Joseph's (North Woodside Road)	Day and evening	Girls (260d/140n) Boys (286d/72n)	Sisters of Mercy Lay master
St John's (Portugal Street)	Day and evening	Girls (250d/130n) Boys (200d)	Franciscan Sisters Lay master
St Vincent of Paul's (Duke Street)	Day	Girls (unknown) Boys (unknown)	Franciscan Sisters Lay master
St Francis' (south side) (Cumberland Street)	Day and evening	Mixed (unknown)	Lay mistress/ master
Charlotte Street Convent School	Boarding and day	Girls (100)	Franciscan Sisters 2 lay assistants

Source: CDS, 1871.

the mid-1860s there were increased efforts to access government grant money by bringing as many Catholic schools as possible under regular government inspection. Sisters in both cities had also begun to push for greater professionalisation among teachers by encouraging a number of their pupil-teachers to train under the Sisters of Notre Dame de Namur in Liverpool.[48] Male religious were less influential in Edinburgh than they were in Glasgow, and although some of the clerics had wanted to establish a community of the Christian Brothers in the capital it never happened.[49]

Despite the advances that had been made, much more needed to be done for the educational needs of Catholic children and young adults to be properly met. Secondary education was almost non-existent and many Catholics were too fearful of government control to make the most of the funds that were

Table 4.4. Educational provision in Edinburgh, 1868–69

School	Type	Teachers
St Patrick's (Market Street)	Boys	Lay Master, John Cavan
Marie Stella (Kirkgate)	Girls?	Sisters of Mercy
St Mary's (Lothian Street)	Girls Infants	Sisters of Mercy
St Andrew's (Canongate)	Boys	Lay Master, Thomas Forbes
St Ignatius' (Hunter's Close, Grassmarket)	Boys	Sisters of Mercy
St Ann's (Niddry Street)	Girls Infants	Sisters of Mercy
St Cuthbert's (Brown's Close, Grassmarket)	Girls?	Sisters of Mercy
Edinburgh United Industrial School (South Gray's Close, High Street)	Mixed (140 total, 100 of whom were Catholic)	1 lay Catholic teacher 1 Protestant teacher
St Ann's (Nicholson Street)	Girls (day)	Ursulines of Jesus
St Margaret's Convent	Girls (boarding, 13)	Ursulines of Jesus

Source: Post Office Directory, Edinburgh & Leith, 1868–69.

available, though accessing grant money was easier said than done since schools that also served as chapels were automatically disqualified from public funding and many parishes were simply too poor to construct purpose-built schools.[50] Teaching quality was also problematic. Women religious, specifically the choir sisters, were generally well educated and benefited from internal community-based mentorship, but lay teachers working outwith the sisters' sphere of influence were at a significant disadvantage because they could not access the same level of collective training or support. This disadvantage was passed on to their pupils and resulted in low attainment levels and in fewer Catholics being able to access the professions. Pervasive poverty, the preference of sending children to work rather than to school, and racial and religious discrimination were significant obstacles, but a narrow curriculum and a fundamental lack of intellectualism impeded the progress of Catholic education beyond the elementary level.[51] The teaching sisters, aided by stringent state-legislated regulations, would play a crucial role in reversing these trends but their influence took time to percolate and it was not until the late 1880s and 1890s that cohorts of well-educated, middle-class female teachers capable of improving the intellectual capacity of the parish school system started to emerge.

The Catholic Poor Schools Committee and Anglicisation

Education was used as a tool to mould the working classes into obedient and respectable citizens, and the recruitment of teaching communities was a crucial part of this standardisation process.[52] The 1877 report in which Her Majesty's Inspector D. Middleton observed that the Catholic schools in Glasgow were doing an 'immense amount of good among a comparatively poor class of children who are, for the most part, of Irish extraction' testifies to the energy being invested in Catholicism's transformation. This energy also represented a Catholic claim to citizenship. Education and other programmes of social reform enhanced the overall standing of the church in Scotland, and school inspectors such as D. Middleton were convinced that a 'sound secular education w[ould] help to make the child, not only a better citizen, but a better Catholic'.[53] It was a fact that bourgeois Catholics wanted to create 'a body of loyal, respectable working-class English and Scottish Catholics of limited social mobility',[54] and so when it was proposed to introduce an inclusive, state-funded and state-controlled education system many breathed a sigh of relief and hoped that this would put an end to the working-class radicalism and social instability that was becoming more commonplace.

In 1839 the Privy Council established a Committee of Council for Education whose aim was to improve the quality of schooling by investing money in teacher training and school buildings. Initially an interdenominational system was trialled, with the Liverpool Corporation schools and Catholic authorities being generally supportive, only objecting to state control over religious education. In 1855 Glasgow's Bishop Andrew Scott had testified to the Poor Law Commission that the establishment of a national system capable of improving the 'feelings, the conduct, the morals, and the loyalty' of Scotland's Irish Catholic poor was desperately needed.[55] Vehement Anglican opposition, influenced by insecurities over the Oxford attrition and an overall loss of political influence in an increasingly 'liberal parliament', quashed any hope of implementing an interdenominational system.[56] Instead, what resulted was an education system divided along sectarian lines and one that excluded Catholic schools from state funding until 1847, though many schools were not in a position to qualify for the grants until much later. The extension of state aid to Catholic education was, according to some scholars, only done in an attempt to maintain social order at the height of Irish Famine migration.[57]

While many British Catholics understood the practical benefits of education, there was division over how it should be administered and funded. In Scotland, the development of a Catholic education system brought into sharper focus the national attachments of the recusants and highlighted their distrust of ultramontanism. Recusants supported the establishment of an education system that would 'denationalise' the Irish and enhance Catholicism's overall image,[58] but they were opposed to a system that would undermine their autonomy or attempt to redefine or Anglicise their identity. In this respect the Scottish recusants were reflecting a more national trend, and in her study of female schooling in nineteenth-century Scotland, Jane McDermid draws attention to the 'plurality of identities' that characterised Scotland during the Victorian era and points out that although Scottish nationalism at the time was unionist, education was a core component of a 'distinct sense of national identity'.[59] Catholicism did not preclude a sense of national identity.

The Catholic Poor Schools Committee (CPSC) was founded in 1847 and was set up to manage the applications for and distribution of the government grant money.[60] It was an English initiative but almost immediately sought to incorporate the Scottish bishops and portray itself as the representative educational body of British Catholics. It was an organisation directed by Oxford-influenced ultramontanes and thus alienated many recusants. It represented a concerted effort to curtail the influence of the laity over education and consolidate the Catholic population under the authority of the clergy. Although the laity would continue to exercise a significant influence over church development, particularly through donations and bequests, their increasing assertiveness, epitomised by men like Frederick Lucas, stimulated a more directed and controlled response to education. A dedicated ultramontane and pro-Irish campaigner, Lucas had converted to Catholicism from Quakerism and had founded the Association of St Thomas of Canterbury for the Vindication of Catholic Rights in 1847 to lobby politicians to support Catholic education.[61] Church authorities in England and Scotland were notorious for their opposition to a politically conscious laity, especially when it was tinged with Irish nationalism.[62] Thus, in the CPSC, lay involvement was permitted at the discretion of the bishops. Charles Langdale, an English layman who had campaigned for emancipation in the 1820s before sitting as an MP for Beverley and Knaresborough in the 1830s and early 1840s, was an important exception. A 'significant figure in Liberal Catholic politics', Langdale had founded the Catholic Institute, the CPSC's predecessor, and had played a crucial role in the negotiations that opened up Privy Council funding for Catholic schools. He chaired the Committee between 1847 and his death in 1868 and was unique because he was one of the few recusant members.[63]

The man who would exert the most influence over Catholic education in Britain was T. W. Allies, the Eton and Oxford educated English Catholic convert who served as the CPSC's Secretary between 1853 and 1890. This 'pugnacious' and highly intelligent man was committed to installing a more uniform and more ultramontane religious culture and to working with the state to improve educational standards.[64] He believed firmly in having properly trained teachers and collaborated with religious congregations and clerics to establish three Catholic teacher training colleges: St Mary's training college for men run by the Brothers of Christian Instruction in Hammersmith (1850); Mount Pleasant college for women run by the Sisters of Notre Dame de Namur in Liverpool (1855); and Sacred Heart, a female college run by the Sisters of the Society of the Sacred Heart in Wandsworth (1874). These colleges were a direct attempt to circumvent lay influence, and the fact that they were in England is not only indicative of the ultramontane commitment to uniformity but also reveals an underlying current of Anglicisation. Despite the passing of the Education (Scotland) Act in 1872 and Scotland's desperate need for trained teachers, a Catholic training college was not established until 1894, when the Sisters of Notre Dame de Namur came up from Liverpool and founded Dowanhill in Glasgow's west end.[65] As a result educational standards in Scotland's Catholic schools lagged far behind those run by the other denominations and, after 1872, the state. The Church of Scotland had three training colleges by 1879, two in Edinburgh and one in Aberdeen. The Free Church had opened a facility in Glasgow in Cowcaddens in 1846, had acquired a property in Edinburgh for a college in 1848, and had opened another in Aberdeen in 1874, and the Episcopalians had been running one in Edinburgh since 1850. Thus before 1894 those Scots Catholics wishing to receive formal and accredited training were obliged to go to England, and not only was this extremely expensive but it exposed those who went to an alien and alternative Catholic culture that promoted a more uniform and Anglicised approach to teaching and learning.

The establishment of a Catholic education system was crucial to the survival of Catholicism in Britain; seen in this light, the CPSC was a protectionist organisation, and yet on another level the energy that it invested in education represents a determined claim to citizenship and equality. While the *Glasgow Free Press* was right to highlight public apathy as a main obstacle to educational advancement and development, it is important to recognise that significant progress had been made with limited resources.[66] Education reform was endorsed by bourgeois liberals intent on improving the social and moral character of British society, and many Catholics, notably the ultramontanes, embraced the opportunity to be involved with such a grand and inclusive social project. The Association of St Margaret was one of the first organisations to push for access to state funding, but given its ultramontane and middle-class slant, this was not too surprising since all of its activities, which included orphan care, the distribution of cheap Catholic literature, emigration

Figure 4.3. The exterior of the Sisters of Notre Dame de Namur's Dowanhill Teacher Training College, Glasgow.

schemes and teacher training, were focused on promoting Catholic unity and a loyalty to 'priests and papacy'.[67] However, as mentioned earlier, there was strong resistance to standardisation and acceptance of state funding among recusants, who feared a loss of control.[68] The Bishop of Birmingham, William Ullathorne, was highly critical of the decision to accept government funding because of the risk it posed to the church's autonomy. The stiffest Scottish resistance came from clerics in the Western District, who were encountering some of the highest levels of Irish migration seen in Britain and who felt that state funding would only serve to erode Scottish Catholic identity. Not only did they object to the Catholic culture of the Irish but they were averse to the Anglicisation that state funding represented. There was an overriding belief among Catholics of recusant stock that education in Scotland should come under the authority of the Scots, not the state and certainly not the laity, and that is why there was such a determined effort to install recusant or Scottish-born women sympathetic to national traditions in convent leadership positions. This resolve is best displayed in a letter that Bishop Alexander Smith drafted to the CPSC secretary, Allies, in 1856:

While you would multiply the secular teachers, I would multiply the religious teachers; while you would train a large staff of pupil teachers, I would train a large staff of religious novices. While you would build training schools, I would build convents; and while you would say that the government would pay a large proportion of the expenses of the education of Catholics without taxing the Catholic body heavily and yet have the Catholics well educated, I would say: The Catholics will get a more efficient education, a better education, both for this world and the next from my plan – and they will get it all at the same time, more, much more economically, more generally, more satisfactorily and absolutely independently![69]

Smith also made a point of highlighting that the Franciscan Sisters' work with approximately 500 children, boys and girls, in preparation for first communion, was 'in a style far superior to what we clergymen have ever been able to instruct'.[70] Whether Allies ever received this letter is not known but its existence is significant because it is recognition of the important role that women religious played in the mission and testifies to the intense frustration and resentment over the dominating role being assumed by the CPSC. Importantly, and paradoxically, women religious in Scotland served both ultramontane and national ends. Their efforts to extend and enhance educational provision were vital to the system's survival in Scotland, particularly after the Education (Scotland) Act was passed in 1872 and the church opted to maintain its own schools despite the crippling expense and the constant stress of trying to meet, with some level of competency, the ever-changing mandatory regulations. The CPSC was committed to improving educational standards by cooperating with the state, whereas the recusant clerics were not, and deep scepticism would remain until they died off or were replaced, as was the case in Glasgow.

The importance of trained teachers was recognised early on by the CPSC, and a key element in the strategy was the imperfect pupil-teacher system. It was the brainchild of James Phillips Kay-Shuttleworth, the renowned educationalist, who believed that properly trained teachers were essential to educational advancement, and when the scheme was formally introduced in 1846 the Privy Council's education grant had to be raised to £100,000 to accommodate it. Young aspirants were to be mentored in school training centres, there was to be a ratio of one pupil-teacher for every twenty-five children, and trainees were to receive one and a half hours of instruction per day from the head teacher.[71] Candidates were to be identified at thirteen, undergo four or five years of in-school training, which included sitting annual exams, and then attend college with a scholarship.[72] The reality in Catholic schools was more dismal. Pupil-teachers were relied upon as instructors, an unhealthy dependency that had developed as a consequence of a chronic lack of funds and the absence of a strong support network. Heavy workloads, inadequate study time and the scarcity of university-educated Catholics reduced the pool of specialist instructors available to coach pupil-teachers through their exams put Catholic schools at a long-term disadvantage. The CPSC held out little hope for improvement in scholarship examinations until there was equal access to resources, but this only came in 1918.[73] The lack of opportunity and support in Scotland had a direct impact upon certification rates, as statistics published in a Report of the Committee of Council on Education in Scotland for 1886–1887 reveal. Whereas 28.9 per cent of women and 24.4 per cent of men were teaching in the board schools without certificates, the percentages in the Catholic schools were 58.5 per cent of women and 38.5 per cent of men.[74] Women religious, whose membership and presence in Scotland had grown significantly since the late 1840s, had offered vital support to many aspiring young women and would have almost certainly helped the majority of the 41.5 per cent of certificated female teachers get to where they were. The 20 per cent difference between certificated male and female teachers did not mean that male teachers outperformed their female colleagues but was rather a consequence of the church's growing reliance upon lay women, who were cheaper to employ and who were beginning to dominate the profession. A point worth mentioning is that it was common for women in the Catholic system to continue to teach after they got married but not after they had a child.[75]

A confidential report to the CPSC in 1875 from the Hammersmith training college highlighted the poor standard of the male pupil-teachers presenting themselves for the Queen's Scholarship Examinations and admission to the college. Only eighteen of the thirty-six boys who sat the exam and applied for entry were successful and sixteen were pupil-teachers of five years' experience; thirteen of those who failed had been experienced pupil-teachers. The Scottish results were even worse and highlight the adverse effect that the lack of a training college was having on Scotland. Out of five Scots, only Robert Niven, a pupil-teacher from St Andrew's Parish, Glasgow, was successful.[76] The report acknowledged that deep problems existed within the 'general condition of the Catholic body' and warned that unless drastic improvements were made standards in Catholic schools would slip far behind those of their Protestant neighbours.[77] The CPSC appointed a special committee to look into the matter and in the report that was prepared by Edward George Fitzalan Howard, first Baron Howard of Glossop, who served as Chairman of the CPSC between 1869 and 1877, a scheme whereby high-achieving male students would be financially rewarded was proposed. It stated that the money previously allocated for building grants would be used to augment the existing annual grants of £3, £4 or £5 (depending on year) and that students entering Hammersmith with a First Class in both secular and religious exams would receive £10 and those who attained a First in one would get £5.[78] Glossop also expressed concern at the fact that females were not only outperforming their male counterparts, but that they were being selected over and above men by school managers. Hinting that the bishops needed to address this, Glossop wrote:

> Again, it is beyond the power of this committee to regulate the proportion in which Masters and Mistresses are severally employed. As a fact, not only are almost all Mixed Schools given to female teachers, but in many cases where a Master and a Mistress should be employed, a Mistress is put over a Mixed School instead ... But this is a matter which can be regulated only by your eminence and their Lordships the Bishops.

He had speculated, rightly, that the male pupil-teachers were unable to compete because they did not have access to anything like the teacher training programme offered by the Sisters of Notre Dame de Namur.[79] Their effect was far-reaching and statistics for the Queen's Scholarship Examinations in 1875 reveal that of the 1,196 women who sat the exam across Britain, nine Catholics were placed in the top 100 at numbers 21, 24, 26, 37, 45, 59, 61, 92 and 96, whereas the top male Catholic candidate was placed 302 out of 977.[80]

Money remained the big problem and the Catholic education system was basically running on empty, but what made matters worse was the fact that a large part of the funds that did exist was regulated by Catholic authorities in London. The Crisis Fund Committee was established by the CPSC in 1869 to distribute money for education, but the only groups eligible were diocesan education councils, which were to be comprised of clerics and prominent laymen. In 1871 the Education Committee for the Eastern District was formed and succeeded in obtaining a grant of £3,000 from the Crisis Fund, but was only able to use it for building new schools or expanding old ones. It could not be used to fix up schools that also served as chapels nor could it be used to pay salaries or to wipe out existing debts. Another catch was that the amount of money granted could never exceed the amount raised by local efforts.[81] What this system did was create a more uniform, more Anglicised education system that was centrally controlled. The 1872 Act sought to consolidate education, but the system of elementary education was alienating to many Scots since the new school age of five, for example, undermined the traditional later starting age in Scotland of between six and eight.[82] For Catholics the Act's Conscious Clause, which ensured that state schools would retain a Presbyterian character, was also deeply concerning. In contrast to what some scholars suggest, sectarianism in the west of Scotland was not less pronounced in the nineteenth century than in the twentieth when one considers education after 1872 and the school board elections, particularly those in Glasgow.[83] School boards, despite the presence of Catholics, were notorious for their sectarian divisions, and while elected Catholics tended to be priests, they were vastly outnumbered and subjected to vicious criticism by anti-Catholic propagandists such as the Knoxites, whose sole purpose was to eliminate Catholic representation on school boards.[84] Although Catholic authorities had opted out of the state system, Catholics were still required to pay the education rates on top of the money they were expected to fork out to support their own system. Thus the necessity of accessing funding was acute and in 1896, under the direction of Archbishop Charles Eyre, senior appointed and elected clerics of the Archdiocese of Glasgow formed their own Board of Education. In addition to tackling the local problem of the dismissal and poaching of lay head teachers by school managers (priests, often newly installed), which had been concerning them since the early 1890s and was starting to concern government inspectors,[85] it also fought for equal access to government funding. They began their campaign for equal access by objecting to their 'voluntary' status, since it was viewed as a 'flagrant misrepresentation' on account of the Education (Scotland) Act's inability to offer Catholics an alternative for providing adequate religious instruction for their children, and scholars such as Callum Brown admit that the education delivered in the state schools had religious overtones.[86] In 1896 the Board of Education submitted a report to the Scotch Education Department, a body that was instituted in 1872 but only made independent of England and Wales after 1885,[87] that outlined the cost differential between the Catholic and state schools. It pleaded for more funding to assist their 45,837 pupils (average attendance):

> [I]f the expenditure on education in Board schools for building and maintenance be a fair measure of what is necessary to provide efficient schooling the same amount ought to be available for our schools also, if they are to be efficient ... Had our schools been built at the same cost they would, at £10 per place, have cost £639,630, and we actually have saved that amount to the rates. Estimating the cost of our schools at £5 per place, they have cost £319,815, and putting the annual cost of interest and depreciation on that sum at 70/0 we have an annual expenditure on that head of £22,386, which sum divided amongst the 45,837 in average attendance gives us an annual cost per scholar of 9/9 in addition to cost of maintenance. But if £10 per scholar be a reasonable cost for providing suitable buildings properly equipped for Board Schools we also wish to be in a position to spend the same amount on our schools. In as far as finance is concerned we are quite willing to submit to any amount of control from any quarter. We merely insist on retaining the proprietary.[88]

The number of schools receiving grants rose from 65 in 1872 to 138 ten years later and to 188 by 1900. Mandatory attendance also increased pupil numbers, which rose from approximately 12,000 in 1872 to over 58,000 by the end of the century. The emergence of this 'national network' is credited to the energy invested by the CPSC and the religious congregations.[89] To cope with the increase in pupil numbers, more emphasis was placed on teacher training, and as a consequence Mount Pleasant and the Sisters of Notre Dame bore a tremendous responsibility, increasing both its intake and output after 1872. One estimate places the annual output at approximately 70, which was more than double the pre-1872 figures, and by 1887 output reached 110. A total of 1,330 trained teachers had been turned out by the late 1880s, but the influence of the sisters was set to expand even more, with their tightly managed pupil-teacher training system and newly built 'House of Residence' for the pupil-teachers living away from home.[90] According to a list produced by Bernard Aspinwall, which he admits is incomplete, of the 1,330 teachers to come out of Mount Pleasant approximately 330 had links to Scotland either as Scots or as teachers in Scotland. He identifies 109 girls who were pupil-teachers in Scotland before going to Mount Pleasant for formal training and estimates that most of the 125 young women who did their pupil-teacher training in England were from families 'domiciled in Scotland', meaning that they were either Irish or Scottish.[91] What is more, 60 of the 330 became women religious and, of them, 30 joined the Sisters of Notre Dame de Namur.[92] There were seventy-one women associated with Scotland who, in addition to attending Mount Pleasant, also trained under the congregation as pupil-teachers at their schools in Liverpool, Manchester, Blackburn, St Helen's and Wigan, and of these approximately 25 per cent (eighteen) entered the religious life. The majority would have served as teachers in Scotland, but a handful joined contemplative orders or congregations that did not specialise in teaching.[93]

The fact that so many of Scotland's Catholic teachers were trained in England from a relatively young age was bound to have consequences for Catholic identity in Scotland, a point that has been raised above. The Sisters of Notre Dame de Namur were tremendously influential in the development of Catholic identity in Scotland because they empowered generations of Catholic women. However, the monopoly they held over teacher training ensured the delivery of a more uniform, more British teaching programme in Catholic schools. This congregation espoused a strong ultramontane and British identity; this was passed on to their students and so in many ways they were Anglicising Catholic culture in Scotland. This process continued with the establishment of Scotland's first Catholic teacher training college at Dowanhill in Glasgow. The committee responsible for organising it included ultramontanes such as Canon Mackintosh, Canon Jochetti, Rev. J. Holder, Mr Ogilvie-Forbes, Mr Hunnybun and Archbishop Eyre. Irish and Highland culture was deeply affected, though for the Highlands it was more a case of a general shortage of trained teachers than a deliberate attempt to undermine Highland culture. In his article on the connections between the Mount Pleasant training college and Scotland, Aspinwall explains that a number of Anglophones, English and Lowland Scots, were recruited to teach in remote districts of the Highlands and Islands. The status of Gaelic was eroded because these teachers did not speak the language and so did not teach it; only one was classed as bilingual by census officials.[94] It is worth pointing out, however, that many of the teachers were appointed with the support of locals who, although they felt strongly about protecting Gaelic, recognised that there were few alternative options for a region still struggling to recover from the mass emigration that had taken place earlier in the century. Irish Catholic culture was specifically targeted and at Mount Pleasant trainee teachers were told to deal 'firmly and professionally with Irish parents who wished their children taught in particular ways'.[95]

After 1872, church authorities were clearly more concerned with the extension of a Catholic education system than with the preservation of cultural diversity, but it is important to emphasise that the Sisters of Notre Dame provided Catholic women with a way of accessing university, and this was a principal tenet of Scotland's educational tradition. In fact Robert Anderson, an educational historian, notes that after secondary education was reorganised in the late nineteenth century Scotland's secondary schools were 'particularly effective at feeding pupils into the universities' when compared to England.[96] When the system of concurrent training was introduced by the revised Scottish Schools Code, Dowanhill students were able to access university courses during their teacher training. In 1897 four students attended classes at the University of Glasgow and in 1899 this number increased to sixty-six. The second woman to receive a PhD from the University of Glasgow was Lucy Carter, one of the first twenty-five students to enrol at Dowanhill in 1895. Interestingly, six of the twenty-five, including Lucy, entered the Notre Dame congregation.[97]

That women religious were instrumental in the development of Catholic education is a crucial yet overlooked point. Admittedly, very little research has been carried out on women religious in Scotland, but some scholars have fallen into the dangerous trap of assuming that because of the prominence of lay teachers in Catholic schools towards the end of the nineteenth century, women religious were not as integral to working-class female education as their counterparts in Ireland.[98] It is important to clarify that, to begin with,

Scotland's Catholic population was much smaller than Ireland's and so the religious life culture was less entrenched and fewer women would have been available. What is more, in the early days, before the Sisters of Notre Dame and Mount Pleasant, women religious were teaching the lay women in Glasgow, Edinburgh, Perth, Inverness, Aberdeen, Dundee, Lanark and Coatbridge who would go on to become teachers in the Catholic system. Many of the urban-based schools that relied upon lay teachers were in fact run by women religious. By 1870 Catholic female schooling in Edinburgh was so dominated by the Sisters of Mercy that many of the young women who grew up there and became teachers had the option of working under them or looking for a job elsewhere. In addition, the Mercies were also in charge of a number of the boys' schools (St Ignatius' on Glen Street, for example) and so even male teachers might have found it difficult to get a job in the capital.[99] This lack of opportunity for lay women may have convinced some to enter the religious life, as the following examples testify. Agnes MacPherson, a Mount Pleasant-trained teacher of Highland heritage but Edinburgh birth, had originally been taught by Miss O'Neil, a woman who had been teaching in Edinburgh before the Sisters of Mercy rose to prominence. In the end both O'Neil and MacPherson joined the Sisters of Notre Dame in England and MacPherson's two younger sisters joined the Sisters of Mercy in Edinburgh.[100] Anne Jenkins had been trained as a pupil-teacher in Liverpool before attending Mount Pleasant, but when she moved to Edinburgh, she too joined the Mercy community. For those women who felt that teaching rather than marriage was their vocation, entering the religious life was often the best way to secure their career.[101]

As can be seen, women religious also dominated Glasgow's Catholic girls' schools. In 1880–81 nine of the fourteen female parish schools were under their control and a decade later in 1891–92 they ran eight out of eighteen.[102] Rather than showing a contracting influence, this demonstrates an extension of their influence through the lay women whom they had taught. When statistics for Glasgow are cross-referenced with the Aspinwall list, what emerges is the fact that at least twelve of the young women who trained as pupil-teachers in Glasgow (including Greenock) did so in schools administered by either the Franciscan Sisters or the Sisters of Mercy. Ten were trained in schools that were not administered by sisters, and details for fourteen cannot be accurately gauged since there was no reference to a particular school.[103] Approximately twenty-five of Mount Pleasant's trainee teachers had served as pupil-teachers in Edinburgh, many of them at St Mary's, and given the Ursuline presence in that school and the overall dominance of the Sisters of Mercy, it is likely that the vast majority would have come under their influence.[104] It can also be assumed that the majority of pupil-teachers in places like Perth, Dundee, Aberdeen or

Table 4.5. Statistics for Edinburgh's Catholic schools, 1877–88

School	Type	Principal teacher	Present on day of religious exam
St Mary's	Girls	Ursuline Nuns	119
	Boys	Marist Brothers	172
St Patrick's	Boys	T. Forbes	205
Lothian Street	Girls	Sisters of Mercy	150
	Infants	Sisters of Mercy	144
Niddrie Street	Girls	Sisters of Mercy	130
	Infants	Sisters of Mercy	112
Sacred Heart	Girls	Sisters of Mercy	102
	Boys	Sisters of Mercy	126
	Infants	Sisters of Mercy	88
St John's	Boys	Unknown	Unknown
St Anne's	Girls	Sisters of Mercy	Unknown
	Infants	Unknown	
St Ignatius'	Boys	Sisters of Mercy	Unknown
St Margaret's Convent School	Girls	Ursuline Nuns	Unknown

Source: SCA, ED9/13/6. *Eastern District Scotland. Report of the Religious Examination of Schools, 1877–1878.*

Inverness were trained by one of these three teaching congregations. Although the influence of male religious was less extensive, they too, particularly the Marist Brothers, were influential in the career development of many young men. In Glasgow, evening classes for pupil-teachers were offered at the Marist Brothers' St Andrew's and St Alphonsus' schools, whereas the Franciscan Sisters and the Sisters of Mercy hosted male and female pupil-teacher classes at their Charlotte Street and Garnethill convents. These classes were given by lay male instructors and focused on English, mathematics, reading, elocution and school management.[105] The efforts being put into improving school and teacher quality did not go unrecognised, and the government inspection reports for 1896–97 and 1898–99 reflected this with both religious and lay-directed schools receiving favourable reports. The Franciscans' Sacred Heart Girls' School was praised for showing great improvement, with inspectors noting that some areas touched on excellence and that the teaching efficiency and the courtesy of the children at St Mungo's were impressive.[106]

Students and pupils also appreciated the energy being invested by their teachers, and in 1894, when the Sisters of Notre Dame de Namur arrived

Table 4.6. Statistics for Glasgow's Catholic schools, 1880–81

School	Type (no. of depts)	Principal teacher	Number on roll	Average attendance	Presented for government exam	Presented for religious exam
St Andrew's	Boys (3)	Marist Bros	479	351	314	371
	Girls	Franciscans	428	255	223	300
	Infants	Franciscans	249	129	79	163
St Alphonsus'	Boys (2)	Marist Bros	263	233	195	238
	Girls	Franciscans	354	220	178	228
	Infants	Franciscans	250	105	64	148
St Francis'	Boys (2)	P. V. Tighe	426	373	295	379
	Girls (2)	M. A. Boyle	430	334	272	366
	Infants	C. Callan	210	214	147	201
St John's	Boys (2)	J. Keenan	351	232	185	257
	Girls	Franciscans	330	242	199	263
	Infants	Franciscans	269	173	145	177
St Joseph's	Boys (3)	W. Moloney	430	301	264	345
	Infant boys	Ellen Moloney	149	110	99	128
	Girls (2)	Srs of Mercy	243	165	163	220
	Infant girls (2)	M. Callaghan	183	158	111	175
St Aloysius'	Boys	Isabella Barrett	220	151	141	160
	Girls	Srs of Mercy	207	120	94	126
	Infants	Srs of Mercy	115	97	68	99
St Mary's	Boys (3)	Marist Bros	492	363	295	424
	Girls (4)	Franciscans	485	349	305	416
	Infants	Franciscans	253	149	78	210
St Michael's	Mixed infants	Mary Bannon	207	149	122	165
		Mary Woods	173	95	57	110
St Mungo's	Boys (2)	Marist Bros	502	376	330	387
	Girls (3)	Annie Lyons	380	218	190	248
	Infants	Mary Brogan	231	113	61	139
Our Lady and	Boys	John Lyons	205	149	131	203
St Margaret's	Girls	Franciscans	195	122	102	160
	Infants	Annie Duff	203	154	139	170
St Patrick's	Boys (2)	James Austin	329	190	135	251
	Girls (2)	Franciscans	357	238	218	242
	Infants	Franciscans	213	183	127	191
Sacred Heart	Boys (3)	Marist Bros	382	287	271	315
	Girls (2)	Franciscans	307	234	200	278
	Infants	Franciscans	296	189	130	160
St Vincent's	Boys (2)	J. Dempsey	229	135	130	144
	Girls	M. Ann O'Neill	236	107	104	171
Govan	Boys (2)	M. Clancy	398	206	171	261
	Girls	M. M'Carron	406	181	135	250

Source: GAA, ED7. The complete Detailed Statistics of each School from July 1880 to July 1881.

to open the Dowanhill Teacher Training College, a stone's throw from the University of Glasgow in the city's affluent west end, they were officially welcomed by a delegation of fifty-two former Mount Pleasant students. They presented an address on the lawn of the new college and stressed the need for Catholics to participate in Scotland's educational tradition:

> The need was urgent, Scottish trained teachers were few, and as Scotland holds a high rank among educated nations, the church recognised the necessity of supplying a long felt want to enable her Catholic children to compete with their Protestant brethren on equal terms without endangering their faith. Many difficulties had to be fought, opposition from various quarters had to be overcome, but Right has triumphed and your presence here today makes our Scottish Catholic Training College an established fact.[107]

Women religious did not just teach their students how to learn, they taught them how to assume responsibility for the institution that would become the lynchpin of Catholic identity in Scotland. Consequently education became a defining element in the self-identification of many Catholic women in whose families teaching would become a tradition. Catherine Kierney recalled how much she had been influenced by her aunt, whose career began as a pupil-teacher under the Sisters of Notre Dame at Dowanhill: 'She taught in St Peter's for over 40 years and, as she brought me up, it was natural for her to have me follow her [to Dowanhill] and for me to do likewise with regards to my daughters.'[108] Another former student recalled a 'long and close connection' with the Sisters of Notre Dame and noted that both of her grandmothers had trained at Mount Pleasant around 1870 and that one of them had encouraged the sisters to establish Dowanhill.[109] Women like these enshrined the educational legacy of the teaching sisters, and their collective ambition testifies to the doors that the sisters helped to open for women in nineteenth- and twentieth-century Scotland. They enabled women to participate in the construction of a national education system, which in turn incorporated them as the key shapers of the nation's Catholic culture.

Looking more deeply at the socio-cultural implications, the work that the women religious undertook was crucial to the expansion of Scotland's middle class and thus the transformation of Catholic culture. It has already been noted that the poor parish schools offered children a basic utilitarian education but for those middle- and upper-class Catholics capable of affording private tuition, the prospects were significantly better. Convent schools were well equipped with secular subjects and at St Margaret's in Edinburgh students were taught English, French grammar, reading, writing, arithmetic, geography, the use of globes, history, outlines of astronomy, and natural history, as well as

Figure 4.4. A group of pupils outside St Margaret's Convent in Edinburgh. Reproduced by permission of the Scottish Catholic Archives, Edinburgh.

plain and ornamental needlework at a cost 36 guineas per year for those over twelve and 28 guineas for those younger. In addition to the music, drawing, Italian, German and dancing classes that were available for an additional charge, the school also boasted a state-of-the-art heating system and 'spacious and well-aired' dormitories.[110] In Glasgow, the Franciscan Sisters offered a similar though less extensive prospectus that included plain and ornamental sewing, reading, writing, arithmetic, geography, history and grammar, and for an additional charge, pupils could also take French, Italian, German, Spanish, drawing, music and singing lessons.[111] Wishing to appeal to improving middle- and upper-class tastes and to accommodate rising pupil numbers, the Charlotte Street convent school underwent an extensive refurbishment in the early 1870s.

Much less has been written on secondary education in nineteenth-century Scotland, especially where Catholics were concerned. The education legislation introduced in 1872 only concentrated on elementary schooling and so the growth of a secondary sector was much slower by comparison. According to an 1871 report by Scotland's Registrar General, William Pitt Dundas, the total number of scholars enrolled in some form of education in Scotland between the ages of sixteen and twenty-five was 10,408 men and 9,450 women. The ration of female to male scholars was higher in Glasgow – 1,684 to 1,539 – which this reflected the city's focus on industry. In Edinburgh it was the reverse, with men numbering 1,939 and women numbering 1,701.[112] The

Figure 4.5. Raffy the dog, a much-loved resident of the Ursulines of Jesus' St Joseph's Convent in Perth. Reproduced by permission of the Scottish Catholic Archives, Edinburgh.

vast majority of these scholars would have been Protestant, since secondary education in the Catholic system remained almost entirely neglected until the mid-1890s, when the religious congregations were finally in a position to deliver it.[113] The point that Jane McDermid makes about the comparatively smaller number of private schools for girls in Scotland when compared to England helps to highlight the pivotal role that women religious played in the expansion of a Catholic middle class.[114] The first convent school in Scotland opened in the mid-1830s and at the time of the census in 1841, the tiny school had nine pupil boarders. Twenty years later the number of pupil boarders at St Margaret's Convent School had doubled to eighteen and by 1871 there were twenty-five pupil boarders.[115] These numbers may appear insignificant but it is important to recognise that in addition to these pupils, there was also an unknown number of day scholars enrolled in the school and other ones elsewhere in Scotland being run by the Ursulines of Jesus and the Franciscan

Sisters. Thus, the corporate spirituality of these communities was being transferred to growing numbers of bourgeois Catholic girls.

In addition to facilitating the expansion of a Catholic middle class, convent schools also guaranteed the future security of the community, since women religious, like their male counterparts, recruited new members from among their own pupils. Steeped in the culture of religious life since childhood, former students made excellent religious candidates. This was a trend wherever teaching communities of women religious operated, and in France, for example, which had the highest number of women religious in the nineteenth century, potential candidates were identified in elementary school.[116] In Scotland, like Ireland, it was the middle and upper classes that came to dominate the religious life and so it is important not to underestimate the influence of women religious. A former pupil of the Ursulines who went on to join the Franciscan Sisters of the Immaculate Conception recalled how influential her time at St Margaret's had been: 'I owe a debt of gratitude to your community as my first desire to become a religious came from the holy example given by the Srs ... I still count myself as one of St Margaret's Children.'[117] Jane and Helen Grant, siblings from Edinburgh, were also educated as little girls by the Ursulines of Jesus before they entered the novitiate of the Sisters of Mercy in Ireland. They had intended to return to Scotland and found a Mercy convent in Edinburgh, and although Jane died before the foundation actually happened, Helen became one of the founding sisters of that community and served as its first Scottish-born superior between 1861 and 1864. In addition to linking back to points made in the previous chapter about the Scottish clerics' desire to install Scottish-born superiors, the lives of these women reveal the influence that sisters and nuns exerted upon their pupils and the Catholic mission in Scotland.

Not only did their private boarding schools provide a much better education than what was on offer at a local parish level, but they offered a Scottish-based alternative and this was absolutely crucial. In *Scottish Nationalism* H. J. Hanham discusses the impact that education reform had upon the self-identification of Scots and notes that in the early 1820s there was a strong desire among some of the nation's (especially Edinburgh) literati to develop a school system that would rival England's public schools and compel more 'Scottish boys' to stay in Scotland. They wanted to raise the bar of educational standards in order to facilitate progress and ensure that Scots got 'the same start in life as their English contemporaries'.[118] In Hanham's opinion, this perspective was inherently patriotic since the liberals who pushed for this change wanted to introduce initiatives that would benefit and sustain the 'traditional Presbyterian democracy of the country'.[119] Hanham's analysis does not take into account the Catholic population or its education system but his points are applicable because they concern Scottish identity and citizenship. Despite Scotland's overarching Presbyterian culture, Catholics espoused many of the same cultural characteristics as their neighbours and sought to negotiate similar means through which to access social citizenship. Mary Hickman argues that the construction of modern Britain 'involved a particular integration of aristocratic values and capitalist institutions which defined a certain notion of what it was to be British'.[120] Educational reform was central to an emerging British identity, and the fact that Catholic authorities (lay and ecclesiastical) engaged with this more and more as the century progressed is strong evidence of their desire to fit in. Private convent boarding schools helped Catholics to do this and to keep in Scotland those upper- and middle-class Catholics who might otherwise have been sent away to school.

These institutions helped to stem the flow of affluent Catholics to the Continent or to England while raising the standards for some students and placing them on a more equal footing. Scottish ultramontanes, like their non-Catholic liberal literati counterparts, wanted a more prosperous, productive, respectable and *British* Catholic body. On the other hand, non-liberal Scots, including many recusants, felt that the kind of educational reform being advocated by those desirous of a deeper affinity between the English and Scottish systems was undermining the uniqueness of Scottish education and culture. Hanham proposes that there was a belief that such change would inhibit the 'expression of a distinctive national point of view' that emphasised 'making education freely available to all'.[121] The fundamental problem with all of this was that before 1779 education was not freely available to all because it was illegal for Catholics to attend school and even for many decades afterwards they were timid and remained detached from Scotland's so-called 'democratic' education tradition.

The Catholic boarding schools also implemented strict sex divisions, and the range of subjects on offer included subjects like needlework, dancing and 'experimental cookery', which served to feminise education. Scholars argue that Victorian feminists supported gender differences in education because it gave middle-class single women career opportunities in a masculine profession.[122] Convent schools certainly served this purpose and while they and many of the female-run parish schools perpetuated a gendered Catholic identity, women religious must be seen as having played a leading role in the feminisation of what had hitherto been a nationally defining masculine profession. They were the main protagonists in the separation of the sexes in education and the role they played in the 'shaping of civil nationality' in this context must be acknowledged and critically examined.[123] They were pivotal to the establishment of a national network of elementary schools and the organisational techniques and methods that they introduced became the template that others would follow, but the problem that would plague the Catholic system was the lack of investment at the secondary level. The educational situation of the late 1840s through to the 1890s and beyond illustrates the centrality of women religious to Catholic education in Scotland and helps to reveal how they bridged the gap between Scottish Catholic identity and ultramontane consolidation. Although many of the women who entered the religious life in Scotland would not have identified with ultramontanism, excepting women like Agnes Trail, the religious communities were pivotal to its implementation. Pioneering educational and social welfare reform, sisters and nuns gave, perhaps unintentionally, ultramontanism a decided advantage, though the extent to which this permeated the working classes is less clear, as the following chapter reveals.

Notes

1. FISCA Box 012.2 'Beginnings and Early History', A Notre Mère. A poem for the Franciscan Sisters of the Immaculate Conception written by Alexander Smith, vicar apostolic of the Western District, 1854.
2. Quoted in Bernard Aspinwall, 'Catholic devotion in Victorian Scotland', Manuscript of paper delivered in May 2003 at the University of Aberdeen. SCA OL2/86/10. Letter from Smith to T. W. Allies on the subject of education by religious – with account of progress, 28 October 1856.
3. Herman Bakvis, *Catholic Power in the Netherlands* (Kingston and Montreal, McGill-Queen's University Press, 1981), pp. 61–2.
4. *Quanta Cura. Encyclical of Pope Pius IX promulgated on December 8, 1964*. http://papalencyclicals.net/Pius09/p9quanta.htm [accessed 27 November 2007].
5. *Ibid.*
6. Jane McDermid, *The Schooling of Working-Class Girls in Victorian Scotland: Gender, Education and Identity* (London, Routledge, 2005), p. 115.
7. *Ibid.*, pp. 115–16. Bernard Aspinwall states that they were the first to introduce any kind of systematic education in Glasgow: 'The formation of the Catholic Community in the West of Scotland: some preliminary outlines', *Innes Review*, 33 (1982), pp. 46–8.
8. *CDS*, 1851, p. 106.
9. *Ibid.*, pp. 71–106.
10. McDermid, *The Schooling of Working-Class Girls*, p. 49. J. H. Treble, 'The development of Roman Catholic education in Scotland, 1878–1978', *Innes Review*, 29 (1978), p. 112.
11. Thomas A. Fiztpatrick, 'Catholic education in Glasgow, Lanarkshire and South-West Scotland before 1872', *Innes Review*, 36:2 (1985), pp. 93–4.

12 Ibid.
13 R. D. Lobban, 'The Irish community in Greenock in the nineteenth century', *Irish Geography*, 6:3 (1971), pp. 270–2.
14 CDS, 1851, pp. 71–106.
15 Raymond McCluskey, *St. Joseph's Kilmarnock, 1847–1997: A Portrait of a Parish Community* (Kilmarnock, St. Joseph's, 1997), p. 5.
16 CDS, 1851, pp. 71–106.
17 Ibid.
18 S. J. Curtis, *History of Education in Great Britain*, 5th edition (London, University Tutorial Press, 1957), p. 243.
19 This is an average based on the number of pupil boarders in the convent listed in the 1841 and 1861 censuses.
20 McDermid, *The Schooling of Working-Class Girls*, pp. 46–7.
21 UGSC, Mu56-i.l, J. G. Morrison, *A word to the young about the Glasgow Industrial or Ragged Schools* (c.1840s).
22 CDS, 1851, p. 131.
23 SCA St. Margaret's Convent, *Annals*. Begun on St Peter and St Paul's Day 1847. Folders marked Annals 1847, 1849 and 1848.
24 Martha Skinnider, 'Catholic elementary education in Glasgow, 1818–1918', in James Scotland (ed.), *History of Scottish Education* (London, University of London Press, 1969), p. 17, and T. A. Fitzpatrick, *Catholic Secondary Education in South-West Scotland before 1972: Its Contribution to the Change in Status of the Catholic Community of the Area* (Aberdeen, Aberdeen University Press, 1986), p. 26.
25 Mark Dilworth, 'Religious orders in Scotland, 1878–1978', *Innes Review*, 29:1 (1978), p. 103.
26 SCA ED9/13/2. Letter from John Cavan to Gillis, 19 January 1860.
27 Ibid.
28 Skinnider, 'Catholic elementary education', p. 15.
29 CDS, 1871, pp. 71–87.
30 Ibid., pp. 71–87 and 130.
31 Ibid.
32 John Watts, *A Canticle of Love: The Story of the Franciscan Sisters of the Immaculate Conception* (Edinburgh, John Donald, 2006), pp. 258 and 262.
33 Dilworth, 'Religious orders', p. 103.
34 SMA, Dundee. Letter from Stephen Keenan to Sr Francis Locke, 18 March 1859.
35 SMA, Dundee. Keenan to Sr Francis Locke, 28 March 1859 and Keenan to M. Francis Locke, 30 March 1859.
36 SMA, Dundee. Keenan to Sr M. Catherine, 6 April and 6 May 1859.
37 CDS, 1871, pp. 81–112 and CDS, 1870, p. 132.
38 CDS, 1870, p. 134.
39 Ibid., p. 91.

40 *CDS*, 1871, p. 131.
41 Peter Mackie, 'Inter-denominational education and the United Industrial School of Edinburgh, 1847–1900', *Innes Review*, 43:1 (1992), pp. 3–17.
42 *Ibid.*, pp. 3–17.
43 SCA St Margaret's Convent Annals. A typhus outbreak in St George's Square was reported in 1847 and one of the sisters who looked after sick children got sick and was in and out of illness for the better part of a year.
44 Mackie, 'Inter-denominational education', p. 16.
45 ECL Minutes of a meeting of the Edinburgh School Board, 12 December 1877.
46 ECL Minutes of a meeting of the Edinburgh School Board, 11 July 1877.
47 ECL *Report of Committee for feeding and clothing destitute children, on condition of their attendance at school, 1884–5*.
48 Ian Stewart, 'Teacher careers and the early Catholic schools of Edinburgh', *Innes Review*, 46:1 (1995), pp. 58–60.
49 *Ibid.*, p. 63.
50 Fitzpatrick, *Catholic Secondary Education*, p. 29.
51 J. H. Treble, 'The development of Roman Catholic education', p. 120. McDermid, *The Schooling of Working-Class Girls*, pp. 66 and 118. Fitzpatrick, *Catholic Secondary Education*, pp. 19 and 32.
52 Francis J. O'Hagan and Robert A. Davis, 'Forging the compact of church and state in the development of Catholic education in late nineteenth-century Scotland', *Innes Review*, 58:1 (2007), pp. 80–2.
53 GAA ED2/10. Extract from 'General Report, for the Year 1877, by Her Majesty's Inspector, D. Middleton, Esq., M.A., LL.D., on the Schools in the Lower Ward of Lanarkshire and Five adjoining Parishes'.
54 Mary Hickman, 'Alternative historiographies of the Irish in Britain: a critique of the segregationist/assimilation model', in Roger Swift and Sheridan Gilley (eds), *The Irish in Victorian Britain: The Local Dimension* (Dublin, Four Courts Press, 1999), p. 249 and Hickman, 'Incorporating and denationalizing the Irish in England: the role of the Catholic Church', in Patrick O'Sullivan (ed.), *The Irish World Wide: History, Heritage, Identity*, Volume 5: *Religion and Identity* (London, Leicester University Press), 1996, p. 200.
55 Quoted in Catherine Jones, *Immigration and Social Policy in Britain* (London, Tavistock, 1977), p. 62.
56 Mary Hickman, *Religion, Class and Identity: The State, the Catholic Church and the Education of the Irish in Britain* (Aldershot, Avebury, 1995), pp. 142–8.
57 Mary Hickman, 'Catholicism and the nation-state in nineteenth-century Britain', in Mary Eaton et. al. (eds), *Commitment to Diversity: Catholics and Education in a Changing World* (London, Cassell, 2000), pp. 52–3.
58 Hickman, 'Incorporating and denationalizing the Irish', p. 200 and 'Alternative historiographies', p. 249.
59 McDermid, *The Schooling of Working-Class Girls*, p. 14.
60 In 1888 its name was changed to the Catholic School Committee and again in

1905 to the Catholic Education Council for England, Wales and Scotland. Francis J. O'Hagan, *The Contribution of the Religious Orders to Education in Glasgow during the Period 1847–1918* (Lewiston, NY, Edwin Mellen Press, 2006), p. 122.
61 Thompson Cooper, 'Lucas, Frederick (1812–1855)', rev. Josef L. Altholz, *Oxford Dictionary of National Biography*, Oxford University Press, 2004. www.oxforddnb.com/view/article/17127 [accessed 2 May 2008].
62 See Martin Mitchell, *The Irish in the West of Scotland, 1797–1848: Trade Unions, Strikes and Political Movements* (Edinburgh, John Donald, 1998).
63 Rosemary Mitchell, 'Langdale, Charles (1787–1868)', *Oxford Dictionary of National Biography*, Oxford University Press, 2004. www.oxforddnb.com/view/article/16009 [accessed 2 May 2008].
64 W. B. Owen, 'Allies, Thomas William (1813–1903)', rev. G. Martin Murphy, *Oxford Dictionary of National Biography*, Oxford University Press, 2004. www.oxforddnb.com/view/article/30393 [accessed 6 May 2008].
65 Alexander Morgan, *Rise and Progress of Scottish Education* (Edinburgh, Oliver & Boyd, 1927), p. 218.
66 *Glasgow Free Press*, 11 June 1860.
67 Bernard Aspinwall, 'The welfare state within the state: the Saint Vincent de Paul Society in Glasgow, 1848–1920', in W. J. Sheils and Diana Wood (eds), *Voluntary Religion* (Oxford, Basil Blackwell, 1986), p. 453.
68 O'Hagan and Davis, 'Forging the compact', p. 77.
69 SCA OL2/86/10. Three attempts at a long letter from Bishop Smith to Mr Allies on the subject of education by religious with account of progress, 28 October 1856.
70 *Ibid.*
71 Curtis, *History of Education*, p. 243.
72 Frank O'Hagan, *Change, Challenge and Achievement: A Study of the Development of Catholic Education in Glasgow in the Nineteenth and Twentieth Centuries* (Glasgow, St Andrew's College, 1996), p. 13.
73 GAA ED9/2. *42nd Annual Report of the Catholic Poor School Committee.*
74 Treble, 'The development of Roman Catholic education', p. 117.
75 Aspinwall, 'Catholic teachers for Scotland: the Liverpool connection', *Innes Review*, 45:1 (1994), p. 51.
76 SCA ED9/18/1. Confidential report to the CPSC about male pupil-teachers presented for the Queen's Scholarship Examination in February 1875.
77 *Ibid.*
78 SCA ED9/18/3. Draft report of the Special Committee of the Privy Council written by Howard of Glossop, 8 April 1875.
79 *Ibid.*
80 *Ibid.*
81 SCA ED9/13/4. *Eastern District of Scotland Education Fund Report, 1871.* Compiled by Bishop John Strain, 18 August 1871.
82 Richard Winters, '"The Empire of Learning": The School Board of Glasgow

and Elementary Education, 1872–1885 with particular reference to the work of William Mitchell'. Unpublished PhD thesis, University of Glasgow, 1997, p. 61 and Morgan, *Rise and Progress*, p. 170.
83 Martin Mitchell, 'Irish Catholics in the West of Scotland in the nineteenth century: despised by Scottish workers and controlled by the Church?' Paper delivered at the 17th Annual conference of the Scottish Catholic Historical Association, University of Glasgow, 7 June 2008.
84 Pamphlet entitled *Reasons for Organising a Protestant Confraternity to be called 'The Knoxites'*. Signed on behalf of the 'Knoxites' by Duncan M'Dermid, 15 February 1881.
85 NAS ED16/1, 1896-7. School Inspection Reports. When examined on 31 October 1896, the inspector blamed the staffing changes that had taken place in 1895-6 for disrupting the efficiency of St Agnes' school which was run by lay female teachers. GAA ED2/10 Education papers. Memorandum from Charles Eyre, 6 October 1893.
86 GAA ED2/10. Education Papers. Archdiocese of Glasgow, Board of Education. Printed Report, 21 February 1896, and Copy of memorandum submitted by Canon Cameron to the Scotch Education Department, April 1896. Callum Brown, 'Faith in the city', in *History Today*, 40 (1990), p. 44.
87 Morgan, *Rise and Progress*, pp. 197–8.
88 GAA ED10/2. Copy of memorandum to Scotch Education Department.
89 Treble, 'The development of Roman Catholic education', p. 113.
90 Aspinwall, 'Catholic teachers', pp. 50–1.
91 Ibid.
92 Ibid., pp. 50 and 52–64.
93 Ibid., pp. 52–64.
94 Ibid., p. 65.
95 Ibid.
96 Robert Anderson, 'Education and society in modern Scotland: a comparative perspective', in *History of Education Quarterly* (1985), p. 477.
97 *Dowanhill Training College Magazine*. The issues consulted were those between 1908, when it began, and July 1914. T. A. Fitzpatrick, *No Mean Service: Scottish Catholic Teacher Education 1895–1995* (Bearsden (Glasgow), St Andrews College, 1995), pp. 45–6.
98 McDermid, *The Schooling of Working-Class Girls*, p. 21.
99 Stewart, 'Teacher careers', p. 59.
100 Ibid., pp. 58–60.
101 Ibid.
102 GAA ED7. Detailed Statistics of each school from July 1880 to July 1881 and July 1891 to July 1892.
103 Aspinwall, 'Catholic teachers', pp. 52–64.
104 Ibid.
105 GAA ED2/10 and ED2/13. Printed letter from St. Alphonsus' secretary, Thomas

O'Reilly, confirming that everything was ready for the classes to begin and poster entitled 'Evening Classes for Pupil Teachers', autumn 1892.
106 NAS ED16/1, 1896–7.
107 Sisters of Notre Dame de Namur, Provincial Archives Office, Liverpool. MPTC 1, Shelf 1, Box 28 marked 'Miscellaneous'. Address presented to Sister Superior of the Liverpool Training College by the old students resident in and around Glasgow on the opening of the Dowanhill Training College. Glasgow, 25 August 1894.
108 Quoted in Beatrice Donnelly, *Hill of Doves: Memories of 100 years of the Notre Dame Dowanhill Schools* (Glasgow, The Notre Dame Centenary Book Project, 1997), pp. 12–13.
109 *Ibid.*, p. 20.
110 *CDS*, 1854, p. 127.
111 *Ibid.*, p. 129.
112 William Pitt Dundas, Registrar General, and James Stark, MD, *Eighth Decennial Census of the Population of Scotland, taken 3D April 1871, with Report*, vol. 2 (Edinburgh, Murray and Gibb, 1874), p. cxlviii.
113 Fitzpatrick, *Catholic Secondary Education*, p. 171 (Appendix II).
114 McDermid, *The Schooling of Working-Class Girls*, p. 51.
115 RGS 1841 Census, RD:685/02 ED:163/000; 1861 Census, RD:685/05 ED:100/000; 1871 Census, RD:685/05 ED:113/000.
116 Sarah A. Curtis, *Educating the Faithful: Religion, Schooling, and Society* (Dekalb, Northern Illinois University Press, 2000), p. 46.
117 SCA MC4/51/8. Letter from Sr. M. Cecilia, Franciscan Sister, Aberdeen to Rev. Mother, June 1886.
118 H. J. Hanham, *Scottish Nationalism* (London, Faber & Faber, 1969), pp. 37–8.
119 *Ibid.*, p. 38.
120 Hickman, *Religion, Class and Identity*, p. 37.
121 Hanham, *Scottish Nationalism*, p. 39.
122 McDermid, *The Schooling of Working-Class Girls*, p. 9. Alison Prentice also comments on this in 'The feminisation of teaching in British North America and Canada, 1845–1875', in J. M. Bumsted (ed.), *Interpreting Canada's Past*, vol. 1: *Before Confederation* (Toronto, Oxford University Press, 1986), pp. 374–86.
123 McDermid, *The Schooling of Working-Class Girls*, p. 13.

5

Consolidating catholicity: Devotion, association and community

Poverty was pervasive in nineteenth-century urban Scotland and was most evident in the housing conditions. Of families living in Edinburgh in 1871, 58.5 per cent lived in two rooms or less and in Glasgow the figure was 78.5 per cent.[1] The majority of people living in the cities were crammed into inadequate dwellings with little privacy and even less dignity. Poor living conditions, illness and disease, low wages, the lack of voting rights and the growing debate over Home Rule gave rise to a working-class consciousness that would grow stronger as the century closed. Land tenure and Home Rule spurred a nationalist energy that united people, and principles of citizenship were being contested by women, who wanted to participate and who were dissatisfied with their marginalised status. This ideological upheaval was threatening to the Catholic Church and forced it to find new ways of engaging people. The development of an associational and devotional culture that would appeal to both sexes and all age groups was prioritised. Catholic education had opened the doors for this by facilitating a process of church modernisation and consolidation.

This chapter considers Scottish associational culture in the Catholic context. The first section investigates the relationship between Catholicism and civil society and looks at how the church mediated social and religious culture through the creation of an extended devotional and associational culture. Civil society was bourgeois-led and functioned for social governance. The growth of this culture in the church and among its followers enhanced religiosity but it also facilitated the inclusion of Catholics in Scottish society. Here, the notion of a Catholic 'ghetto' is challenged by the assertion that although Scotland's tradition of anti-Catholicism had enshrined a sense of separateness, Catholics participated willingly in the civic community and consistently demonstrated a desire to engage with the values and corporate aspirations of Scottish society. Thus, one of the points this chapter will specifically emphasise is that Catholicism precluded neither Scottishness nor Britishness. The second section examines how Catholic associational culture in urban Scotland created closer links with the nation and with the ambitions of the British state by looking at the kinds of organisations being established. There was a marked increase in the number and variety of societies and associations after 1870 that enhanced people's spiritual commitment to the church and promoted community consolidation. The roots of the devotional initiatives had been sown by the religious communities through their education and social welfare work, and they helped to connect people more closely with the local parish and the wider church. Societies and associations were supposed to provide an alternative to those deemed subversive.

Civic culture

Defining civil society is difficult but it centres on communication and association and can be defined as 'institutions in the *public* sphere, arrangements in the *private* sphere' or both.[2] Civil society is how society is governed and organised, in whatever form, beyond the state, and it encompassed minority groups such as Catholics because of their ability to create organisational structures. The incorporation of religion and religious interests in discussions about civil society is complicated because some groups such as religious dissenters can be viewed as the 'potential subverters of civil society' as well as its 'supporters and beneficiaries' simultaneously.[3] The 'propensity' of the nineteenth-century British bourgeoisie to 'organise clubs, societies and associations in the "spaces" in civil society left untouched by the central and local state . . . was the essential mediating structure' between local government and the state.[4] Graeme Morton's investigation of urban governance in mid-nineteenth-century Scotland emphasises that people living during that time viewed civil society as their 'public-life' and understood that it existed in an 'acknowledged framework outwith the formal structures of the state'.[5] Towards the end of the nineteenth century, as national governments across Europe were increasingly focused on restricting the influence of the church, the Catholic hierarchy in Scotland, which was re-established in 1878, was actively seeking new ways of working with the institutions that governed society. Despite having undergone a significant process of Romanisation in the second half of the century, Catholic culture in Scotland remained distinct from many of its European neighbours on account of its geographic isolation and because it had to accommodate two peoples, the Irish and the Scots, with distinctive cultural characteristics. Ethnic loyalties remained an important consideration, particularly since the Irish tended to be more interested in Irish issues, like Home Rule, than in religious ones.[6] The effectiveness of Catholic associations and societies, therefore, rested upon their ability to be culturally sensitive while engaging with the key issues affecting Scotland, such as poverty, drink, crime, child welfare and education. The development of these kinds of organisations enabled their members to emulate the ideal of the 'active citizen' and the church to be portrayed as an institution that took responsibility for its own fate and made valuable contributions towards an 'open and prosperous society'.[7]

Some scholars suggest that the growth of associational culture implies the development of a Catholic 'ghetto', but this ignores the desire that the majority of Catholics had for social and political incorporation. Others, such as Tom Gallagher, suggest that it was the issues like Home Rule and land reform that provided the links to Scotland's broader working-class consciousness and brought alienated groups such as the Irish and the Scottish Highlanders closer together for a common cause.[8] There can be little doubt that the 'pervasive prejudice' and anti-Catholicism that existed in Scotland encouraged a sense of separateness that was enhanced by the church's doctrine of 'no salvation outside the Church',[9] but the tendency for scholars to view the Catholic experience as one of ghettoisation reduces the important role that the church played in the extension of civil society through the mediation of the social and religious culture. In a book appraising life in an Ayrshire parish community, Raymond McCluskey explains that the participation of Catholics in Scotland's civic culture was necessary if they hoped to achieve any 'long-term improvement' in their condition.[10]

Their involvement in education, the temperance movement and child welfare are perhaps three of the most obvious examples that highlight the church's willingness and desire to take an active role in defining the identity of local communities and national institutions.[11] The Catholic education system, despite being regulated by the Education Acts, operated nationally beyond the state through a local parish network and was enhanced by a vast network of societies, clubs, associations and confraternities that encouraged loyalty to the church, the community and the nation. Catholics were involved in the temperance crusade from the beginning and this was crucial since it was a movement that intervened directly in the 'public life of Victorian Britain' by 'set[ting] its own agenda and enact[ing] its own solutions'.[12] Although this movement tends to be associated with evangelical dissenters, temperance rallies offered the chance for Catholics and Protestants in Scotland to commingle for a common cause. Temperance, as a movement, was especially important for Catholics because it provided the opportunity to show that they, the majority of whom were Irish or of Irish descent and thus regularly linked with or blamed for the social effects of alcohol abuse, were taking responsibility. It also gave women a public role in social improvement initiatives, and their devotion to temperance gave them the opportunity to organise public events that were alcohol-free. The 1892 New Year's Eve celebration of music and dancing in Saltcoats, for example, had been organised by the Ladies' Committee of the League of the Cross.[13]

The management of child welfare was another critical juncture for Catholics and non-Catholics, though the plight of the urban street child united as much as divided groups. Glasgow's White Vale Refuge, which was opened by Archbishop Eyre in 1887 and run by the Sisters of Charity, provided temporary shelter to vulnerable street children and those who had been removed from broken or abusive homes. It helped to re-home them with families or in industrial schools and, in 1892, 276 children had passed through its doors and had received food, clothing, religious and secular instruction and training in 'industrial work' (sewing, knitting, washing, cleaning, mat making and embroidery).[14] Described as an institution that was dedicated to saving destitute children from the 'clutches of kidnapping faith-destroyers', this refuge did work with outside agencies including the Society for the Prevention of Cruelty to Children when it came to child rescue and parental rehabilitation.[15] This kind of cooperation, albeit limited, demonstrates a commitment to social improvement and a willingness to take responsibility for the problems affecting urban Scotland.

On a broader level, these examples reveal that by the 1880s the church had achieved a level of organisation that was making it integral to Scotland's civil society and which, apart from contributing to social governance, was working to protect and enshrine an identity for the nation that was distinctively Scottish as a way of maintaining the British union. The expansion of associational and devotional culture was part of the Continental trend of cementing church authority, but it was crucial to British society because it sought to further integrate a population that was predominantly Irish and working class, though the extent to which the working-class participated in this before 1900 was limited. It represented a more determined attempt to curb the more subversive elements by reaching out to those who might be classed as Irish nationalists but who opposed violence or direct action. Volatile nationalist movements such as Fenianism and Ribbonism that endorsed and perpetrated acts of sabotage damaged the church's campaign to improve its image. The dynamite explosions at the Tradeston Gas Works, the Buchanan Street train station and the canal bridge at Possil Road in Glasgow during the winter of 1883 dented social confidence, and the fallout from these and other events such as the Phoenix Park murders in Dublin was severe. Phoenix Park was linked to a particularly dangerous group known as the Invincibles and it is most likely that they had some form of representation in Glasgow. According to court reports printed in Glasgow's *Evening Times*, it was a group that resembled the Irish Patriotic Brotherhood in their preference for 'strategic' assassinations. The local press followed the trial of the accused closely and even carried a detailed account of the execution of Daniel Curley.[16]

Even though the Irish Republican Brotherhood and other volatile elements were on 'the margins of the expatriate Irish political scene',[17] its presence in Scotland was concerning enough to prompt an official church inquiry in 1882. In early May Archbishop Eyre appointed a committee of four senior priests to investigate secret societies in the Western District.[18] There had been growing concern about the 'nature and working' of three societies in particular, the St Patrick's Hibernian Society, the St Patrick's Fraternal Society and the Molly Maguires. When the committee issued its report it concluded that Ribbonism was continuing to exist through the auspices of these societies but that it was adept at staying under the radar. What also concerned the committee was that these were oath-bound societies where 'obedience promised is not limited or qualified' and where members could be subjected to 'arbitrary' acts of violence by leaders if the rules of the societies were seen to have been breached. The report relied heavily upon the evidence provided by three informants, who revealed that at least one man had been murdered for 'giving trouble' to an unnamed society.[19] Apart from the obvious societal consequences, at an ecclesiastical level there was concern that these societies undermined the family and a person's ability to carry out his or her religious duties. It was also felt that their membership prevented them from being completely loyal to the church and state because of the oaths. In 1883 the church issued an official condemnation of these societies and the Ancient Order of Hibernians (AOH).[20] The most problematic aspect of the ban was that anyone identified as belonging to one of these societies was to be refused the sacraments, and while the majority of clerics complied, some priests willingly offered communion and confession to known members. The ban was strongly opposed by the AOH, which argued that it was a friendly society that had supported the church in every way that it could, including providing financial loans. Despite an energised and prolonged letter-writing and lobbying campaign, members of the AOH were not able to get the ban reversed until 1907.[21] An underlying fear of grassroots political power was at the heart of this controversy. There was intense suspicion of organisations that had the potential to attract an active and sizeable following and, if left unchecked, would undermine the church's ability to consolidate and direct the growing Catholic vote.[22]

Support for Home Rule among the Irish in Scotland was significant, but many of its supporters, including those who comprised the 'Irish petty bourgeoisie' and belonged to organisations such as the Home Government Association and the Glasgow Shamrock Association, did their best to distance themselves from militant radicalism.[23] It was thought that the growth of Irish nationalist militancy and working-class activism could be contained, or at least directed, by providing alternative social and religious forums. Groups such as the Catholic Young Men's Society (CYMS) in Edinburgh, for example, were introduced by clerics who were concerned for the reputation of their congregations. They and other groups and organisations like them enabled 'some Irish' the opportunity to access socialising networks that plugged them into Victorian respectability.[24] When reporting on the activities of the Catholic Young Men's Society, the *Glasgow Observer*, which was founded in 1885 as an Irish national and Catholic newspaper in Scotland,[25] referred to the high Irish membership and stressed that the purpose of such groups was to help these young men 'take a leading part in public life'.[26] What is also clear is that there were consistent attempts by members of the clergy to stress that Irish Catholics in Scotland were valuable members of a self-improving, respectable class of citizens. The founder of the CYMS in Edinburgh, Canon Edward Hannan, said that he was

> determined upon advancing his Irish flock through moral self-improvement, and while anxious not to harshly subvert fringe ethnicity was equally determined that the purpose of such self-improvement should be the production of respectable, law abiding and ultimately loyal and useful citizens.[27]

The religious dimension of these groups was emphasised as a way of demonstrating Catholicism's role in civil and societal progress. In Glasgow, the St Francis' Young Men's Society was also overseen by male clerics, and the *Glasgow Observer* made a point of mentioning that its members were recruited into the Savings Bank, the Saint Vincent de Paul Society and the Gregorian Choir, and stressed that the spirit of this society aimed to instil within youth the 'courage to sacrifice everything rather than depart from the principles of the Catholic religion'.[28] The message being emphasised was that these young men were Catholic and respectable.

The restoration of the Scottish Catholic Hierarchy in 1878 was an attempt by Rome to achieve greater community consolidation and suppress, once and for all, the ethnic divisions that had been so damaging to church stability. On some levels it worked and after this period the church did experience significant consolidation, but the campaign for Irish Home Rule had stimulated a very real debate about governance, identity and nationhood. While nationalist outbursts were strongly condemned by the church, it recognised that it could not silence the debate over Home Rule and so it sought some sort of accommodation by supporting those organisations that it felt were intellectual and moral, groups like the Edinburgh branch of the Home Government Association, and permitted them the use of church property for meetings and events.[29] Those groups with overt Fenian connections were denied the use of church property and were condemned outright. Where the church could not suppress the volatile energy of Irish nationalism, it acted as a steward to popular protest. A good example of this was the Home Rule procession which took place on 15 August 1873 and snaked its way from Glasgow Green through the Saltmarket, attracting approximately 7,000 participants and spectators. Walking behind the dignitaries were the priest-led parish delegations, men and women from St Vincent's, Duke Street, St Patrick's, Anderston, St Alphonsus', London Road, St Joseph's, North Woodside Road, St Mungo's, Townhead, and St John's, Gorbals, decked out in 'green ribbons, sashes, rosettes and neckties'.[30] Behind them were the United Labourer groups and a contingent of Fenians who followed conspicuously under a black flag. The deliberate contrast between the brightly coloured and heavily decorated parish contingents and the Fenians reveals the estrangement that existed between militant nationalism and a Catholic community that was predominantly Irish in urban Scotland. Canon Hannan, like many of his colleagues in Scotland, was an outspoken critic of Fenianism and Ribbonism and was involved in the establishment of Edinburgh's Hibernian Football Club in 1875 in an effort to divert nationalist energy. It was a similar case in Glasgow with the establishment of Celtic Football Club in 1887. In addition to building a loyal fan base, these clubs worked to improve the social condition of the poorer sections of the Catholic population by making contributions to poor parishes, schools, poor houses, care facilities for children, including the Glasgow Child Refuge and the White Vale Refuge, and organisations such as the Saint Vincent de Paul Society.[31] On another level, their entry into the Scottish League in 1890 was a critical turning point, because although they were Catholic organisations, this formal connection strengthened the Scottish League and enabled Catholics to become part of the nation's official sporting culture. What this also did was distance the Scottish Catholic clubs from Irish nationalist sporting organisations such as the Gaelic Athletic Association which had been founded in Ireland in 1884. The Association had a strong Fenian element, and while its first club was only established in Scotland in 1897, it was never able to attract a sizeable following among the Irish migrants.[32]

The functioning of associational culture

The myriad of Catholic confraternities, sodalities, associations and societies that emerged in Scotland during the second half of the nineteenth century was a significant accomplishment and testified to the influence that bourgeois devotional activity had been increasingly exercising since the 1830s. Member organisations like Saint Vincent de Paul and the Association of St Margaret were pioneers, but growth had been slow due to a few factors, namely the newness of these initiatives, the embryonic state of parish structure, persistent financial hardship and the lack of an adequate supply of religious personnel before the 1860s and 1870s. Where they were able, women were strongly represented in associational and devotional organisations, and scholars such as Lynn Hollen Lees and Paul O'Leary stress that the significant rise in devotional activity and mass attendance that was witnessed towards the end of the century had been the result of their influence and the role they had played in cultivating closer ties between their families and the church.[33] Conversely, Mary Heimann is more hesitant to endorse the notion of a 'gender-linked piety', despite acknowledging that women were 'disproportionately prominent in every aspect of Catholic practice from attendance at church services to participation in the extra-liturgical devotions and enrolment in devotional societies'. She argues that because men and young boys were involved as well what actually existed was an inclusive Catholic piety.[34] This argument would carry more weight if piety and the associational culture that was developing in the late nineteenth century had not been so strictly divided by sex, between boys and girls and men and women. Umbrella societies such as the League of the Cross, which was committed to temperance, had separate branches for men, women and children, whereas the majority of the rest were single-sex.

The *CDS* reveals the rapid progress being made by membership organisations in the latter part of the century. In 1863, for example, the only sodalities listed for Edinburgh were the Living Rosary and Bona Mors in St Patrick's Parish, and in Glasgow the only ones shown as having existed were the Children of Mary, the Children of the Angels and the Young Men's Society in St Mungo's Parish. It is likely that there were a few more but these have yet to be identified. The lack of associational culture at this time was linked to the limited presence of the religious communities and to the fact that those who had settled in urban Scotland had prioritised education and were working their way through the teething pains of settlement. The Sisters of Mercy, for example, had only been established in Edinburgh in 1858, and the community in Glasgow had endured a wave of disease (typhus and consumption) in the early 1860s that killed at least three of the community's twelve sisters and made a number of others sick.[35] Thirty years later, it was a very different story, with the total number of religious congregations in these cities topping ten (many ran more than one house in each city) and the number of devotional and associational organisations exceeding 150.[36] By the early 1890s, most of

Figure 5.1. A photograph of Roderick Grant, who became a Catholic priest and whose father was none other than James Grant, co-founder of Scotland's pioneer nationalist organisation, the National Association for the Vindication of Scottish Rights. Reproduced by permission of the Scottish Catholic Archives, Edinburgh.

the parishes in Scotland had established an effective structure and were supported by an army of sisters, nuns, brothers and priests. Tables 5.1 and 5.2 show the distribution of parish organisations and highlight those parishes with the most active associational life.

Many of the associations and societies of the mid-nineteenth century focused on improving the working classes by combining Christian instruction with practical assistance, whereas the confraternities and sodalities did more to emphasise piety and devotion. A few of the more common ones in Scotland were the Confraternity of the Holy Family, Bona Mors, the Children of Mary and the Society of the Angels. Bona Mors, a Jesuit foundation dating back to 1648 in Rome, sought to prepare people for death through a life of prayer and good works. The Children of Mary and the Society of the Angels, on the other hand, were popular movements for children. The Children of Mary had originally been established by the Sisters of Charity in France in the 1830s,

Table 5.1. Parish organisations in Edinburgh, 1893

Society	St Mary's	St Patrick's	The Sacred Heart of Jesus	St Columba's	St Cuthbert's	St Mary, Star of the Sea (Leith)	St John's (Portobello)
Saint Vincent de Paul	•						
Sacred Heart	•	•					
Living Rosary	•	•	•	•			
Bona Mors	•		•				
Children of Mary	•	•	•	•		•	•
Guild of St Joseph	•	•	•	•	•	•	•
Association of the Angels	•			•	•	•	•
Crusade of Temperance	•						
Catholic Boys' Brigade	•						
Catholic Club	•						
Holy Family		•					
Children of the Angels		•					
St Aloysius Guild			•				
Immaculate Heart for Conversion of Sinners			•				
Guild of Sacred Heart			•				

Organization							
Sodality of Blessed Virgin Mary	•						
Christian Mothers	•	•					
League of the Sacred Heart	•	•					
Patronage Club							
Catholic Benefit Society							
Apostleship of Prayer				•	•		
League of Prayer							
Immaculate Conception					•	•	•
Young Men's Society							
Angels for Children							
Temperance Guild						•	•
Altar Society							

Table 5.2. Parish organisations in Glasgow, 1893

Society	Parishes											
	St Andrew's	St Mary's	St John's	St Alphonsus'	St Joseph's	St Aloysius'	St Patrick's	St Mungo's	St Vincent of Paul's	St Francis'	Sacred Heart	Our Lady and St Margaret's
Saint Vincent de Paul	•	•										
Sacred Heart		•	•	•				•	•		•	•
Living Rosary	•	•	•	•	•	•		•	•		•	•
Bona Mors				•	•	•						
Children of Mary	•	•	•	•	•		•	•	•	•	•	•
St Joseph's Guild	•											
St Patrick's Guild	•											
Holy Family							• •					
Children of the Angels	•	•				•	•					•
St Aloysius' Guild						•						
Christian Mothers					•							
Apostleship of Prayer		•	•		•		•					
Young Men's Society				•							•	
Altar Society			•		•				•		•	
Mount Carmel	•		•	•		•					•	• •

- League of the Cross
- Clothing Society
- Guardian Angel
- Perpetual Adoration Society
- Boys' Guilds
- Girls' Guilds
- Christian Doctrine Society
- Holy Cross and Passion
- Blessed Sacrament Guild
- Immaculate Conception Guild
- Juvenile Societies
- Sacred Heart Guild
- Third Order of St Francis

but branches of it and the Society of the Angels were overseen throughout Scotland by a variety of religious communities. In Kilmarnock they were supervised by the Sisters of Nazareth after their arrival in the town in 1890, whereas in Dundee they were run by the Sisters of Mercy. Full membership in the Children of Mary could only be secured after a three-month probation period. Duties included the recitation of morning and evening prayers, regular attendance at mass and confession, weekly communion and attendance at an annual four-day retreat.[37] Its members also did a lot of practical work in the community, including the making of altar materials for poorer churches, organising collections for orphans and visiting hospital patients. Another sodality, the Children of the Sacred Heart, was for older girls, and its foundress, Mother Sophie Barat of the Sisters of the Sacred Heart, stressed good mothering, since she believed it was the 'foundation of many noble Christian homes'.[38] Sacred Heart guilds, presumably of the same kind, existed in both Edinburgh and Glasgow, but they were not as common as some of the others. Class was an important element and many organisations like this functioned to secure and expand the Catholic middle class, which meant that overall membership was small and dominated by the bourgeoisie. However, outreach to the working class came from groups such as the Children of Mary through the elementary schools. The activities that they undertook were more inclusive and were ones that would enhance the public profile of Catholicism; crucially, they also elevated the status of women in the public sphere. By stressing practical, community-based activities, many sodalities worked to accommodate the growing desire that many women had to move beyond the home and into the community.

The bourgeois culture that emphasised visibility and display through activities such as promenades, civic processions and exhibitions were as appealing to Catholics as they were to their non-Catholic neighbours. Many Catholic associations and societies, including the Children of Mary, participated in parades and processions, the civic events that symbolised 'leadership and authority', and their involvement reaffirmed their commitment to civic culture and reinforced their claim to citizenship.[39] Home Rule processions, such as the one described above, despite being antagonistic to unionists, were just as important to Catholic identity as the Corpus Christi processions featuring collections of immaculately dressed sodality children.[40] They were both symbolic assertions of citizenship and showcased a desire to organise and participate and a growing confidence within the Catholic community in general. Many events were initially male-only and were described as symbolic 'ritual acts of integration in urban culture', but the participation of women steadily increased.[41] In Dundee, where church authorities had allowed the Catholic culture of

Figure 5.2. Members of the Children of Mary sodality at St Margaret's Convent, Edinburgh, c.1870. Reproduced by permission of the Scottish Catholic Archives, Edinburgh.

the Irish to flourish to a greater extent than in Glasgow, the procession that marked the laying of the foundation stone for the Sisters of Mercy convent had a strong Irish nationalist presence. Each parish was led by a branch of the Irish National Foresters (INF), who, marching four abreast, were followed by the resident confraternities and guilds that included the Children of Mary, the Holy Angels, Immaculate Conception, the League of the Cross, the Catholic Union, Holy Family and the various boys' and girls' guilds. Behind them were the members of the Saint Vincent de Paul Society followed by the Marist Brothers, two carriages for the priests and one for the Bishop that was flanked by six members of the INF. The Sisters met the procession at the site for the official ceremony.[42] The Mercy community had built a good reputation in Dundee and received significant support from 'all classes and denominations' because of their commitment to social welfare and educational work.[43] The reputation of these women helped to elevate that of the Catholic community

Figure 5.3. Mabel Gould, a pupil at St Margaret's Convent in Edinburgh. On the cover photo, she is the child at the bottom left. Reproduced by permission of the Scottish Catholic Archives, Edinburgh.

as a whole, and it is significant that this procession was led by the INF, who were former nationalist radicals. This procession and the manner in which it was organised reveals that groups like the Foresters were aligning themselves, or being aligned, with pious respectability.[44]

The previous chapter argued that the emergence of a Catholic elementary education system enabled Catholics to connect with one of the defining institutions of Scottish society. On another level, the cooperation between church and state gave both greater access to the working classes, thereby facilitating the promotion and extension of a stronger associational culture. While this was a natural progression for a consolidating church, recognising the mutual dependence of education and associational culture is crucial when trying to understand how the church functioned in a nineteenth-century urban environment. Parish schools were seen as the best way to ensure the survival of

Catholicism in Scotland because they established the foundation from which all other associations, confraternities and the like could grow and take 'doctrinal conformity' to the next level.[45] In Scotland, as in England, the influence that communities of women religious had upon the upsurge in devotional activity in the second half of the nineteenth century was integral to the 'new and distinctively Catholic environment' that was developing. A burgeoning material culture was a crucial facet since the new buildings, statues, medals, pictures, vestments and other artefacts represented the intense visual transformation of Catholicism. The process of building a new religious environment created a more gendered Catholic culture as women spearheaded the design of an innovative and stimulating material culture. Not only did the visual impact of decoration increase devotion, but it was also thought to have encouraged conversions. In the 1850s an English nun criticised the unappealing plainness of a church because it had 'not one decent thing in the place' to attract potential converts.[46] That women in the churches recognised the 'evangelising potential' of visual stimuli showed their desire to influence the development of popular Catholicism. The female sewers, embroiderers, knitters, weavers and painters who promoted the Virgin Mary and other female saints in their banners, tapestries, sashes and statues influenced how Catholicism was practised on an everyday level. The aesthetic revolution that took place in convents, chapels, schools and colleges prioritised the 'devotional preferences' of women, which were then transferred to the younger generations in schools and through sodalities such as the Children of Mary.[47]

Women were also involved in designing the public spaces that conveyed civic and national pride. In his work on civic spaces in Victorian England Simon Gunn explains that the function of squares, statues, monuments, clocks and public buildings such as museums was to 'impose a symbolic identity that would stand for the city as a whole'.[48] The urban landscape of mid-to-late nineteenth-century Scotland was awash with testaments to civic pride, and Edinburgh still displays an excellent collection, including Calton Hill and the striking monument to Sir Walter Scott on Princes Street. While very few of these reflect the experience of Catholics in Scotland, the National Portrait Gallery exhibits three statues on the centre of its east wall that do: Mary, Queen of Scots, and her supporters, William Maitland of Lethington, and John Leslie. Crafted by William Birnie Rhind in 1896, these carvings were commissioned by a committee of bourgeois Catholic Edinburgh women. Both the fundraising campaign and the statues were viewed as significant accomplishments for Scotland's Catholic women and for British Catholics in general, and yet the work that women did for the church behind the scenes and the public role that many were beginning to assume as the twentieth century dawned did not translate into equality.⁴⁹ When Archbishop Eyre addressed a crowd at the first annual meeting of the Catholic Union of Glasgow (an organisation founded in 1885 to direct the Catholic vote for school board elections and to assist eligible voters in registering for parliamentary elections), the *Glasgow Observer* reported that he amused his predominantly male audience with a comment about the conspicuous absence of women:

> [There was] only one thing he regretted, and that was that they were nearly all men who were present (laughter). He thought that many of them had been very hard on their wives and daughters and sisters in leaving them at home to sit, listless, by the fireside – (laughter) – while the men had come to the city hall to be interested and instructed by the very agreeable proceedings... However, when the men went back to their homes he was sure they would give their female relatives a full account of what had taken place.⁵⁰

Not only does this statement reveal that many of those in attendance still felt that a public meeting was not a place for women but, somewhat conversely, it also hints at Eyre's awareness of the importance of female agency within the church, society and politics. Provided they met the property qualifications, they had been able to vote in school board elections since they were first introduced with the Education (Scotland) Act of 1872 and in municipal elections since 1885. In order for the church to be able to achieve its electoral aspirations it had to recognise the value of the female vote, especially when events such as the female suffrage rally at Glasgow Green in 1872 were beginning to reveal the growing influence of the women's movement in the urban centres where the Catholic population was most concentrated.⁵¹ Leah Leneman, in an article examining how the Scottish churches responded to the campaign for votes for women, pointed to a letter in favour of the female vote published in *The Scotsman* in 1913 by the chairwoman of the Catholic Suffrage Society in Scotland.⁵² Although Catholic women were more reserved in their overt support for female suffrage, the ripples were beginning to break the surface by the 1870s.

The growing desire of some women to move beyond their prescribed domestic role is evidenced by the increase in public and printed debates about the position of women in society during the 1880s and 1890s. Writing in 1885, one anonymous columnist for the *Glasgow Observer* attempted to discourage women from moving beyond their 'natural' sphere by stressing the responsibilities of a 'good mother':

> [N]ature has marked the paths they are to tread. It is rare indeed for a man to leave his; and when a woman is led from hers by some ism, she seems less like a woman than before, just as she looks less like one in anything approaching a

masculine costume. The same education, the same work, the same pleasures, the same experience are not meant for woman and her brother, and unerring childhood teaches us this lesson.[53]

Two years later the paper ran a front-page story entitled 'Woman's Sphere of Labour', which informed people of the qualities that made a good Christian woman:

> In the Church, it is true, they can only, like Magdalen, sit at the feet of Christ and hear His words yet in the houses, like Martha, they are bound to make their influence felt... we expect of them that they will be gentler, purer, more sympathetic... we expect from their voices words of sympathy rather than reproach... we expect the Christian woman to be more perfect than ourselves. The woman who has a coarse and abusive tongue, the woman who is intemperate or immoral excites disgust even in men who have the same failings themselves.[54]

In yet another article, the higher calling of women was stressed in the hope that it would dissuade them from competing with men for jobs.[55] This bourgeois perception of women in the home could accommodate neither the labouring classes, who relied upon paid female employment for survival, nor the increasing number of unmarried, middle-class women who were required to be self-supporting. Factory work had always welcomed women's labour but increasingly middle-class women were training for fields that had previously been dominated by men, with the most obvious example being teaching. Interestingly, just two years after the above article went to press, the *Glasgow Observer* ran another one that emphasised the value of female teachers and in particular stressed the value of those who had been educated in convent schools. This background, coupled with certification would, it was felt, enable a young woman from a 'struggling middle-class Catholic family' to 'earn a decent livelihood in an independent manner'.[56] This contradiction testifies to a changing dynamic and highlights the value placed on the education being delivered by women religious and those they trained.

Domesticity and morality were linked female virtues, but by the late 1880s this ideal was being openly challenged by young Catholic women who were no longer willing or able to accept this role. Female morality had been a concern throughout Victorian Scotland, with illegitimacy causing significant concern. Illegitimacy was often linked to female employment patterns in the more densely populated districts, and James Drummond, Burgh Assessor in Greenock, speculated in 1871 that his town's low illegitimacy rates stemmed from the low number of marriageable women because of the focus on skilled male rather than unskilled female labour. He boasted that Greenock's illegitimacy rate was just 4.9 per cent when other densely populated towns like

Dundee, Aberdeen, Glasgow and Edinburgh had rates of 11.2, 12.3, 9.5 and 9 per cent respectively.[57] In Dundee, the inspector of local registrars also made a point of mentioning that most of the illegitimate children were born to factory girls or domestic servants. In some ways this was linked to Scotland's unbalanced sex ratio and in his official report of the 1871 census, William Pitt Dundas, Registrar General for Scotland between 1854 and 1880, noted that for every 100 males there were 114 females.[58] He proposed a large-scale emigration scheme for the 'excessive female Population', though it is worth pointing out that he also felt that the Irish were a 'body of labourers of the lowest class' that diluted the quality of the 'native Scots' who mixed with them.[59]

As women gained greater access to educational opportunities, much of which was provided by communities of women religious or those trained by them, they began to see themselves, their abilities and their needs differently, and this was an uncomfortable shift for some. The best evidence of this grassroots resistance comes from the Correspondence section of the *Glasgow Observer*, where in 1889 it showcased a spirited debate that began when a young man, who attempted to pass himself off as female in his letter, criticised the morality of Catholic girls. His letter provoked a flurry of angry responses, with one woman writing that young Catholic men were 'not fit to be trusted with the happiness of any woman'.[60] The young man replied that he and his peers were at a significant social and economic disadvantage and blamed the priests, who treated them with a 'spirit of distrust', the church, for not organising mixed-sex social gatherings, and young women, for seeming to 'delight in the company and conversation of the better dressed and more fortunate Protestant youth of their neighbourhood'.[61] Suspecting that this outburst had come from a 'youth who has sown his wild oats, and now, conscience-stricken, seeks to pose as a moralist', he was attacked for daring to speak on women's behalf. One woman wrote that 'In this enlightened century of higher education ... we are perfectly able to give voice to our own woes without masculine aid, and when we see fit, we will.'[62]

The establishment of girls' clubs in every parish was proposed as a way of offering young women additional support and it was felt, by one correspondent, that these would 'improve the large number of girls between the ages of fourteen and twenty who are so frequently to be seen parading the streets after nightfall', whereas another declared that it was 'only fair' for these to be offered to young women since so many were already devoted to the needs of young men.[63] Tremendous energy had been invested in founding groups for young men because in the eyes of the church they were the ones who would secure its prosperity and spread it 'over the land'. It was felt that they required help to 'tide them over the dangerous interval between the school and manhood', but what had happened was the neglect of the needs of young working-class women.[64]

Opinions about gender difference and gender roles underpinned the construction of Catholicism's associational culture in the urban centres. When this printed exchange occurred, despite the existence of groups such as the Children of Mary and the League of the Cross, which had branches for girls and women, there were very few organisations that focused directly on the needs of teenage girls. Some in the wider community had obviously paid attention to these letters, because by 1893 at least three new groups for young women had been established in Glasgow: a Sacred Heart Guild for girls in Our Lady and St Margaret's parish and two other girls' guilds in the parishes of St Joseph's and St Mungo's. This was mostly likely the work of the religious communities, since the Franciscan Sisters, the Sisters of Mercy and the Marist Brothers were active in all three of these parishes.[65] The only parish in the city to have had guilds for working boys and girls since the 1880s was that of St Francis and, interestingly, this was one of only three parishes where the religious communities did not run the schools. The parishes that developed the strongest associational culture, such as St John's and St Joseph's in Glasgow and Sacred Heart of Jesus and St Mary's in Edinburgh, were those in which the Franciscan Sisters and the Sisters of Mercy were active. The Marist Brothers and the Jesuits were also influential in promoting associations and societies in Glasgow, but in Edinburgh there was a lack of male communities, with an exception being St Patrick's Parish, where the Brotherhood of St Vincent de Paul ran a chapter of the St Aloysius Society for boys who had left school.[66]

Some scholars have rightly questioned the overall effectiveness of these organisations, since their membership was relatively small and confined, for the most part, to the middle class. Steven Fielding, for instance, suggests that in Manchester many of the young people who joined, especially males, were only attracted by the material benefits, but notes that most were turned off by the costs associated with membership.[67] Groups such as the Catholic Boys' Brigade, an organisation that aimed to transform 'irreligious roughs into devout citizens', were simply beyond the reach of most working-class boys, since the cost of a full uniform equalled nearly a week's wages.[68] Consequently, the number of youth gangs increased and although Scotland's nineteenth-century urban gang culture is relatively unexplored, gangs such as the San Toy Boys and the Tim Malloys in Glasgow tended to be organised along sectarian rather than ethnic lines.[69] Most members were from the lower-middle or working class and were kids who had no real disposable income that would have permitted them to join the Catholic Boys' Brigade, and this is probably why there was just one unit in Edinburgh and none in Glasgow in 1893. In his study of Irish republicanism in Scotland, Máirtín Ó Catháin adds that as the militancy of the Ribbonmen dropped off and its members defected to friendly societies such as the Irish National Foresters, youth gang activity (male and female) rose dramatically.[70] He also believes that despite gangs having been a persistent feature in Scotland throughout the nineteenth century, they took on a 'new life from the late 1870s' and adopted a more sectarian Irish Catholic/ Irish Protestant identity.[71]

The rise in gang culture was symptomatic of an increasingly frustrated working class that extended far beyond Scotland and touched a deep nerve within the church. Social inequality and the growing activism of the working classes provoked the publication of Pope Leo XIII's *Rerum Novarum* in 1891. This dictum outlined the church's official position on the relationship between labour and capital and was a critique of the growing tension between the classes. It argued that inequality was necessary as the only way to sustain social and public life and that, because of this, the upper and lower classes had a responsibility to co-exist peacefully.[72] Resting as it did upon ecclesiastical and social hierarchy, the church refused to support any movement or ideology that threatened to overturn this balance. *Rerum Novarum*'s publication came at a time when there was a growing fear in church circles that socialist elements were infiltrating an increasingly disenchanted and non-enfranchised working poor.[73] However, no serious moves towards socialism began until after the turn of the century when John Wheatley, an Irish migrant from County Waterford and Scottish miner and publisher, founded the Catholic Socialist Society in 1906. The church came down hard on Wheatley and his followers but did not excommunicate them, because he and people like him 'embodie[d] the convergence of immigrant Irish nationalism with the aspirations of a Scottish working class'.[74]

John McCaffrey reflects that a distinctive heritage and the need to be part of Scottish society have 'jostled uneasily side by side'.[75] An in-depth examination of politics and the Catholic community is beyond the scope of this work but it is important to emphasise that although Catholic political activity was largely subdued before 1900, certain issues, such as Home Rule, were crucial in mobilising Catholic political thought from the 1880s.[76] In his appraisal of politics and the Catholic community since 1875, McCaffrey suggests that political activity 'aided . . . integration with Scottish society' and allowed Catholics the opportunity to share a 'political allegiance' with those outwith their faith.[77] What he also emphasises is that this helped many of the Irish living in Scotland who, at the end of the nineteenth century, were caught between two worlds, being neither Scottish nor purely Irish. A re-established hierarchy, a strong parish structure, an educational system and a developing associational culture would support the church as it worked to integrate itself, on its own terms, with Scottish society.

Notes

1. William Pitt Dundas and James Stark, *Eighth Decennial Census of the Population of Scotland, taken 3D April 1871, with Report*, vol. 2 (Edinburgh, Murray and Gibb, 1874), p. xxxiv.
2. Jose Harris (ed.), *Civil Society in British History: Ideas, Identities and Institutions* (Oxford, Oxford University Press, 1999), p. 5. Graeme Morton, 'Civil society, municipal government and the state: enshrinement, empowerment and legitimacy. Scotland, 1800–1929', in *Urban History*, 25:3 (1998), p. 350.
3. Harris (ed.), *Civil Society*, p. 10.
4. Graeme Morton, *Unionist Nationalism: Governing Urban Scotland, 1830–1860* (East Linton, Tuckwell Press, 1999), p. 64.
5. *Ibid.*
6. Hugh McLeod, 'Building the "Catholic Ghetto": Catholic organisations 1870–1914', in W. J. Sheils and Diana Wood (eds), *Voluntary Religion* (Oxford, Basil Blackwell, 1986), p. 416.
7. Brian Harrison, 'Civil society by accident? Paradoxes of voluntarism and pluralism in the nineteenth and twentieth centuries', in Harris (ed.), *Civil Society*, p. 87.
8. Tom Gallagher, 'A tale of two cities: communal strife in Glasgow and Liverpool before 1914', in Roger Swift and Sheridan Gilley (eds), *The Irish in the Victorian City* (London, Croom Helm, 1985), p. 121.
9. McLeod, 'Building the "Catholic Ghetto"', pp. 417–18.
10. Raymond McCluskey, *St. Joseph's Kilmarnock 1847–1997: A Portrait of a Parish Community* (Kilmarnock, St Joseph's, 1997), p. 111.
11. The *Glasgow Herald* reported on 20 June 1885 that many of the regulations of the Education Acts, especially those regarding compulsory attendance, could not be implemented without the cooperation of Catholics and other minorities.
12. Morton, *Unionist Nationalism*, pp. 72–3.
13. *Glasgow Observer* (*GO*), 9 January 1892.
14. *GO*, 12 March 1892.
15. *Ibid.*
16. On 18 April 1883 the reporter covering the execution for the *Evening Times* described the scene outside Kilmainham Jail and noted rosaries were being said in 'all directions' before breaking off and admitting that the whole scene was 'exceedingly painful to witness'. See chapters 4 and 5 of Máirtín Seán Ó Catháin, *Irish Republicanism in Scotland 1858–1916: Fenians in Exile* (Dublin, Irish Academic Press, 2007) for a discussion on the activities of these groups in Scotland.
17. Ó Catháin, *Irish Republicanism*, p. 84.
18. GAA RI3/6. Small black notebook, 1882.

19 GAA RI3/6. *Report to His Grace the Archbishop of Glasgow, on Secret Societies by the Commission appointed by His Grace, 1882.*
20 GAA RI3/1. Episcopal Circulars. Circular printed 15 December 1883 and reprinted 18 December 1888 and 15 December 1894 regarding the censure of certain societies.
21 GAA RI3/1. Episcopal Circulars. Circular printed 15 December 1907.
22 GAA RI3/7. *Report of Commission on the Society of the Ancient Order of Hibernians, Glasgow, 25 October 1907.*
23 Ó Catháin, *Irish Republicanism*, pp. 85–90. There were Home Government Association branches in Barrhead, Glasgow, Edinburgh and Dundee.
24 Paul O'Leary, 'Networking respectability: class, gender and ethnicity among the Irish in South Wales, 1845–1914', *Immigrants and Minorities*, 23:2–3 (2005), p. 256.
25 *GO*, First Issue, 18April 1885.
26 *GO*, 2 January 1892.
27 Ó Catháin, *Irish Republicanism*, p. 90.
28 *GO*, 31 December 1892.
29 Ó Catháin, *Irish Republicanism*, p. 90.
30 *Ibid.*, p. 94.
31 *GO*, 26 January 1889 and 12 March 1892. Celtic continues to support this organisation: see www.celticfc.net/home/charityFund/beneficiaries.aspx.
32 Ó Catháin, *Irish Republicanism*, p. 143 and Joseph M. Bradley, 'The Gaelic Athletic Association in Scotland, 1948–2007: diaspora and immigrant identity', *The International Journal of the History of Sport*, 24:10 (October 2007), p. 1316. A useful history of the Gaelic Athletic Association in Ireland is provided by the University College Cork, see http://multitext.ucc.ie/d/History_of_the_Gaelic_Athletic_Association_GAA#7TheGAAandtheIRB.
33 Lynn Hollen Lees, *Exiles of Erin: Irish Migrants in Victorian London* (Manchester, Manchester University Press, 1979), p. 182.
34 Mary Heimann, *Catholic Devotion in Victorian England* (Oxford, Clarendon Press, 1995), p. 127.
35 SMA, Glasgow. History of the Sisters of Mercy, Glasgow. Handwritten account dated 12 December 1881 prepared for the Jubilee of the Mercy Congregation. S. Karly Kehoe, 'Nursing the mission: the Franciscan Sisters of the Immaculate Conception and the Sisters of Mercy in Glasgow, 1847–1866', *Innes Review*, 56:1 (2005), pp. 52–3.
36 *CDS*, 1893, pp. 124–7 and 177–83 and Mark Dilworth, 'Religious orders in Scotland, 1878–1978', *Innes Review*, 29:1 (1978), pp. 103–4.
37 Heimann, *Catholic Devotion*, pp. 128–9.
38 www.newadvent.org/cathen/03659e.htm and www.newadvent.org/cathen/14120a.htm [accessed 3 and 4 September 2008].
39 Simon Gunn, *The Public Culture of the Victorian Middle Class: Ritual and Authority and the English Industrial City* (Manchester, Manchester University Press, 2000), p. 163.

40 O'Leary, 'Networking respectability', p. 267.
41 Gunn, *Public Culture*, p. 172.
42 SMA, Dundee. Handwritten directive: Order of Procession for the laying of the Foundation Stone of the Convent of Our Lady of Mercy, October 10th 1892. The procession began at West Port and then went along Scouring Burn, Pole Park and Lochee Road to Lawside.
43 SMA, Dundee. Printed leaflet, *Convent of the Sisters of Mercy, Blackness Road, Dundee*. 7 April 1884.
44 SMA, Dundee. Order of Procession.
45 Steven Fielding, *Class and Ethnicity: Irish Catholics in England, 1880–1939* (Buckingham, The Open University Press, 1993), pp. 51 and 61.
46 Susan O'Brien, 'Making Catholic spaces: women, décor, and devotion in the English Catholic Church, 1840–1900', in D. Wood (ed.), *The Church and the Arts* (Oxford, Blackwell, 1992), pp. 455–6.
47 *Ibid.*, p. 458.
48 Gunn, *Public Culture*, pp. 50–2.
49 James Holloway, *A Companion Guide to the Scottish National Portrait Gallery* (Edinburgh, National Galleries of Scotland, 1999), p. 67. *GO*, 2 January 1892.
50 *GO*, 26 December 1885.
51 www.theglasgowstory.com/story.php?id=TGSDC09 [accessed 19 September 2008].
52 Leah Leneman, 'The Scottish Church and "Votes for Women"', *Records of the Scottish Church History Society*, 24 (1992), p. 251.
53 *GO*, 2 May 1885.
54 *GO*, 10 December 1887.
55 *GO*, 13 July 1889.
56 *GO*, 19 January 1889.
57 James Drummond, *Report upon the Census of Greenock, 1871*, by the Burgh Assessor (Greenock, Orr, Pollock & Co., 1871), p. 7.
58 NAS GRO3/8/1. Inspection of Registrars' Offices. Notebook 1, beginning 1872, p. 25.
59 William Pitt Dundas and James Stark, *Eighth Decennial Census of the Population of Scotland taken 3D April 1871, with Report*, vol. 1 (Edinburgh, Murray and Gibb, 1872), pp. xviii–xix.
60 *GO*, 10 August 1889.
61 *Ibid.*
62 *Ibid.*
63 *GO*, 31 August 1889 and 21 September 1889.
64 *GO*, 2 May 1885.
65 *CDS*, 1892, p. 173.
66 *Ibid.*, p. 115.
67 Fielding, *Class and Ethnicity*, pp. 65–8.
68 *Ibid.*, p. 66.

69 *Ibid.*, pp. 66–8. James Patrick, *A Glasgow Gang Observed* (London, Eyre Methuen, 1973), p. 150.
70 Ó Catháin, *Irish Republicanism*, p. 108.
71 *Ibid.*
72 *Rerum Novarum. On Capital and Labour.* Encyclical of Pope Leo XIII, 15 May 1891. www.papalencyclicals.net/Leo13/l13rerum.htm [accessed 2 November 2007]. Irene Collins, *Liberalism in Nineteenth-Century Europe* (London, The Historical Association, 1957), p. 16.
73 *Rerum Novarum.*
74 Ian S. Wood, 'Wheatley, John (1869–1930), politician'. *Oxford Dictionary of National Biography*, Oxford University Press, 2004. www.oxforddnb.com/view/article/36848 [accessed 2 May 2008].
75 John McCaffrey, 'Politics and the Catholic community since 1878', *Innes Review*, 29:2 (1978), p. 151.
76 *Ibid.*, p. 151. Gallagher, 'A tale of two cities', pp. 121–3.
77 McCaffrey, 'Politics', pp. 140–2.

Conclusion

One of the interviewees who participated in an oral history project entitled Religion and Worship on the Home Front in 2006 was an elderly nun who had grown up in Glasgow. For a question designed to illuminate perceptions of national identity, when asked whether she thought that the Scots who had fought as soldiers, sailors and airmen and those who had toiled in the factories and plants at home had done it for Scotland or for Britain, her response was this: 'Well if they were doing it for anybody, it would be for Scotland rather than Britain', and then she added 'a lot of Scottish people are still Irish at heart'.[1] This statement, more than any other, brings home the reality of the complexity of Catholic identity in Scotland. It also testifies to the resilience of Irishness in Scotland and how it has been grafted to a broader Scottish identity.

Sitting just thirteen miles apart at their closest points, Scotland and Ireland have pasts that are closely linked, from language and clan networks to the development of agriculture and industry. Given the intense connections between the two, it is surprising that their histories are treated so separately by scholars on both sides of the water.[2] This book, by contrast, has sought to bring their mutual dependence and influence to the fore through the study of religiosity, gender and ethnicity. The Catholic Church in Scotland became a multi-faceted institution that was neither purely Scottish nor purely Irish. Nor was it wholly British. It was characterised by a fusion of cultures and peoples with differing values and priorities. The church, as it exists today, could not have developed without the mass Irish migration that shook its foundations, the guarded and protectionist recusant population, nor the wealthy, ambitious and idealistic convert class of the nineteenth century. Instead of remaining a broken and underground church on the periphery of Scottish society, the Catholic Church emerged from the Victorian era as an empowered and mobilised force on the nation's religious and political landscape.

This book has considered the transformation of Catholicism and the

Catholic Church in the nineteenth century and in doing so it has prioritised the role that women played in this process and in the active mission of the church as a cultural and religious institution. In Scotland, as in Ireland, religion was an instrument of imperialism and Britain's imagined identity was grounded in a Protestant union, with Scotland's identity being anchored to Presbyterianism. Given this context, the fact that Catholicism was used as an imperialist tool might be surprising, but it was the only way for church and state authorities to incorporate the Irish. The development of a Catholic education system was a partnership between the Catholic Church and the state, and was the most obvious example of incorporation and assimilation.[3] The Irish tended to be perceived as culturally, religiously and racially inferior, as a people whose influence would undermine the progress of the Scottish nation and its people. The fact that well-known government officials such as William Pitt Dundas, Scotland's first Registrar General, suggested that the Irish were corrupting the morals, habits and future prospects of Scotland and its people is a case in point. In his report for the 1871 census he wrote that 'This invasion of Irish is likely to produce far more serious effects on the population of Scotland than even the invaders of the warlike hordes of Saxons, Danes or Norsemen.'[4] This way of thinking was carried on in the twentieth century by other influential individuals like Andrew Dewar Gibb, Regius Professor of Law at the University of Glasgow, whose 1930 mission statement, *Scotland in Eclipse*, described the 'Irish trek to Scotland [as] a national problem and a national evil of the first importance'.[5]

As has been pointed out, much of the impetus required to stimulate change in the early stages of the nineteenth century had come from those who were seen as outsiders, those who were either converts to Catholicism or had been born outside Scotland. England's Oxford Movement, which was a critique of the perceived growing secularisation of the Church of England, sparked a Catholic revival that had significant ramifications for Catholicism north of the border, particularly in the conversion of a number of prominent individuals who would inject both money and passion into reforming and rebuilding a tired and beaten church. Sr Agnes Xavier Trail, the convert daughter of a Church of Scotland minister from Forfarshire, had co-founded the first convent to be re-established in Scotland since the Reformation with Bishop James Gillis, a Montreal-born cleric of Scottish Catholic parentage. Gillis had unlimited enthusiasm, family connections, and the experience of living as a Catholic outside Scotland, and was unusual in his ability to secure support from both converts and recusants. Similarly, others such as Robert Monteith and James Stothert, with their convert status and political influence, represented a new demographic in the church. Armed with money, influence and friends in high places, they envisioned a Catholic utopia, where a united British Catholicism stretched from one end of the island to the other. The old Scottish Catholics, those whose families had learned how to survive intense religious persecution, property confiscation and banishments, were resentful of the newcomers, who they felt lacked a basic understanding of what it was to be a Scottish Catholic.

The collision of old and new Catholics forced a reappraisal of the state of the church which intensified as the number of Irish in Scotland increased. Despite coming from very different backgrounds, recusant and convert elements were united in their mutual aversion to the Irish and in their commitment to Scotland and the British state. They were keen to demonstrate their worth and loyalty as citizens and subjects through the expansion of a Catholic middle class, a commitment to community building and an enhancement of social responsibility. The impact that the Irish had upon Catholicism in Scotland was, of course, profound. Conscious of the negative impact that the Irish were having upon the image of Catholics and Catholicism in Scotland and concerned about the overt political radicalism of some, Scottish church authorities were deeply suspicious and largely unwelcoming of the Irish. Like the Highland Catholics, the Irish were coming from a religious cultural tradition that was considered less sophisticated than what church authorities desired for their followers. Political conservatism and loyalty to crown and country had been a key feature in how the church had been operating and would continued to operate in Scotland.

This book, while being a history of Catholicism in nineteenth-century Scotland seeks to place a particular emphasis on the influence that women religious had over church development. Women religious, as teachers, social welfare workers and role models, played a crucial role in the church's complex though not entirely successful campaign to dilute the Irishness of the Catholic migrants in Scotland. Though the first two chapters do not concentrate specifically on women religious, they map out the religious landscape and highlight the developments that preceded and necessitated their arrival. The first chapter reveals that before the late nineteenth century, widespread diversity characterised European Catholicism. In nations such as Scotland, where the Reformation had delivered a devastating and almost deadly blow, the religious culture was quiet, private and conservative. As the nineteenth century dawned, changes started to be felt that mirrored the broader social, economic and political changes that were sweeping through Scotland. Legislative action was key, particularly the expansion of the electorate and incorporation of an increasingly powerful and wealthy bourgeoisie. The passing of the Catholic Relief Act in 1829, despite being primarily designed to appease a growing tide of discontent in Ireland, signalled the broader reappraisal of those groups and communities that existed outwith the national churches and ushered in a new era of social and political inclusion for Catholics.

The second chapter highlights the progressive lay element that emerged in the 1830s and 1840s and worked to inject money, time and energy into the church, and shows the development of a framework for a new church infrastructure that would serve the needs of a growing and modernising population. Networks complementing burgeoning civil society were forged which granted middle- and upper-class Catholics a more direct role in the overall moral improvement of society as teachers, community visitors, care workers and fundraisers. All of this was in response to the growing spirit of voluntarism that was characterising the evangelical churches, but in all circles these changes succeeded in elevating and emphasising the active agency of women. The push to recruit women religious came predominantly from the laity, though a handful of clerics, specifically James Gillis in Edinburgh, Peter Forbes in Glasgow and, somewhat later, Stephen Keenan in Dundee, were instrumental in the process of establishing women religious in Scotland. The laity put up the money for the first convents and then filled them with their daughters, sisters and nieces. This was an important legacy for successive generations of women even though the influence of the laity would be reined in by the early 1860s by a clergy that was more in touch with the Roman mandate.

In the third chapter the focus shifts more directly to sisters, and links are made between the kinds of work they undertook and the development of a Catholic culture that would suit the needs of a church that existed within a stateless and predominantly Presbyterian nation. Their identity as pious women with religious authority complemented the broader middle-class preoccupation with the resurrection of a Christian society through social and moral improvement of the working classes. Statistics highlighting nationality and family connections within the convent leadership structure and the wider membership reveal the extent to which ethnicity influenced the development of these religious. Additionally, the scrutiny to which leadership positions were subjected demonstrates a precise clerical understanding of the sisters' corporate spirituality and the influence they could exert. The decision to select, where possible, Scottish and English women to run the communities was taken by an indigenous clergy anxious to ensure the transmission of a religiosity that preserved the authority of Scottish Catholic culture and complemented the ambitions of a Romanising church.

Part of the fourth chapter's aim is to challenge the notion of a Catholic 'ghetto' by asserting that the energy invested in transforming Catholic culture had actually served to liberate Catholics from the periphery of Scottish society.

It also argues that the communities of teaching sisters were actively renegotiating the boundaries of education by committing themselves to the development of elementary and female education. It is true that on one level the Catholic education system fostered a culture of insularity and exclusivity, but on another it enabled the church to participate in the production of a civil society. Education was a crucial component of the transformation of Catholic culture and despite provoking significant sectarian opposition Catholic schools gave the Catholic community the opportunity to participate in the maintenance of a distinctive Scottish identity. Scotland's imagined tradition of a democratic education culture was enhanced by these schools because they permitted the inclusion of a previously excluded minority and placed significant emphasis on the schooling of girls and young women, a feature distinctively lacking in the Protestant tradition.[6]

The final chapter considers the rise in devotional activity and associational or organisational culture between 1870 and 1900. The confraternities, sodalities, societies and associations that were introduced, largely by the middle class, worked to further consolidate the Catholic population. Although Irish culture would remain a distinctive element in the character of Catholicism, an increasingly united Scottish working-class consciousness and activism was beginning to emerge that would preoccupy the church's leadership. The establishment of an associational culture, much of which was largely managed by the religious communities, would, it was hoped, connect the local parish more closely with the wider church and combat subversive elements.

Catholics wanted to participate as equals in Scotland's civil society, in the voluntary structures, associational culture and institutions that were deemed nationally defining, as a way of demonstrating their commitment to the Scottish nation and to Britain. A theme running through the book is the parallel between Catholicism's position in Scotland and Scotland's position within Britain. Although the idea of the British state was built upon what Linda Colley describes as an 'uncompromising Protestantism',[7] its Catholic population sought recognition as equal and important citizens. The Catholic desire for social inclusion mirrored Scotland's efforts to claim recognition as a full and vital partner in union, for like their fellow countrymen and women, indigenous and convert Catholics in Scotland were in possession of a dual national identity, one that was Scottish and British. They did not see their Catholicity as precluding either one. Scotland's civic atmosphere permeated every level of society and relied upon the moral responsibility and authority of women. Sisters dedicated themselves to producing good Catholics and to making the Catholic community as a whole respectable, obedient and loyal to church and state.

Notes

1. Interview conducted by S. Karly Kehoe on 30 January 2006 with a Franciscan Sister of the Immaculate Conception for the Religion and Worship on the Home Front Oral History Project. Transcripts are held with the Scottish Catholic Archives.
2. Frank Ferguson and James McConnel's edited book, *Ireland and Scotland in the Nineteenth Century*, published in 2009 by Four Courts Press in Dublin, represents an important departure.
3. Mary Hickman, 'Incorporating and denationalizing the Irish in England: the role of the Catholic Church', in Patrick O'Sullivan (ed.), *The Irish World Wide: History, Heritage, Identity*, Volume 5: *Religion and Identity* (London, Leicester University Press), 1996, pp. 196–216.
4. William Pitt Dundas and James Stark, *Eighth Decennial Census of the Population of Scotland taken 3D April 1871, with Report*, vol. 1 (Edinburgh, Murray and Gibb, 1872), pp. xviii–xix.
5. Andrew Dewar Gibb, *Scotland in Eclipse* (London, Humphrey Toulmin, 1930), p. 53. See ch. 4, 'The Irish immigration', pp. 53–62.
6. Jane McDermid, *The Schooling of Working-Class Girls in Victorian Scotland: Gender, Education and Identity* (London, Routledge, 2005), p. 9.
7. Linda Colley, *Britons: Forging the Nation, 1707–1837*, 2nd edition (London, Pimlico, 2003), p. 18.

Appendix: the patrons of the Holy Gild of St Joseph and the St Andrew's Mortuary Gild, Edinburgh, c.1849

Her Grace Duchess of Leeds
The Most Noble, the Marchioness of Wellesley
The Honourable Mrs. Macdonnell
Mrs. Hutchison
Mrs. Collingwood of Lilburn Tower
Mrs. Gillespie of Cambus-Wallace
Mrs. Kirsopp of the Spital
Mrs. Edgar
Mrs. Macdonald of Glenaladale
Mrs. Glassford Bell
Mrs. Arnott
Mrs. John Stewart
Mrs. Glendonwyn of Parton
Miss Gibson of Spital
Miss Kirsopp of the Spital
Miss Maxwell, Greenholl Cottage
Miss Gladstone of Fasqué
The Rt. Honourable Earl of Shrewsbury
Sir James Gordon, Baronet of Letter Fourie
Sir Charles Gordon of Drimmin
Lt. Col. George Macdonnell
Captain Mann
Captain Kyle of Binghill
Captain Mitchell
Captain Dick
John Menzies, Esq of Pitfodels
John Sobieski Stuart, Esq

William Constable Maxwell, Esq
Joseph Constable Maxwell, Esq of Milhead
James Hamilton, Esq
Henry Thornton Marie Witham, Esq of Larington
Alexander Penrose Miller, Esq 92nd Regiment
Thomas Hogg, Esq Mount Vernon

Source: SCA, *Book of the Holy Gild of St. Joseph*. Red velvet book with ornate bronze corners, clasp and centre feature.

Bibliography

Repositories

Edinburgh City Library
Minutes of a meeting of the Edinburgh School Board, 11 July 1877.
Minutes of a meeting of the Edinburgh School Board, 12 December 1877.
Report of Committee for feeding and clothing destitute children, on condition of their attendance at school, 1884–5.

Franciscan Sisters of the Immaculate Conception Archives, Glasgow
Box 011, Mother Adelaide and Mother Veronica. Copy of manuscript sent from Tourcoing, 1930.
Box 012.2 'Beginnings and Early History', A Notre Mère, by Alexander Smith, 1854.
Cochrane, Dolores, Franciscan Sisters of the Immaculate Conception. In the Beginning. Part One. Unpublished manuscript, 1986.
Rule of the Community of the Immaculate Conception of the Third Order of St. Francis, Glasgow; as Revised and Modified by the Sacred Congregation of Bishops and Regulars at Rome and Approved by his Holiness, Pius IX A.D. 1853.
Obituary Book.
Sister Professions and Receptions, Volumes 1 and 2.
The Franciscan Sisters of the Immaculate Conception: Celebrating 150 years in Glasgow. Produced by the community, 1997.

Registrar General for Scotland (General Register House, Edinburgh)
1841 Census, RD:685/02 ED:163/000.
1861 Census, RD:685/05 ED:100/000.
1871 Census, RD:685/05 ED:113/000.
1871 Census, RD:685/04 ED:094/000.
1891 Census, RD:685/04 ED:074/000.
1891 Census, RD:685/05 ED:110/000.
1901 Census, RD:685/04 ED:060/000.

Glasgow Archdiocesan Archives

ED2/10. Extract from 'General Report, for the Year 1877, by Her Majesty's Inspector, D. Middleton, Esq., M.A., LL.D., on the Schools in the Lower Ward of Lanarkshire and Five adjoining Parishes'.

ED2/10. Copy of memorandum submitted by Canon Cameron to the Scotch Education Department, April 1896.

ED2/10. Education papers. Memorandum from Charles Eyre, 6 October 1893.

ED2/10. Education Papers. *Archdiocese of Glasgow, Board of Education*. Printed Report, 21 February 1896.

ED2/10. Printed letter from St. Alphonsus' secretary, Thomas O'Reilly.

ED2/13. Poster entitled 'Evening Classes for Pupil Teachers', autumn 1892.

ED7. Detailed Statistics of each school from July 1880 to July 1881 and July 1891 to July 1892.

ED9/2. *42nd Annual Report of the Catholic Poor School Committee.*

RI3/1. Episcopal Circulars, 15 December 1883, 18 December 1888, 15 December 1894, 15 December 1907.

RI3/6. Small black notebook, 1882.

RI3/6. *Report to his Grace the Archbishop of Glasgow, on Secret Societies by the Commission appointed by His Grace, 1882.*

RI3/7. *Report of Commission on the Society of the Ancient Order of Hibernians, Glasgow, 25 October 1907.*

WD5. Condon Memoirs. Note for 19 May 1874.

WD12/43. *Report on the State of Religion in the Western District*. John Gray, 1866.

Hannah McCarthy's Personal Collection

Letter from Mary Margaret Brewster to Mrs Kyle, 13 October 1849.

Letter from Brewster to Kyle, 29 December 1849.

Mercy International Centre Archives, Dublin

Record Group 100-3.2. Xeroxed copies of Letters, set 2 of 2.

Record Group 300-2.5 England/G. B. Glasgow. Statement of the Convent of Mercy. Written by Bishop Alexander Smith, Glasgow 1857.

National Archives of Scotland

ED16/1, 1896–7. School Inspection Reports.

GRO3/8/1. Inspection of Registrars' Offices. Notebook 1, beginning 1872.

Scottish Catholic Archives, Edinburgh

BL6/625/1. Letter from Garden to Smith, 2 October 1851.

ED9/13/2. Letter from John Cavan to Gillis, 19 January 1860.

ED9/13/4. *Eastern District of Scotland Education Fund Report, 1871*. Compiled by John Strain, 18 August 1871.

ED9/18/1. Confidential report to the CPSC about male pupil-teachers presented for the Queen's Scholarship Examination, February 1875.
ED9/18/3. Draft report of the special committee of the Privy Council by Howard of Glossop, 8 April 1975.
MC3/3. Memorandum with reference to Properties of St. Margaret's Convent, Edinburgh.
MC4. General correspondence.
MC 4/2/7. Letter to the Ursuline Sisters from James Gillis, 1 January 1844.
MC4/50/13. Letter to Rev. Mother from M. M. Bernard Garden, 8 June 1886.
MC4/51/8. Letter from Sr. M. Cecilia, Franciscan Sister, Aberdeen to Rev. Mother, June 1886.
OL2/83/5. Letter from Kyle to Murdoch, 3 May 1852.
OL2/86/10. Letter from Smith to T. W. Allies, 28 October 1856.
OL4/6/1. Alexander Smith: Report on 'clergy and convent' in his mission, c.1858–60.
SM4/47/1. *Sawney's Defence against the Beast Whore Pope and Devil.*
SM14/5. A catalogue of the Missionaries of the Secular Clergy in Scotland from the year 1653, when they first formed into a regular Body until the present year 1767.
SM15/1/3. Pastoral Letter from Bishop James Gordon, Vicar Apostolic, 9 December 1740.
An antidote against the infectious contagion of popery and tyranny. Presbyterian Society in Edinburgh, 1745.
SM15/2/7. Pastoral Letter, 12 July 1793.
SM15/2/13. Pastoral Letter, 1798.
SM15/2/14. Pastoral Letter, 7 May 1798.
SM15/3/2. Pastoral Address by George Hay, John Chisholm and Alexander Cameron, 1803.
SM15/3/15. Pastoral Address by George Hay, John Chisholm and Alexander Cameron, 1813.
Uncatalogued, Annals of St. Margaret's Convent.
Uncatalogued, Dowry Book for St. Margaret's Convent.
Uncatalogued. Interview with Sr. A. M., Glasgow. January 2006. Religion and Worship on the Home Front Oral History Project.

Sisters of Mercy Convent Archives, Bermondsey

Mother Mary Bernard Garden. Paper produced for a congregational meeting, 15 November 2003.
400/2/19. Letter from Sr. M. Clare McNamara to the sisters of St. Mary's Convent, Limerick. 12 September 1867.

Sisters of Mercy Convent Archives, Birmingham

List of the Edinburgh Sisters compiled by the archivist.

Sisters of Mercy Convent Archives, Dundee

Handwritten directive: Order of Procession for the laying of the Foundation Stone of the Convent of Our Lady of Mercy, October 10th 1892.

List of the names of the sisters who entered the Dundee foundation. Provided by the community.

Letter from Stephen Keenan to Sr. Francis Locke, 18 March 1859.

Letters from Stephen Keenan to Sr. Francis Locke, 28 March 1859.

Letter from Stephen Keenan to M. Francis Locke, 30 March 1859.

Letter from Stephen Keenan to M. Catherine, 6 April 1859.

Letter from Stephen Keenan to M. Catherine, 6 May 1859.

Printed leaflet, *Convent of the Sisters of Mercy, Blackness Road, Dundee.* 7 April 1884.

Sisters of Mercy Convent Archives, Glasgow

History of the Sisters of Mercy, Glasgow. Handwritten account dated 12 December 1881 prepared for the Jubilee of the Mercy Congregation.

Names of the Sisters who entered in Glasgow.

Anonymous, handwritten chapter entitled 'On the necessity of dying to self and not taking too much care of our health'. 'Instructions of St. Theresa' on the cover of a soft-back jotter, *c*.mid-nineteenth century.

Sisters of Mercy Convent Archives, Limerick

Annals of the Sisters of Mercy, Limerick, vol. 1, 1838–58.

Sisters of Notre Dame de Namur Provincial Archives Office, Liverpool

MPTC 1, Shelf 1, Box 28 marked 'Miscellaneous'. Address presented to Sister Superior of the Liverpool Training College by the old students resident in and around Glasgow on the opening of the Dowanhill Training College. Glasgow, 25 August 1894.

University of Glasgow Special Collections

Mu56-i.l, J. G. Morrison, *A word to the young about the Glasgow Industrial or Ragged schools. c.*1840s.

Newspapers and directories

Blackwood's Edinburgh Magazine
Catholic Directory for Scotland (*CDS*)
Dowanhill Training College Magazine
Evening Times
Glasgow Free Press
Glasgow Herald
Glasgow Observer (*GO*)
The Scotsman

Contemporary commentaries and histories

A Bill for the Relief of His Majesty's Roman Catholic Subjects, Hansard, 24 March 1829.

A Narrative of the late riots at Edinburgh; and a vindication of its magistracy against the charges advanced in the memorial for the papists of Scotland. London, 1779.

A report, &c. with an account of the speeches delivered, and of the gild premiums awarded for the cleanest and tidiest kept houses. Edinburgh, 21st October 1842.

A report, &c. with an account of the speeches delivered, and of the gild premiums awarded for the encouragement of domestic comfort. Edinburgh, 31st January 1845.

Account of Ceremonial, &c. at Laying the Foundation Stone of Knox's Monument, in the Merchant's Park. Glasgow, Khull, Blackie, and Co., 1825.

Appeal in reference to the extension of the Edinburgh Irish Mission and Protestant Institute, addressed to the friends of Protestantism. Edinburgh, c.early 1850s.

Brotherhood of Saint Vincent of Paul; Conference of Edinburgh. Report of the first general meeting, held in Saint Marie's school, April 30, 1846.

Census of Great Britain, 1851.

Cockburn, Henry, *Journal of Henry Cockburn being a continuation of the memorials of his time, 1831–1854*, vols 1 and 2. Edinburgh, 1874.

Declaration of the Catholic Bishops, the Vicars Apostolic and their coadjutors in Great Britain. London, Keating and Brown, 1826.

Drummond, James, *Report upon the Census of Greenock, 1871, by the Burgh Assessor*. Greenock, Orr, Pollock & Co., 1871.

Dundas, William Pitt and Stark, James, *Eighth Decennial Census of the Population of Scotland taken 3D April 1871, with Report*, vol. 1. Edinburgh, Murray and Gibb, 1872.

Dundas, William Pitt and Stark, James, *Eighth Decennial Census of the Population of Scotland, taken 3D April 1871, with Report*, vol. 2. Edinburgh, Murray and Gibb, 1874.

Gillis, James, *Objects of St. Catherine's Institute of our Lady of Mercy, Lauriston Gardens, Edinburgh*. 1861.

Glasgow Past & Present, vol. 1. Glasgow, David Robertson & Co., 1884.

Hay, George, *A memorial to the public, in behalf of the Roman Catholics of Edinburgh and Glasgow; containing an account of the late riot against them on the second and following days of February, 1779*, 2nd edition. London, 1779.

Hints to Romanizers: No. 1. The Confessional, and the Conventual System. Extracted from Michelet's 'Priests, Women and Families'. London, Seeleys, 1850.

Martin, Martin, *A Description of the Western Isles of Scotland*, reprinted. Edinburgh, J. Thin, 1976.

O'Sullivan, Mortimer (ed.), *Romanism as it Rules in Ireland: A Full and Authentic Report of the meetings held in various parts of England and Scotland in which the Theology secretly taught, the commentary on the Bible clandestinely circulated, the law of the Papal States surreptitiously set up to govern Ireland, and the secret Diocesan Statutes of the Province of Leinster*, vols. 1 and 2. London, R. B. Seeley, 1840.

Reasons for Organising a Protestant Confraternity to be called 'The Knoxites'. Signed on behalf of the 'Knoxites' by Duncan M'Dermid, 15 February 1881.

Report (taken from the Caledonian Mercury) of the speeches of Sir James W. Moncrieff, Bart. Dean of Faculty, Dr. Chalmers, and other distinguished individuals at the meeting held at the Assembly Rooms on Saturday the 14th March 1820, in order to petition parliament for the removal of the disabilities affecting the Roman Catholics.

Roman Catholic fidelity to Protestants ascertained or, an answer to Mr. W. A. D's letter to G. H. In which the conduct of government, in mitigating the penal laws against papists is justified, 2nd edition. London, 1779. Sold by C. Elliot, Edinburgh.

Sawney and Bonaparte, a dialogue. Stirling, 1807.

The true way of dealing successfully with Popery; being the report of the Edinburgh Irish Mission with the list of subscriptions. Edinburgh, 1851.

Trail, Agnes, *Revival of conventual life in Scotland. History of St. Margaret's Convent, Edinburgh, the first religious house founded in Scotland since the so-called Reformation; and the autobiography of the first religious, Sister Agnes Xavier Trail*. Edinburgh, 1886.

Unpublished dissertations and papers

Aspinwall, Bernard, 'Catholic devotion in Victorian Scotland', Manuscript of paper delivered in May 2003 at the University of Aberdeen.

Kehoe, S. Karly, 'Special Daughters of Rome: Glasgow and its Roman Catholic Sisters, 1847–1913'. Unpublished PhD thesis, University of Glasgow, 2005.

Mitchell, Martin, 'Irish Catholics in the West of Scotland in the nineteenth century: despised by Scottish workers and controlled by the Church?' Paper delivered at the 17th Annual Conference of the Scottish Catholic Historical Association, University of Glasgow, 7 June 2008.

O'Brien, Susan, 'Coda – missing missionaries: where are the Catholic sisters in British missiology?' unpublished paper delivered at the 4th annual Consecrated Women Conference, Divinity Faculty, Cambridge University, 16–17 September 2005.

Winters, Richard, '"The Empire of Learning": The School Board of Glasgow and Elementary Education, 1872–1885 with particular reference to the work of William Mitchell'. Unpublished PhD, University of Glasgow, 1997.

Biographies from *Oxford Dictionary of National Biography*

Aspinwall, Bernard, 'Trail, Ann Agnes (1798–1872).' [www.oxforddnb.com/view/article/45566]

Aspinwall, Bernard, 'Gillis, James (1802–1864)'. [www.oxforddnb.com/view/article/10750]

Carter, Philip, 'Menzies, John, of Pitfodels (1756–1843)'. [www.oxforddnb.com/view/article/18566]

Clough, Monica, 'Finlay, Kirkman (1773–1842)'. [www.oxforddnb.com/view/article/9467]

Comerford, R. V., 'O'Connell, Daniel (1775-1847)'. [www.oxforddnb.com/view/article/20501]
Cooper, Thompson, 'Lucas, Frederick (1812-1855)'. [www.oxforddnb.com/view/article/17127]
Haydon, Colin, 'Gordon, Lord George (1751-1793)'. [www.oxforddnb.com/view/article/11040]
Kilburn, Matthew, 'Geddes, John (1735-1799)'. [www.oxforddnb.com/view/article/10489]
McKean, Charles, 'Graham, James Gillespie (1776-1855)'. [www.oxforddnb.com/view/article/11203]
Mitchell, Rosemary, 'Langdale, Charles (1787-1868)'. [www.oxforddnb.com/view/article/16009]
Phillipson, Nicholas, 'Dalrymple, Sir John, of Cousland, fourth baronet (1726-1810)'. [www.oxforddnb.com/view/article/7055]
Owen, W. B., 'Allies, Thomas William (1813-1903)'. [www.oxforddnb.com/view/article/30393]
Reynolds, K. D., 'Stuart, John Patrick Crichton, third marquess of Bute (1847-1900)'. [www.oxforddnb.com/view/article/26722]
Wood, Ian S., 'Wheatley, John (1869-1903)'. [www.oxforddnb.com/view/article/36848]

Internet sources

www.celticfc.net/home/charityFund/beneficiaries.aspx
http://multitext.ucc.ie/d/History_of_the_Gaelic_Athletic_Association_GAA#7TheGAAandtheIRB
www.nls.uk/catalogues/resources/sbti/rae_reynolds.html
www.newadvent.org/cathen/03659e.htm
www.newadvent.org/cathen/07113b.htm
www.newadvent.org/cathen/14120a.htm
www.papalencyclicals.net/Leo13/l13rerum.htm
www.papalencyclicals.net/Pius09/p9quanta.htm
www.sisters-of-charity.org/history.htm
http://stat-acc-scot.edina.ac.uk/link/1834-45/Edinburgh/Edinburgh/
www.theglasgowstory.com/story.php?id'TGSDC09
www.yale.edu/lawweb/avalon/amerrev/parliament/stamp_act_1765.htm

Articles and chapters

Anderson, Robert, 'Education and society in modern Scotland: a comparative perspective', *History of Education Quarterly* (1985), pp. 459-81.
Anderson, William James, 'The autobiographical notes of Bishop John Geddes', *Innes Review*, 18:1 (1967), pp. 36-57.

Aspinwall, Bernard, 'A Glasgow pastoral plan 1855–1860: social and spiritual renewal', *Innes Review*, 35:1 (1984), pp. 33–6.

Aspinwall, Bernard, 'A long journey: the Irish in Scotland', in Patrick O'Sullivan (ed.), *The Irish World Wide: History, Heritage, Identity*, Volume 5: *Religion and Identity*. Leicester, Leicester University Press, 1996, pp. 146–82.

Aspinwall, Bernard, 'Anyone for Glasgow? The strange nomination of the Rt. Rev. Charles Eyre in 1868', *Recusant History*, 23:4 (1996–7), pp. 589–601.

Aspinwall, Bernard, 'Catholic teachers for Scotland: the Liverpool Connection', *Innes Review*, 45:1 (1994), pp. 47–70.

Aspinwall, Bernard, 'Some aspects of Scotland and the Catholic revival in the early nineteenth century', *Innes Review*, 26 (1975), pp. 3–26.

Aspinwall, Bernard, 'The formation of a British identity within Scottish Catholicism, 1830–1914', in Robert Pope (ed.), *Religion and National Identity: Wales and Scotland, c.1700–2000*. Cardiff, University of Wales Press, 2001, pp. 268–305.

Aspinwall, Bernard, 'The formation of the Catholic community in the West of Scotland: some preliminary outlines', *Innes Review*, 33 (1982), pp. 44–57.

Aspinwall, Bernard, 'The welfare state within the state: the Saint Vincent de Paul Society in Glasgow, 1848–1920', in W. J. Sheils and Diana Wood (eds), *Voluntary Religion*. Oxford, Basil Blackwell, 1986, pp. 445–60.

Bartlett, Thomas, 'Ireland, Empire and Union, 1690–1801', in Kevin Kenny (ed.), *Ireland and the British Empire*. Oxford, Oxford University Press, 2004, pp. 61–89.

Belchem, John, 'Nationalism, republicanism and exile: Irish emigrants and the revolutions of 1848', *Past & Present*, 146 (1995), pp. 103–35.

Black, Eugene Charlton, 'The tumultuous petitioners: the Protestant Association in Scotland', *Review of Politics*, 25:2 (1963), pp. 183–211.

Bradley, Joseph M., 'The Gaelic Athletic Association in Scotland, 1948–2007: diaspora and immigrant identity', *The International Journal of the History of Sport*, 24:10 (2007), pp. 1302–19.

Brosnan, Kathleen A., 'Public presence, public silence: nuns, bishops and the gendered space of early Chicago', *The Catholic Historical Review*, 90 (2004), pp. 473–96.

Brown, Callum, 'Faith in the city', *History Today*, 40 (1990), pp. 41–7.

Corr, Helen, 'An exploration into Scottish education', in W. Hamish Fraser and R. J. Morris (eds), *People and Society in Scotland*, vol. 2: *1830–1914*. Edinburgh, John Donald, 1990, pp. 290–309.

Craig, Béatrice, 'La structure de l'emploi féminin dans une ville en voie d'industrialisation: Tourcoing au XIX siècle', *Canadian Journal of History*, 27:2 (1992), pp. 299–330.

Dilworth, Mark, 'Canons regular and the Reformation', in A. A.MacDonald, Michael Lynch and Ian B. Cowan (eds), *The Renaissance in Scotland*. Leiden, E. J. Brill, 1994, pp. 164–82.

Dilworth, Mark, 'Religious orders in Scotland, 1878–1978', *Innes Review*, 29:1 (1978), pp. 92–109. Also printed in David McRoberts (ed.), *Modern Scottish Catholicism, 1878–1978*. Glasgow, John S. Burns & Sons, 1979.

Donovan, Robert Kent, 'Sir John Dalrymple and the origins of Roman Catholic Relief', *Recusant History*, 17:2 (1984), pp. 188–96.

Donovan, Robert Kent, 'The military origins of the Roman Catholic Relief programme of 1778', *The Historical Journal*, 28:1 (1985), pp. 79–102.

Fitzpatrick, Thomas A., 'Catholic education in Glasgow, Lanarkshire and South-West Scotland before 1872', *Innes Review*, 36:2 (1985), pp. 86–95.

Forbes, F. and Anderson, W. J., 'Clergy lists of the Highland district, 1732–1828', *Innes Review*, 17:2 (1966), pp. 129–84.

Hickman, Mary, 'Catholicism and the nation-state in nineteenth-century Britain', in Mary Eaton et. al. (eds), *Commitment to Diversity: Catholics and Education in a Changing World*. London, Cassell, 2000, pp. 48–66.

Hickman, Mary, 'Incorporating and denationalizing the Irish in England: the role of the Catholic Church', in Patrick O'Sullivan (ed.), *The Irish World Wide: History, Heritage, Identity*, Volume 5: *Religion and Identity*. London, Leicester University Press, 1996, pp. 196–216.

Kehoe, S. Karly, 'Nursing the mission: the Franciscan Sisters of the Immaculate Conception and the Sisters of Mercy in Glasgow, 1847–1866', *Innes Review*, 56:1 (2005), pp. 46–60.

Kehoe, S. Karly, 'The Venerable Margaret Sinclair: an examination of the cause of Edinburgh's twentieth-century factory girl', *Feminist Theology*, 16 (2008), pp. 169–83.

Kidd, Colin, 'Race, Empire and the limits of nineteenth-century Scottish nationhood', *The Historical Journal*, 46:4 (2003), pp. 873–92.

Kidd, Colin, 'Senitment, race and revival: Scottish identities in the aftermath of Enlightenment', in Laurence Brockliss and David Eastwood (eds), *A Union of Multiple Identities: The British Isles, c. 1750–1850* (Manchester, Manchester University Press), pp. 110–25.

Leneman, Leah, 'The Scottish Church and "Votes for Women"', *Records of the Scottish Church History Society*, 24 (1992), pp. 237–51.

Lobban, R. D., 'The Irish community in Greenock in the nineteenth century', *Irish Geography*, 6:3 (1971), pp. 270–81.

Lynch, Michael, 'Preaching to the converted? Perspectives on the Scottish Reformation', in A. A. MacDonald, Michael Lynch and Ian B. Cowan (eds), *The Renaissance in Scotland*. Leiden, E. J. Brill, 1994, pp. 301–43.

McCaffrey, John F., 'Irish immigrants and radical movements in the west of Scotland in the early nineteenth century', *Innes Review*, 39:1 (1988), pp. 46–60.

McCaffrey, John, 'Politics and the Catholic community since 1878', *Innes Review*, 29:2 (1978), pp. 140–55.

McCaffrey, John, 'Reactions in Scotland to the Irish famine', in Sewart J. Brown (ed.), *Scottish Christianity in the Modern World*. Edinburgh, T. & T. Clark, 2000, pp. 155–75.

McCaffrey, John, 'Roman Catholics in Scotland in the 19th and 20th centuries', *Records of the Scottish Church History Society*, 21 (1983), pp. 275–300.

MacDonald, Roderick, 'Bishop Scott and the West Highlands', *Innes Review*, 17:2 (1966), pp. 116–28.

McGloin, James, 'Some refugee French clerics and laymen in Scotland, 1789–1814', *Innes Review*, 16 (1965), pp. 27–55.

Mackie, Peter, 'Inter-denominational education and the United Industrial School of Edinburgh, 1847–1900', *Innes Review*, 43:1 (1992), pp. 3–17.

McLeod, Hugh, 'Building the "Catholic Ghetto": Catholic organisations 1870–1914', in W. J. Sheils and Diana Wood (eds), *Voluntary Religion*. Oxford, Basil Blackwell, 1986, pp. 411–44.

McMahon, Timothy G., 'Religion and popular culture in nineteenth-century Ireland', *History Compass*, 4:3 (2007), pp. 845–64.

McMillan, J. F., 'The root of all evil? Money and the Scottish Catholic Mission in the eighteenth century', in W. J. Sheils and Diana Wood (eds), *The Church and Wealth*. Oxford: Basil Blackwell, 1987, pp. 267–82.

McRoberts, David, 'The restoration of the Scottish Catholic hierarchy in 1878', *Innes Review*, 24:1 (1978), pp. 3–29.

MacWilliam, Alexander, 'Catholic Dundee: 1787 to 1836', *Innes Review*, 18:2 (1967), pp. 75–87.

Megel, Thomas, 'Ultramontanism, liberalism, moderation: political mentalities and political behaviour of the German Catholic Bürgertum, 1848–1914', *Central European History*, 29:2 (2001), pp. 151–74.

Morton, Graeme, 'Civil society, municipal government and the state: enshrinement, empowerment and legitimacy. Scotland, 1800–1929', *Urban History*, 25:3 (1998), pp. 348–67.

Muirhead, Ian A., 'Catholic Emancipation: Scottish reactions in 1829. Part One', *Innes Review*, 24:1 (1973), pp. 26–42.

Muirhead, Ian A., 'Catholic Emancipation in Scotland: the debate and aftermath. Part Two', *Innes Review*, 24:1 (1973), pp. 103–20.

O'Brien, Susan, 'French nuns in nineteenth-century England', *Past & Present*, 54:1 (1997), pp. 142–80.

O'Brien, Susan, 'Lay sisters and good mothers: working-class women in English convents, 1840–1910', in W. J. Sheils and Diana Wood (eds), *Women in the Church*. Oxford, Basil Blackwell, 1990, pp. 453–65.

O'Brien, Susan, 'Making Catholic spaces: women, décor, and devotion in the English Catholic Church, 1840–1900', in D. Wood (ed.), *The Church and the Arts*. Oxford, Blackwell, 1992, pp. 449–64.

O'Day, Alan, 'Imagined Irish communities: networks of social communication of the Irish diaspora in the United States and Britain in the late nineteenth and early twentieth centuries', *Immigrants and Minorities*, 23:2–3 (2005), pp. 399–424.

O'Hagan, Francis J. and Davis, Robert A., 'Forging the compact of church and state in the development of Catholic education in late nineteenth-century Scotland', *Innes Review*, 58:1 (2007), pp. 72–94.

O'Leary, Paul, 'Networking respectability: class, gender and ethnicity among the

Irish in South Wales, 1845–1914', *Immigrants and Minorities*, 23:2–3 (2005), pp. 255–75.

Prentice, Alison, 'The feminisation of teaching in British North American and Canada, 1845–1875', in J. M. Bumsted (ed.), *Interpreting Canada's Past*, vol. 1: *Before Confederation*. Toronto, Oxford University Press, 1986, pp. 374–86.

Raedts, Peter, 'The Church as nation state: a new look at ultramontane Catholicism', *Dutch Review of Church History*, 84 (2004), pp. 476–96.

Roberts, Alasdair B., 'The role of women in Scottish Catholic survival', *Scottish Historical Review*, 70:190 (1991), pp. 129–50.

Skinnider, Martha, 'Catholic elementary education in Glasgow, 1818–1918', in James Scotland (ed.), *History of Scottish Education*. London, University of London Press, 1969, pp. 13–25.

Stewart, Ian, 'Teacher careers and the early Catholic schools of Edinburgh', *Innes Review*, 46:1 (1995), pp. 52–66.

Szechi, Daniel, 'Defending the true faith: kirk, state, and Catholic missioners in Scotland, 1653–1755', in *Catholic Historical Review*, 82 (1996), pp. 397–411.

Treble, J. H., 'The development of Roman Catholic education in Scotland 1878–1978', *Innes Review*, 29 (1978), pp. 111–39. Also printed in David McRoberts (ed.), *Modern Scottish Catholicism, 1878–1978*. Glasgow, John S. Burns & Sons, 1979.

Walsh, James, 'Archbishop Manning's visitation of the Western District of Scotland in 1867', *Innes Review*, 18:1 (1967), pp. 3–17.

Wilby, Noel MacDonald, 'The "Encreasce of Popery" in the Highlands, 1714–1747', *Innes Review*, 17:2 (1966), pp. 91–115.

Yonke, Eric, 'The problem of the middle class in German Catholic history: the nineteenth-century Rhineland revisited', *The Catholic Historical Review*, 88:2 (2002), pp. 263–80.

Books

Anderson, R. D., *Scottish Education since the Reformation*. Stirling, Economic and Social History Society for Scotland, 1997.

Anson, Peter F., *Underground Catholicism in Scotland, 1622–1878*. Montrose, Standard Press, 1970.

Bakvis, Herman, *Catholic Power in the Netherlands*. Kingston and Montreal, McGill-Queen's University Press, 1981.

Bloch, Ruth, *Visionary Republic: Millennial Themes in American Thought, 1756–1800*. Cambridge, Cambridge University Press, 1988.

Bowen, Desmond, *Paul Cardinal Cullen and the Shaping of Modern Irish Catholicism*. Dublin, Gill and Macmillan, 1983.

Brown, Callum, *The Death of Christian Britain: Understanding Secularisation, 1800–2000*. London, Routledge, 2001.

Brown, Stewart J., *The National Churches of England, Ireland and Scotland, 1801–1846*. Oxford, Oxford University Press, 2001.

Brown, Stewart J., *Thomas Chalmers and the Godly Commonwealth in Scotland*. Oxford, Oxford University Press, 1982.

Burnstein, Miriam Elizabeth, *Narrating Women's History in Britain, 1770-1902*. Aldershot, Ashgate, 2004.

Campbell-Jones, Suzanne, *In Habit: An Anthropological Study of Working Nuns*. London, Faber & Faber, 1979.

Carlyle, Thomas, *Thomas Carlyle: Selected Writings*. London, Penguin Books, 1971.

Clapperton, William, *Memoirs of Scotch Missionary Priests compiled from original letters, formerly preserved at Preshome, now at Blairs College*, vol. 2. Elgin, 1901.

Coburn, Carol K. and Smith, Martha, *Spirited Lives: How Nuns Shaped Catholic Culture and American Life, 1836-1920*. Chapel Hill, University of North Carolina Press, 1999.

Colley, Linda, *Britons: Forging the Nation, 1707-1837*, 2nd edition. London, Pimlico, 2003.

Collins, Irene, *Liberalism in Nineteenth-Century Europe*. London, The Historical Association, 1957.

Collins, Kevin, *Catholic Churchmen and the Celtic Revival in Ireland, 1848-1916*. Dublin, Four Courts Press, 2002.

Cooke, Anthony et al. (eds), *Modern Scottish History 1707 to the Present*, vol. 1: *Transformation of Scotland, 1707-1850*. East Linton, Tuckwell Press, 1998.

Curtis, L. Perry, *Apes and Angels: The Irishman in Victorian Caricature*, revised edition. Washington, Smithsonian Institution Press, 1997.

Curtis, S. J., *History of Education in Great Britain*, 5th edition. London, University Tutorial Press, 1957.

Curtis, Sarah A., *Educating the Faithful: Religion, Schooling, and Society*. Dekalb, Northern Illinois University Press, 2000.

Devine, T. M., *Irish Immigrants and Scottish Society in the 19th and 20th Centuries*. Edinburgh, John Donald, 1991.

Donnelly, Beatrice, *Hill of Doves: Memories of 100 Years of the Notre Dame Dowanhill Schools*. Glasgow, The Notre Dame Centenary Book Project, 1997.

Donoughue, Bernard, *British Politics and the American Revolution: The Path to War, 1773-75*. London, Macmillan, 1964.

Doyle, William, *Jansenism: Catholic Resistance to Authority from the Reformation to the French Revolution*. London, Macmillan, 2000.

Evangelisti, Silvia, *Nuns: A History of Convent Life*. Oxford, Oxford University Press, 2007.

Farmer, David, *Oxford Dictionary of Saints*, 5th edition. Oxford, Oxford University Press, 2004.

Fay, Terrence J., *A History of Canadian Catholics, Gallicanism, Romanism and Canadianism*. Montreal and Kingston, McGill-Queen's University Press, 2002.

Fenyő, Krisztina, *Contempt, Sympathy and Romance: Lowland Perceptions of the Highlands and the Clearances during the Famine Years, 1845-1855*. East Linton, Tuckwell Press, 2000.

Fielding, Steven, *Class and Ethnicity: Irish Catholics in England, 1880-1939*. Buckingham, The Open University Press, 1993.
Fitzgerald, Maureen, *Habits of Compassion: Irish Catholic Nuns and the Origins of New York's Welfare System, 1830-1920*. Urbana, University of Illinois Press, 2006.
Fitzpatrick, T. A., *Catholic Secondary Education in South-West Scotland before 1972: Its Contribution to the Change in Status of the Catholic Community of the Area*. Aberdeen, Aberdeen University Press, 1986.
Fitzpatrick, T. A., *No Mean Service: Scottish Catholic Teacher Education 1895-1995*. Bearsden (Glasgow), St Andrews College, 1995.
Foster, R. F., *Paddy & Mr Punch: Connections in Irish and English History*. London, Penguin Books, 1993.
Fraser, W. Hamish and Maver, Irene (eds), *Glasgow*, vol. 2. Manchester, Manchester University Press, 1996.
Geser, Fintan, *The Canon Law Governing Communities of Sisters*. London, B. Herder Book Co., 1950.
Gibb, Andrew Dewar, *Scotland in Eclipse*. London, Humphrey Toulmin, 1930.
Gough, Austin, *Paris and Rome: The Gallican Church and the Ultramontane Campaign, 1848-1853*. Oxford, Clarendon Press, 1986.
Gunn, Simon, *The Public Culture of the Victorian Middle Class: Ritual and Authority and the English Industrial City*. Manchester, Manchester University Press, 2000.
Handley, James Edmund, *The Irish in Modern Scotland*. Cork, Cork University Press, 1947.
Hanham, H. J., *Scottish Nationalism*. London, Faber & Faber, 1969.
Harris, Jose (ed.), *Civil Society in British History: Ideas, Identities and Institutions*. Oxford, Oxford University Press, 1999.
Harvie, Christopher, *Scotland and Nationalism: Scottish Society and Nationalism, 1707-1994*, 2nd edition. London, Routledge, 1994.
Heimann, Mary, *Catholic Devotion in Victorian England*. Oxford, Clarendon Press, 1995.
Henderson, Lizanne and Cowan, E. J., *Scottish Fairy Belief: A History*. East Linton, Tuckwell Press, 2001.
Hickman, Mary, *Religion, Class and Identity: The State, the Catholic Church and the Education of the Irish in Britain*. Aldershot, Avebury, 1995.
Holloway, James, *A Companion Guide to the Scottish National Portrait Gallery*. Edinburgh, National Galleries of Scotland, 1999.
Hunt, Tamara L., *Defining John Bull: Political Caricature and National Identity in Late Georgian England*. Aldershot, Ashgate, 2003.
Johnson, Christine, *Developments in the Roman Catholic Church in Scotland, 1789-1829*. Edinburgh, John Donald, 1983.
Jones, Catherine, *Immigration and Social Policy in Britain*. London, Tavistock, 1977.
King, Imelda, *Sisters of Mercy of Great Britain: Brief Historical Sketches*. Glasgow, John S. Burns, 1978.

Kirk, James (ed.), *The Scottish Churches and the Union Parliament, 1707–1999.* Edinburgh, Scottish Church History Society, 2001.

Lees, Lynn Hollen, *Exiles of Erin: Irish Migrants in Victorian London.* Manchester, Manchester University Press, 1979.

Luddy, Maria, *Women and Philanthropy in Nineteenth-Century Ireland.* Cambridge, Cambridge University Press, 1995.

McBride, Terrence, *The Experience of Irish Migrants to Glasgow, Scotland 1863–1891: A New Way of Being Irish.* Lewiston, NY, Edwin Mellen Press, 2006.

McCluskey, Raymond, *St. Joseph's Kilmarnock, 1847–1997: A Portrait of a Parish Community.* Kilmarnock, St. Joseph's, 1997.

McDermid, Jane, *The Schooling of Working-Class Girls in Victorian Scotland: Gender, Education and Identity.* London, Routledge, 2005.

MacDonald, Fiona. *Missions to the Gaels: Reformation and Counter-Reformation in Ulster and the Highlands and Islands of Scotland, 1560–1760.* Edinburgh, John Donald, 2006.

MacDonald, Lesley Orr, *A Unique and Glorious Mission: Women and Presbyterianism in Scotland, 1830–1930.* Edinburgh, John Donald, 2000.

McFarland, Elaine, *Protestants First: Orangeism in 19th Century Scotland.* Edinburgh, Edinburgh University Press, 1990.

McFarland, Elaine, *Ireland and Scotland in the Age of Revolution: Planting the Green Bough.* Edinburgh, Edinburgh University Press, 1994.

McIntosh, John R., *Church and Theology in Enlightenment Scotland: The Popular Party, 1740–1800.* East Linton, Tuckwell Press, 1998.

McNamara, Jo Ann Kay, *Sisters in Arms: Catholic Nuns through Two Millennia.* Cambridge, MA, Harvard University Press, 1996.

McRoberts, David (ed.), *Modern Scottish Catholicism, 1878–1978.* Glasgow, John S. Burns & Sons, 1979.

Magray, Mary Peckham, *The Transforming Power of the Nuns: Women, Religion, and Cultural Change in Ireland, 1750–1900.* Oxford, Oxford University Press, 1998.

Mangion, Carmen, *Contested Identities: Catholic Women Religious in Nineteenth-Century England and Wales.* Manchester, Manchester University Press, 2008.

Maver, Irene, *Glasgow.* Edinburgh, Edinburgh University Press, 2000.

Mitchell, Martin, *The Irish in the West of Scotland, 1797–1848: Trade Unions, Strikes and Political Movements.* Edinburgh, John Donald, 1998.

Morgan, Alexander, *Rise and Progress of Scottish Education.* Edinburgh, Oliver & Boyd, 1927.

Morton, Graeme, *Unionist Nationalism: Governing Urban Scotland, 1830–1860.* East Linton, Tuckwell Press, 1999.

Mumm, Susan (ed.), *All Saints Sisters of the Poor: An Anglican Sisterhood in the 19th Century.* Woodbridge, The Boydell Press, 2001.

Mumm, Susan, *Stolen Daughters, Virgin Mothers: Anglican Sisterhoods in Victorian Britain.* London, Leicester University Press, 1999.

Ó Catháin, Máirtín Seán, *Irish Republicanism in Scotland 1858–1916: Fenians in Exile.* Dublin, Irish Academic Press, 2007.

O'Hagan, Francis J., *Change, Challenge and Achievement: A Study of the Development of Catholic Education in Glasgow in the Nineteenth and Twentieth Centuries*. Glasgow, St Andrew's College, 1996.

O'Hagan, Francis J., *The Contribution of the Religious Orders to Education in Glasgow during the Period 1847–1918*. Lewiston, NY, Edwin Mellen Press, 2006.

O'Sullivan, Patrick (ed.), *The Irish World Wide: History, Heritage, Identity*, Volume 5: *Religion and Identity*. London, Leicester University Press, 1996.

Paterson, Lindsay, *The Autonomy of Modern Scotland*. Edinburgh, Edinburgh University Press, 1994.

Patrick, James, *A Glasgow Gang Observed*. London, Eyre Methuen, 1973.

Schiltz, Nancy Lusignan (ed.), *Veil of Fear: Nineteenth-Century Convent Tales by Rebecca Reed and Maria Monk*. West Lafayette, Notabell Books, 1999.

Smith, Charles J., *Historic South Edinburgh*. Edinburgh, John Donald, 1978.

Swift, Roger, *Irish Migrants in Britain, 1815–1914: A Documentary History*. Cork, Cork University Press, 2002.

Swift, Roger, and Gilley, Sheridan (eds), *The Irish in Victorian Britain: The Local Dimension*. Dublin, Four Courts Press, 1999.

Swift, Roger and Gilley, Sheridan (eds), *The Irish in the Victorian City*. London, Croom Helm, 1985.

Vidler, Alec R., *The Church in an Age of Revolution: 1789 to the Present Day*. London, Penguin Books, 1990.

Walsh, Barbara, *Roman Catholic Nuns in England and Wales, 1800–1937: A Social History*. Dublin, Irish Academic Press, 2002.

Watts, John, *A Canticle of Love: The Story of the Franciscan Sisters of the Immaculate Conception*. Edinburgh, John Donald, 2006.

Whatley, Christopher A., *Scots and the Union*. Edinburgh, Edinburgh University Press, 2006.

Woodbridge, George, *The Reform Bill of 1832*. New York, Thomas Y. Crowell Company, 1970.

Yates, Nigel, *The Oxford Movement and Anglican Ritualism*. London, The Historical Association, 1983.

Index

Aberdeen 11, 76, 84–5, 91, 113, 118–19, 127, 135, 168
Aberdeenshire 27, 28, 49, 99, 101, 118
active religious communities 10–12, 55, 65, 69, 74–5, 85, 88, 96
Airdrie 113
alcoholism 69, 122, 151–2
Allies, T. W. 126, 128–9
American Revolution 29
Ancient Order of Hibernians 153
Anglican (ism) 29, 53, 68, 125
Anglican sisterhoods 68–9
Anglicisation 16, 112, 125–8, 133–4
anti-Catholicism 9, 15, 22, 24–5, 28–9, 31, 33, 38, 40, 50, 53, 58, 124, 131–2, 149
  see also anti-popery
anti-Christ 39
  see also Pope
anti-clericalism 4
anti-conventualism 68, 79–80, 91–2
anti-Irish 38, 53, 84–5, 87, 92, 97–103, 168, 176
anti-Scottish 103
Apostolines of the Immaculate Conception 84, 119
Arbroath 113
Arisaig 112, 120
Association of St Margaret 58, 127, 156
Association for Improving the Condition of the Poor 122

Australasia 10–11
Australia 104
Ayr 113
Ayrshire 7, 151

Badenoch 112
Balfron 112
Banffshire 24, 28, 57, 83, 113
  Enzie 24, 57
Barrhead 113
Bathgate 117
Bavaria 75, 94
Beaton, Fr. James 23
Belgium 10, 94
Benedictine monks 118
Benedict XIV, Pope 11
Birmingham 91
Bishopbriggs 11, 76, 85
Black, Sr M of the Cross 102
Blairgowrie 117
Blairs Seminary 49
Board of Education 132
Bothwell 11, 85
Braemar 113
Brothers of the Christian Instruction 127
Buckie 113
Butler, Sr M. Joseph 86
Bulwark 59

Cameron, Fr Alexander 38
Campbell, Fr Colin 26–7

Canada 10–11, 78, 92, 95, 104
Carfin 120
Carlyle, Thomas 6
Carruthers, Fr Andrew 63
Castle Douglas 117
Catholic Boys' Brigade 169
Catholic Directory for Scotland 59, 63, 112, 156
Catholic Emancipation 15, 34–9, 177
Catholic 'ghetto' (debate) 16
Catholic Poor Schools Committee 16, 111, 125–30, 133
   Crisis Fund 131
Catholic relief 14, 23, 28–1, 33–4, 36, 39, 177
Catholic Schools Committee 60–1
Catholic Socialist Society 170
Catholic Suffrage Society 166
Catholic Union of Glasgow 166
Catholic Young Men's Society 154, 156
Celtic Football Club 155
Chalmers, Thomas 39, 54–5, 63
Charlotte Street Convent 83
childbirth (avoidance of) 11
child reformatories 75
choir nuns 57, 77, 97, 124
cholera 81, 83, 86–7
Christian Brothers 123
Church of England 53, 176
   see also Anglican
Church of Ireland 40
Church of Scotland 28–9, 31, 50, 54, 58, 81, 127
   see also Presbyterian
civil rights 38
civil society 2, 5, 15–16, 51, 149–51, 178–9
Clapperton, Sr Margaret Teresa 77, 98
Coatbridge 113, 119–20, 135
Committee of Council on Education 117, 125, 130
Committee for Feeding and Clothing Destitute Children 122

Committee for the Protestant Interest 14, 31, 33
Condon, Fr Michael 91
confraternities /sodalities 48, 155, 179
   Bona Mors 156–9
   Children of Mary 59, 156–63, 169
   Children of the Angels 156–9
   Holy Family 157–9, 163
   Living Rosary 156, 158–9
   Society of Sacred Heart 162
Connaught 40
consumption 81, 86, 156
contemplative religious communities 11, 74–5
Cordier, Sr M. Veronica 81–3, 92, 100–1, 110, 118
Council of Trent 11
convent 14, 16, 51, 57, 74, 87, 100
   life in 13–14, 55, 57, 84–5, 87–8, 91–7, 100–1, 104, 112, 178
   tensions with priests 98–103
converts (to Catholicism) 5, 27, 50–1, 53–7, 67, 83, 89, 126, 165, 176–7, 179
Corpus Christi processions 116, 162
Crichton-Stuart, John Patrick 5, 54
Cunningham Hutchison, Isabella 89, 181

Dalbeth 121
Dalkeith 90, 117, 119
Dalry 120
Dalrymple, John 31
Daughters of Charity 56, 75–6, 84, 119–20
Demerara 90
devotion 16, 17
devotional revolution 12
disruption 54
Dominicans 4
domesticity 64–5, 68, 167
Dornie 118–19
dowries 77, 86, 97
Dublin 11, 89, 96, 99, 152

Index

Duke Street Prison 85
Dumfries 76, 113, 118

Dundas, Henry 31
Dundases (political managers) 29
Dundas, William Pitt 139, 168, 176
Dundee 3, 28, 64, 67, 76, 84, 104, 118–20, 135, 162–3, 168, 178
Dunfermline 117

Eastern District 48, 55, 67, 76–7, 80, 93, 113, 117, 131
Edinburgh 3, 10–11, 13, 15, 23, 32, 39, 48–9, 52, 55–60, 62, 67, 70, 76, 80, 84, 89–90, 93, 96–8, 104, 113–14, 118–24, 127, 135–8, 149, 154, 155–8, 162–5, 168–9, 175
  whitehouse 77
  university 31
Edinburgh Irish Mission 58–9
Edinburgh United Industrial School 117, 121–2
Education Committee for the Eastern District 131
Education (Scotland) Act 16, 111, 117, 127, 129, 131–2, 139, 151, 166
Elgin 118–19
empire 8, 29, 81
England 3–4, 23, 25, 31–3, 37, 53, 63, 66, 75, 77, 86, 94–6, 98–9, 104, 126–7, 132–4, 140
enlightenment 8, 51
Episcopalian (ism) 40, 56, 127
  non-juring 28
Evangelical (ism) 12, 38–9, 48, 54, 55, 68, 178
Evening Times 153
Eyre, Charles (archbishop) 99, 103, 132, 152–3, 166

Falkirk 117
Fenian (ism) 152, 155
Fingal's Cave (Staffa) 52

Fochabers 113
Forbes, Peter 88, 178
Fort Augustus 112, 118, 120
Fort William 112
France 3, 5, 10, 11, 25–7, 33, 63, 75, 76, 86, 81–3, 94, 96, 98, 102, 141
  Chavagnes-en-Paillers 10, 75
  Tourcoing 10, 81–2
Franciscans (Irish Regulars) 23–4
Franciscan Sisters of the Immaculate Conception 10, 13, 15, 61, 74–5, 81–7, 91–3, 101–3, 110, 114–16, 118–19, 123, 129, 136–7, 139–41, 169
Free Church 54, 59, 127
Free Press 103, 127
French 14, 55, 58, 92, 97, 101
French Revolution 3, 10, 33, 35, 52

Gaelic 24, 134
Gaelic Athletic Association 155
Galashiels 113, 117, 119
Gallicanism 2, 3, 4
gangs 169–70
Garden, Sr M. Bernard 80, 99–100, 118
Gatherer, Mary 83
Gatherer, Sr M. Margaret 83–4
Geddes, Fr John 24
gender difference (teaching) 130–3, 135, 142
General Assembly 58
George III 32, 36
Gibb, Andrew Dewar 176
Gibraltar 75, 94
Gibson, William 36
Gillis, Fr James 3, 55–6, 63, 67, 76, 80, 88, 176, 178
Girvan 11, 85
Glasgow 3, 15, 23, 28, 32–3, 36, 39, 48–9, 55, 61–2, 65–7, 70, 76, 80–90, 93, 96, 98, 100, 103–4, 113, 116–23, 125, 129, 132, 135–8, 149, 152–3, 155–6, 159, 162–4, 168–9

Glasgow (*cont.*)
  cathedral 37
  green 50, 82–3, 155, 166
  necropolis 37
  university 54, 134, 176
Glasgow Catholic Association 37
Glasgow Child Refuge 155
Glasgow Courier 38, 40
Glasgow Free Press 58, 61
Glasgow Herald 7, 38
Glasgow Observer 61, 154, 166, 168
Glasgow Shamrock Association 153
Good Shepherds 75, 84, 121
Govan 120
Grant, Helen 80, 89, 141
Grant, James 52
Grant, Jane 80, 141
Grant, Roderick 156
grants (education) 58, 60, 117, 120, 123–6, 129–33
Grant, Sr M. Julia 80, 89, 98
Gray, Fr John 8, 83, 103
Greenock 3, 11, 85, 113, 135, 167
Greenock women's prison 85
Guernsey 94

Haddington 117
Hamilton 113
Hannan, Fr Edward 154–5
Hawick 113
Hay, Fr George 30, 33–4
Highland District 26–8, 38, 48
Highlanders 8, 134–5, 177
Highlands 14, 23–8, 41
  anti-Highland 26
  fairy belief 27, 28
  soldiers 29, 34
Highland Seminary 25
Home Government Association 153, 155
Holy Family 84, 119
Holy Gild of St Joseph 58, 63, 65–6, 68, 181–2

Home Rule 53, 149–55, 162, 170
Hope-Scott, J. R. 52, 78
Hume, David 8
Huntly 113

illegitimacy 167–8
India 11, 90, 95
Inellen 11, 85
Institute of the Blessed Virgin Mary (Loreto) 76, 84, 119
Inverness 10, 85, 91, 113, 118, 135–6
Invincibles 152
Ireland 11, 31, 33, 39, 63, 77, 86–7, 93–6, 98–100, 102, 134–5, 141, 155
  famine 7, 54, 61, 81, 87, 93
  soldiers 29
Irish labourers 7, 39, 41, 50, 113, 119, 168

Irish National Foresters 163–4, 170
Irish Patriotic Brotherhood 153
Irish Republican Brotherhood 153
Isle of Barra 27, 112
Isle of Canna 112
Isle of Eigg 27, 112
Isle of South Uist 112

Jacobite (ism) 14, 23, 26–9, 34
Jamaica 75, 90, 94–5, 101–3
James, Fr Gordon 26
James VI & I 23
James VII & II 34
Jansenism 26
Jedburgh 117
Jesuits 4, 24–5, 28, 52, 118–19, 157
John Bull 32

Keenan, Stephen 67, 104, 119, 178
Keith 113, 118
Kelso 117
Kerrin, Sr M. Clare 86
Kilmarnock 113

Index

Kilsyth 112, 117
Kirkcaldy 67
Kirkcudbrightshire 24, 60, 67, 100
Kirkintilloch 112
Knox Monument 37
Knox, John 38
Knoydart 112
Kyle, Fr James 100

Lanark 11, 76, 119–21, 135
Langdale, Charles 126
lay sisters 57, 76–7, 92, 97
League of the Cross 152, 156, 161, 163, 169
Leinster 93
Leith 84, 93, 113, 119
Leo XIII, Pope 170
liberal (ism) 6, 15, 48, 51, 55, 63, 110–12, 125–6
Limerick 11, 86, 89, 96, 99
Linlithgow 67, 90
Little Sisters of the Poor 75–6, 84
Liverpool 96, 99, 123, 127, 133
Liverpool Corporation schools 125
Lochaber 112
Locke, Sr M. Catherine 104
Locke, Sr M. Francis 104
London 24, 32, 39, 91, 98, 131, 155
 Gordon riots 32
Londonderry (Derry) 104, 119
Lothians 7, 31
Lowland District 26, 28, 31, 48
Lowlands 23–5, 40–1, 134
Loyola, Ignatius 25
Lucas, Frederick 126
Lynch, Fr Lynch 103

MacDonell, Fr Alexander 78
Mackintosh, Sr M. Aloysius 101–2
Magdalen homes 55, 121
male orders 25, 49, 56, 67–8, 70, 112, 116–18, 123, 169
Manchester 133

Manning, Fr Henry Edward 5, 53, 103
Marchand, Sr M. Francis 81, 84
Marist Brothers 116, 118–19, 123, 136–7, 169
marriage 28, 69, 75
 avoidance of 11
Maryhill 120
material culture 165
McAuley, Catherine 11, 86
McNamara, Sr M. Clare 86, 89–90, 98, 100
McSwinney, Sr M. Angela 101–4
McNamara, Sr M. Catherine 86
Menzies, John (of Pitfodels) 49, 53, 56, 65, 77–8, 181
Middleton, D. (HM Inspector) 125
Milngavie 117
missionary (ies) 11, 25, 55–7, 74
mixed religious communities 74–5
Moidart 112
Molly Maguires 153
Monk, Maria 79
Monteith, Robert 5, 52–3, 67, 83, 176
Montreal 4, 176
Moore, Sr M. Elizabeth 86, 87, 89, 98
Morar 112
Munster 93
Murdoch, Fr John 37, 87, 99–100, 110, 113

National Association for the Vindication of Scottish Rights 53, 156
national identity 37, 41, 138–43
 Scotland 25, 32, 75, 104, 111–12, 125–6
nationalism 13–14
 Scotland 9–10, 53, 65, 67, 175
 Ireland 152–4, 170, 175–6
navvies 7
Netherlands, The 6
Newman, Fr. John Henry 5, 53
New York 76
Nicholson, Fr Thomas 25

Northern District 36, 48, 100, 112–13, 118
novice mistress 16, 97
novices (religious) 16, 78–9, 97, 100, 129

Oban 76
O'Connell, Daniel 15, 36–7, 40, 50, 52
orphanage 15, 48, 55, 86, 113, 121
orphans 58, 63, 70, 162
Ossian 33, 52
Oxford 125–6
Oxford Movement 5, 53–4, 68, 176

Paisley 3, 80, 113
Paris 4, 23–4
parlour borders 83–4
Partick 120
Paterson, Fr Alexander 38, 76
patronage 29, 54
Peebles 113, 117
penal legislation 22
Pericluso 11, 69
Perth 10, 76–7, 117–18, 135
Phoenix Park murders 152
piety 12, 23, 156
Pius IX, Pope 6, 110
Poor Law (Scotland) Act 54, 75, 81
Poor Sisters of Nazareth 84, 113, 162
Pope 29, 38, 51, 53, 69, 91
  see also anti-Christ
popery 8, 28, 33, 40, 59
  anti-popery 15
Papists 38, 66
Port Glasgow 86, 120
Presbyterian (ism) 12, 28–30, 33, 51, 54, 59, 67, 74, 131, 141–2, 176–7
Preshome 113
Privy Council grants 60
proselytise 49, 81, 104
prostitution 69, 79
Protestant Association 31

pupil teachers 59, 90, 114–15, 123, 129–31, 133, 135–6, 138
Punch 6

Quamvis Iusto 11, 69
Quanta Cura 6, 110
Quebec 3, 29, 56
Quebec Act (1774) 31

race 8, 9, 23, 36, 40, 41, 66, 92, 103, 124
radicalism (political) 4, 8, 9, 35–7, 111, 125, 154, 164, 177
Raffy 140
recusant 41, 48, 50, 65, 99–100, 113, 125–6, 142, 177
Reform Act (1832) 50, 51
reformation 1, 5, 15, 22, 23, 24, 37, 48, 50, 57, 76, 112, 176–7
religious life 10, 11, 69, 75, 81, 84–7, 91–2, 96, 104, 133, 135, 141, 143
  convent 10, 11
republicanism (Irish) 7
Rerum Novarum 170
ribbonism 152–3, 155, 170
Rigg, Fr. George 60, 67
Rigg, Sr M. Aloysius 100
Restoration of Roman Catholic Hierarchy (Scotland) 5, 150, 154, 170
Romanisation 150
Rome 3, 4, 8, 24–7, 31, 48, 50, 52, 59, 69, 74, 81, 92, 99, 101, 103, 157, 178
Roswell 76
Rothesay 120

Sacred Heart Guild 169
Sacred Heart of Jesus 113
Sacred Heart training college 127
Saint Vincent de Paul 58, 63–7, 84, 155–6, 169

Saltcoats 120, 152
Sawney Scot 31–2, 34
Scalan Seminary 25, 27
schools
   adventure 114
   convent 61, 89–90, 104, 116, 118–20, 123–4, 136, 140, 142
   day 59, 61, 89, 104, 113, 115, 123
   evening 113, 115, 119, 123
   industrial 116, 121–3, 152
   poor parish 116–17, 165
   ragged 55, 113, 116
   Sunday 60–1, 66, 89, 104
   see also Edinburgh Industrial School
Scotch Education Department 132
Scots Colleges 24, 26, 27, 34

Scotsman 38–40, 80, 166
Scott, Fr Andrew 37, 125
Scottish Mission 22–3, 34
   Prefect Apostolic (1653) 23
Scottish Friends of the People 35
Scott, Sir Walter 52
Secondary education 123, 134, 140
Sinclair, Margaret 13
Sisters of Charity 56, 58, 152, 157
   see also Daughters of Charity
Sisters of Mercy 11, 13, 15, 67, 74–5, 80, 85–100, 104, 115–16, 118–24, 135–7, 141, 156, 162–4, 169
Sisters of Notre Dame de Namur 97, 112, 123, 127, 131, 133, 135–8
   Dowanhill teacher training college 112, 127–8, 133–4, 138
   Mount Pleasant teacher training college 127, 133–5, 138
Sisters of St Joseph 14, 76
Smith, Fr Alexander 83–4, 87–8, 92, 100–3, 110, 128–9
Society for the Prevention of Cruelty to Children 152

Society for the Propagation of Christian Knowledge (SSPCK) 112
Society of the Sacred Heart 57
Spain 95
Stamp Act (1765) 31
St Andrew's Society 66–7, 117
St Columba 52
St Francis' Young Men's Society 154
St Helena 95
St Margaret's Convent 60, 80, 89, 97, 115, 124, 136–41, 164
St Mary's teacher training college 127
St Patrick's Fraternal Society 153
St Patrick's Hibernian Society 153
Stirling 117
Stothert, James Augustine 5, 52, 63, 67, 176
Strain, Fr John Menzies 90
Strathblane 112
Sulpicians 3, 56
superior 14, 16, 81, 86–7, 90–3, 96–104, 141

Temperance 36, 151–2
   see also League of the Cross
Teutonic 8
Tomintoul 113, 118
Toronto 76
Trail, Sr Agnes Xavier 56, 57, 58, 77, 79, 84, 143, 176
tuberculosis *see* consumption
typhus 81, 86, 122, 156
Tyrie, Fr John 26–7

Ullathorne, William 128
Ulster 40
ultramontane (ism) 4, 6, 13, 15–16, 48, 50–4, 58, 63, 70, 74–5, 99, 112, 126–7, 133–4, 142–3, 177
Uunion (1707) 8, 14, 22, 32
unionist 8
United Irishmen 35

United States 10, 11, 14, 31, 75–6, 104
Ursulines of Jesus 10, 15, 55–8, 63, 67, 70, 74–80, 83–4, 88–9, 93, 97–8, 115–16, 118–19, 124, 135–41, 163–4

Vaast, Sr M. Adelaide 81, 83–4
Vatican 13
Vicentians (Irish Regulars) 23
voluntarism 1, 49, 54, 58–9, 178

Wales 132
Western District 8, 48–9, 57, 66–7, 91, 93, 103–4, 112, 128, 153
Western District Fund 66–7
West Indies 75, 77
Wheatley, John 170
White Vale Refuge (street children) 152, 155
William III 50
women (morality debate) 166–8
World War I 4

EU authorised representative for GPSR:
Easy Access System Europe, Mustamäe tee 50,
10621 Tallinn, Estonia
gpsr.requests@easproject.com

www.ingramcontent.com/pod-product-compliance
Ingram Content Group UK Ltd.
Pitfield, Milton Keynes, MK11 3LW, UK
UKHW021942200326
4879IPUK00004B/51